SECOND
EDITION

HANDBOOK OF
Diversity
Management

INCLUSIVE STRATEGIES
FOR DRIVING
ORGANIZATIONAL EXCELLENCE

D1563523

DEBORAH L. PLUMMER

EDITOR

ISBN-13 978-0-9966720-5-4
LCCN: 2018957781

Copy Editor: Chip Cheek
Managing Editor: Holly R. Brown
Cover and Interior Design: www.TeaBerryCreative.com

Foreword

SIXTEEN YEARS AGO I was asked to write a foreword for the first edition of this handbook that was published in 2003. At that time the field of diversity management was still in the early stages of development, and I wrote of my hopes for its further refinement and enrichment. Now, as I reflect on where we are in 2018, I recognize many ways in which the field has changed. Some of these changes are related to shifts in the social and political landscape of the world. In the United States, the immigration debate, increasing polarization between conservatives and liberals, and greater activism of persons from the LGBT community have brought greater attention to the social identities of national origin, political affiliation, and sexual orientation, while highly publicized and controversial racial interactions between young African American men and police officers and ubiquitous incidents of alleged sexual harassment by public figures have reenergized traditional points of focus regarding race and gender. As the above-referenced present-day challenges make clear, the work on managing diversity has never been more critical to the societal well-being of all forward-thinking nations. To these and other contemporary diversity-related challenges, writers such as those included in this volume have responded with cogent ideas, and an increasing array of research, advice, and analytical tools.

Another major change to the field of diversity management has to do with a deeper uncovering of what is required to leverage diversity as an organizational resource. One example of this change is that offices and councils charged with diversity management are now commonly referred to by the dual labels of *diversity and inclusion*. While inclusion was always a part of the diversity-management agenda, recent developments have added a much richer understanding of what the term means. For example, we now have insight into the importance of self-inclusion behaviors and the personal willingness of group and organizational members to act authentically. These concepts are dealt with extensively here in chapter one by Deborah Plummer, chapter three by Bernardo Ferdman and Laura Morgan Roberts, and chapter four by Herb Stevenson. This recent work rightly points out that inclusion is a joint responsibility of the organization—composed of people, systems, policies, etc.—and the individual people who seek to be included. The authenticity message is reminiscent of earlier work on the concept of *valuing diversity*, which warned that the potential benefits of diversity are lost unless members actually bring their differences to the table when creative and problem-solving processes are underway.

Another example of newer work in the field that adds substance to our understanding of inclusion is the theory, research, and practice on microaggressive behaviors (e.g., see chapter eight on building inclusion by Patricia Bidol-Padva). This area highlights subtle ways in which diversity-related negativity or disparagement of people creates barriers to diversity competence. (To illustrate, when a colleague heard that I was moving from the faculty of the Fuqua School of Business at Duke to the Ross School at The University of Michigan, his only comment was, "Yes, I hear they are really pushing affirmative action at Michigan." Typical of microaggressions, he was unaware of the negative impact of his comment on me.)

The chapters in this book span the three major areas of diversity-management activity: teaching, theory/research, and practice. While readers will find this edition of the handbook especially helpful for guiding the practice of diversity management, it is clear that these three areas greatly overlap and mutually reinforce one another.

As you explore the volume, take note of the diversity among the contributors on such dimensions as race, gender, age, and field of specialization. Other strengths of the book include: (1) significant attention to making diversity management strategic and institution-alized (e.g., Katz and Miller, chapter ten, and Plummer and Jordan, chapter nine), (2) help with the important but often shortchanged area of metrics (see Castillo-Page, Eliason, and Poll-Hunter, chapter six), (3) a full chapter on diversity management in faith-based and other nonprofit organizations, and (4) the message that well-developed models for diversity management can and should be applied across many dimensions of human differences. The advice offered by my dear friend R. Roosevelt Thomas to go "Beyond Race and Gender" is indeed honored here.

As the field continues to evolve, it will be important for diversity scholars and practitioners to give more explicit attention to specific contextual aspects of diversity dynamics such as immigration policy, how to more effectively apply diversity education to interactions between police and citizens, and using diversity-management tools to reduce political polarization. In addition, as called for in my foreword sixteen years ago and reinforced here by Judith Katz and Fred Miller, we still need more partnerships between internal professionals (e.g., diversity and inclusion executives) and external professionals (e.g., diversity scholars). Such partnerships are needed for the design and implementation of high-quality research as well as organizational interventions. The knowledge base on diversity and inclusion will also benefit from more interdisciplinary work, such as the merger of complex systems and organizational behavior inherent in the writings of Scott E. Page (see *The Diversity Bonus*, 2017, Princeton University Press). Finally, as the field continues to expand and extend itself to address broader and broader definitions of what it means to *manage diversity*, let us not forget that there is still important work to be done on more traditional issues such as gender equity, racial justice, pluralistic acculturation, and navigating cultural differences. Indeed, the field presents a challenging and complex agenda, which experts like those assembled here must remain diligent to address. There is too much at stake to do otherwise.

—Taylor Cox, Jr., Ph.D.

Preface

IN 1997, THE FIRST master of arts degree program in diversity management began at Cleveland State University, in the Department of Psychology. Since that time, the faculty for this program, comprised of CSU professors and local and national diversity practitioners, has had the opportunity to work with over six hundred students. Developing the curriculum for diversity management as a degree program reinforced for me, as a psychologist and founding director of the program, that the practice had burgeoned into a field of academic inquiry as well as organizational practice. The CSU program continues, and other diversity management graduate degree programs and diversity and inclusion certificate programs now exist across the United States, serving as an impetus for the revision of this text.

In addition to the increasing numbers of academic programs devoted to advancing diversity scholarship, the public struggles around race, LGBT equality, and immigration reform demonstrate that diversity issues will not be relegated to obscurity in society or work environments. Hiring individuals with disabilities, supporting transgender individuals in the workplace, and integrating faith traditions to work life are now essential components of an organizational people strategy. As a result, the need is even greater to develop and disseminate the base knowledge on diversity management and give serious consideration to diversity management as its own field of study with proven methodologies, strategies, and frameworks. In response to the current need in organizations to design effective people strategies, the second edition of *Handbook of Diversity Management* focuses specifically on diversity management as a part of the mainstream of organizational work.

As in the first edition, the content of *Handbook of Diversity Management* is divided into three sections: "Theoretical Foundations," "Skill-Based Learning," and "Professional Issues." The chapters can be read in sequence for a snapshot of each of the components of diversity management that together present a comprehensive picture of the field. The *Handbook* can also be read on a need-to-know basis by selecting specific chapters. The section entitled "Chapters at a Glance" is a handy guide for the reader and supports the use of the *Handbook* for either a comprehensive overview or a specific understanding of a component.

Contributors to the book are eminent scholars in the field of diversity management: Taylor Cox, Jr., Judith Katz, Frederick Miller, Marilyn Loden, Bernardo Ferdman, and Ollie Malone. They are authors of best-selling books and seminal works in diversity and inclusion. A chapter from the first edition by noted scholar and diversity pioneer R. Roosevelt Thomas (now deceased) is revised and edited by his long-time mentee and former executive director of Dr. Thomas's American Institute for Diversity, Melanie Harrington, along with Dr. Thomas's daughter, April Thomas, who carries on the legacy of her father in developing cutting-edge, substantive ideas on leveraging differences in the workplace. Other contributors to the text include distinguished university faculty and seasoned global diversity management consultants—Laura Roberts, Herbert Stevenson, Laura Castillo-Page, Jennifer Eliason, Norma Poll-Hunter, Patricia

Bidol-Padva, C. Greer Jordan, Jim Henkelman-Bahn, and Jacqueline Bahn-Henkelman. A brief biographical sketch of each of the contributors is included at the end of this text.

Handbook of Diversity Management makes a valuable contribution to the scholarship of diversity not only because of its contributors, but because of the comprehensive, integrative way in which the subject is presented. Rather than a collection of essays or articles, the book is a conceptualization of the arena of diversity management. This integrative presentation helps define diversity management as an academic field of study—and builds a strong business case, too, for diversity management as a professional practice.

From this perspective, the first section of the book, "Theoretical Foundations," begins with an overview chapter that outlines the overarching themes present in a study of human differences and diversity management's history and theoretical roots in organizations. With conceptual clarity for diversity and inclusion outlined, the focus turns to diversity strategies as ways to create conditions that leverage differences to achieve the mission and goals of an organization. What follows is a chapter that examines culture and social group identities and explores differences as key drivers of organizational excellence. As diversity has moved from the social justice domain to the business agenda, the final chapter of the first section focuses on global diversity.

The book proposes that diversity management is an area of systematic study and scientific inquiry as well as a field of professional practice. The second section, "Skill-Based Learning," demonstrates this concept. It begins with a chapter on diagnosing diversity and addresses the myriad ways in which diversity is approached and operationalized in organizations. The old adage is true, "What doesn't get measured, doesn't get done." Thus, the focus of the next chapter is on how diversity is assessed, measured, and analyzed.

If measurement is a necessity when managing diversity, then building relationships is the key to effectively doing the work. Transforming organizations and managing conflict are the foci of the next two chapters, which explore how to manage the tensions that are inherent when differences are leveraged to create new ideas, new products, and new processes. The "Skill-Based Learning" section concludes with a chapter on how diversity and inclusion work can be integrated into business strategy, talent management, and work design.

The third and final section, "Professional Issues," brings together the theory and practice aspects of diversity management. Whether you are internal to an organization as a chief diversity officer or external to an organization as a consultant, diversity skills are necessary to move organizations forward. These concepts will be explored in the chapter on consultation skills.

The book primarily focuses on corporate organizations, yet we know that diversity is equally important to the work in nonprofits, educational institutions, faith-based organizations, and service organizations. To that end, a chapter on practicing diversity in specialized settings is included. The final chapter turns special attention to leading diversity effectively in contemporary society.

The breadth and depth of the concepts expressed in each of the chapters in all three sections are characterized by the subtitle of the book—*Inclusive Strategies for Driving Organizational Excellence.* In sum, the book serves as a standard discourse about diversity management and the great potential it has for adding value to engaged, high-performing organizations.

—Deborah L. Plummer, PhD, Editor

Acknowledgements

AS A PSYCHOLOGIST who began her professional career in clinical work with an emphasis in multicultural counseling, I relied on pioneers in the field of diversity management to understand how to apply what I knew about human differences to the organizational level. Many of the contributors to this text have been my teachers, either by attendance at their professional workshops or through reading their writing. Other contributors have been colleagues and mentees who have sharpened my thinking, challenged my assumptions, and helped to expand my worldview. As we work together to create inclusive organizations and communities, I have learned from and continue to learn with all of the contributors in this text. I am profoundly grateful to each of them for past, present, and future learning. I am especially grateful to Taylor Cox for writing the Foreword. His wisdom adds value to the learning.

Getting a book from idea to print is a mammoth task, and for this edition I depended upon the organizational skills of Managing Editor Holly Brown. Holly was able to build on the expertise, drive, and energy of Veronica Cook Euell, managing editor for the first edition. I am grateful to you both for your support for this project. Everyone who worked on this edition loved working with copyeditor Chip Cheek, whose brilliance with syntax and attention to detail are outstanding. Thank you, Chip. The design work of Tara Mayberry captured our hopes for bringing to the reader a book that could not only inform but inspire. Thank you, Tara.

I am lovingly grateful to my husband, Michael Bussey, for his unyielding support in my professional career along with my family, my first and forever diversity management teachers!

Onward and upward,
Deborah L. Plummer, PhD

Chapters at a Glance

SECTION I: THEORETICAL FOUNDATIONS

CHAPTER ONE
Overview of the Field of Diversity Management
Deborah L. Plummer

This chapter addresses the overarching themes that are present in the study of human differences. It provides an introduction to diversity management—exploring its nature and processes, assumptions and values, the forces that have shaped its contemporary form, and the professional practice of diversity. As an evolving field of theory, research, teaching, and practice, diversity management has its historical and theoretical roots in many disciplines. The chapter includes the historical and theoretical roots of diversity management and defines the parameters, the values, and the relationship of diversity management to social justice.

Frameworks and a glossary of diversity terms are contained in the chapter to assist the reader toward a collaborative understanding of the field and for conceptual clarity of these concepts throughout the book. It engages the reader through exercises and case studies for understanding diversity. This is an expanded and updated chapter from the first edition.

CHAPTER TWO
Moving to Strategic Diversity Management: A Necessary Shift
Melanie Harrington and April Thomas

The process of preparing a diversity strategic plan is complex and requires a number of essential tasks beyond creating a solid business case and rationale. It starts with conceptual clarity on the broad nature of diversity and the business case for making meaningful, sustainable progress toward an inclusive work environment.

The chapter presents four approaches to workforce mixtures: managing workforce diversity, managing strategic diversity, understanding differences, and managing pluralism. The goals and motives of each approach are examined. With this differentiation, the diversity practitioner can use these approaches as analysis tools to design a diversity strategic plan. The authors describe this as a dynamic process and provide ways for the practitioner to assess and change their diversity strategies to reflect shifting organizational realities.

Written by Dr. Roosevelt Thomas's longtime mentee and Dr. Thomas's daughter, who continues his work, this chapter builds on the noted work of the recently deceased diversity scholar and pioneer. Dr. Thomas was the author of the original chapter in the first edition.

CHAPTER THREE
Creating Inclusion for Oneself: Knowing, Accepting, and Expressing One's Whole Self at Work
Bernardo M. Ferdman and Laura Morgan Roberts

This chapter addresses the multiple and intersecting identities that comprise how one understands oneself as a cultural being. It addresses the work that individuals, including leaders, must do to foster inclusion for themselves and others. The authors explore how individuals understand and express themselves in their full identity at work while distinguishing between personality traits and those dimensions of diversity that are immutable and integral to the self.

This is a new chapter for this edition and is an updated chapter from work previously published in *Diversity at Work: The Practice of Inclusion*. Copyright permission has been obtained from the publisher to reprint and revise the chapter for publication in this text.

CHAPTER FOUR
Global Inclusion: The Mandate for Successful Organizations
Herbert Stevenson

This chapter explores global diversity, how it is viewed within and beyond the United States. Through the lenses of responsibility, accountability, and core values, the chapter explores how cultural differences shape daily perceptions and impact the effectiveness of achieving diversity and inclusion goals. It examines how values are embedded within these perceptions and discusses how they lead to the clashes between cultures.

The premise of this chapter is that there is no universally shared model of what defines diversity. As a result, how organizational cultures advance inclusion in a global society is culture-specific. It requires attention to a process of implementation that is aligned with the organization's values, needs, and business objectives.

This is a new chapter about a critical body of work in the field over the past ten years.

SECTION II: SKILL-BASED LEARNING

CHAPTER FIVE
Diagnosing Diversity in Organizations
Deborah L. Plummer

The aim of this chapter is to help practitioners understand the process of analyzing diversity in organizations. It focuses on the process of identifying the current state of an organization and the methods for analysis. Topics explored in this chapter include the process of organizational diagnosis through the lens of diversity, diagnostic tools that support inclusion, application of the process of data-gathering and analysis to diversity, feeding back diagnostic diversity information, and the challenges in diagnosing organizations in a diversity context.

This is a revised and updated chapter from the first edition.

CHAPTER SIX
Assessing, Measuring, and Analyzing Diversity
Laura Castillo-Page, Jennifer Eliason, and Norma Poll-Hunter

Diversity is often viewed as a "soft" and sometimes unclear contributor to an organization's performance and bottom line. This chapter demonstrates how assessing, measuring, and analyzing the impact of diversity initiatives can generate a wealth of resources for improved performance and enhanced productivity. The purpose of this chapter is to identify a brief sample of tools and procedures to assess, measure, and analyze diversity initiatives in quantitative and qualitative methodologies. It is designed to help outline methods to tie diversity to an organization's bottom-line performance outcomes. Assessing, measuring, and analyzing the impact of diversity initiatives is a critical link for success in diversity management and organizational performance, today and in the future.

This is a completely revised, reader-friendly chapter, discussing metrics in a manner that can benefit those without a deep statistical background. The chapter is written by authors who are directly and routinely engaged in diversity metrics as part of their work for a large professional organization.

CHAPTER SEVEN
Transforming Organization Cultures: Notes from the Field
Marilyn Loden

Heightening awareness of issues about human differences, particularly race and gender, has been the primary goal of diversity facilitation in the past. The author, a well-respected diversity thought leader and pioneer in the field, takes stock of the impact of past diversity educational efforts and charts the course for future diversity facilitation. By challenging us to redefine our priorities and the arena of diversity work, the author moves the field of diversity management beyond awareness. In addition, the chapter provides frameworks and tools that can take the work of facilitation to the next level of consolidating support and bridge-building.

This is a revised chapter from the first edition by the same author and is updated with several revised models and frameworks.

CHAPTER EIGHT
Building Inclusion Through Conflict-Resolution Mechanisms
Patricia Bidol-Padva

This chapter presents a conceptual framework for managing conflicts that result from the dynamics of differences. It distinguishes conflict that is rooted in human differences versus conflict that stems from systemic organizational issues. Organizational conflict occurs when one or more individuals are dissatisfied. The sources of the dissatisfaction in organizations with a diverse workforce often include such factors as unclear communications, the negative impact of policies and procedures, incompatible interests, cultural differences, power discrepancies, and the perception that someone is not respected.

As a framework for differentiating diversity conflict, this chapter describes a conflict-escalation cycle and offers a conflict-resolution system to aid organizations in collaborative resolution of diversity conflict.

This is a revised and updated chapter from the first edition by the same author, who is a seasoned and noted consultant in the field of diversity management.

CHAPTER NINE
Going Plaid: Integrating Diversity Into Business
Strategy, Talent Management, and Work Design
Deborah L. Plummer and C. Greer Jordan

Progressive organizations have taken heed that diversity needs to be woven into the overall business strategy and integrated into every aspect of an organization, very much like producing a vibrant plaid fabric. Yet most organizations are clueless as to how to make it happen and continue to manage diversity as a separate work function of human resources. This chapter explores the integrated nature of diversity as a critical function of talent acquisition, talent management, contemporary work design, leadership development, employee engagement, innovation, and globalization.

This is a new chapter that replaces two chapters from the first edition—one on internal and external relationship-building and one on diversity as a way of doing business. This chapter captures the topics of those two chapters concisely and provides more application of the frameworks.

SECTION III: PROFESSIONAL ISSUES

CHAPTER TEN

Consultation Skills: Creating Inclusive Cultures That Leverages Diversity for Higher Performance
Judith H. Katz and Frederick A. Miller

We live in challenging times, with organizations going through massive change and uncertainty. Organizations rely on the specialized skills of subject matter experts to help them achieve their business objectives. A workforce that is reliable, talented, and diverse, that is willing and able to contribute new thinking and ideas, and that collaborates and partners effectively among and across differences requires practitioners with seasoned judgment, visionary thinking, financial acumen, and influencing and negotiating skills.

This chapter outlines the key approaches and skills that change agents need to create and implement strategies that ensure people feel included, differences are leveraged, and people are able to do their best work in order to achieve organizational goals and higher levels of performance. It describes some of the assumptions on which the work of building inclusion and leveraging diversity is based, and outlines some of the skills, competencies, and behaviors that are essential for individuals involved in creating a culture of inclusion that leverages diversity.

This is a revised chapter from the first edition by the same authors. The chapter offers the current perspectives of two eminent professionals in the field of diversity and inclusion.

CHAPTER ELEVEN
Diversity Management in Specialized Settings:
Nonprofit and Faith-Based Organizations, Schools,
Communities, and Government Agencies
Jim Henkelman-Bahn and Jaqueline Bahn-Henkelman

The work of the diversity professional in nonprofit, faith-based, school, or other community organizations and government agencies resembles the work of the diversity professional in any organization. Talent acquisition and retention, leadership development, employee engagement, and conflict management are functions that are within the portfolio of diversity practitioners in all settings. The differences about nonprofit organizations and government agencies are their service orientation and the mission-driven emphasis that guides the work. These differences can either boost diversity goals or create barriers to diversity work.

Transforming nonprofit organizations and government agencies into truly diverse organizations is not a simple task and often is more challenging than working in corporate settings. This chapter presents the characteristics of these specialized settings, which require varied skill sets on the part of diversity practitioners, and presents case studies for application.

This is a revised chapter from the first edition by the same noted authors whose life work has been advancing diversity and inclusion in specialized settings.

CHAPTER TWELVE
Diversity Leadership: There's More
Ollie Malone

When organizations undertake diversity as a culture-change initiative, leaders have to be more than champions and advocates. In this chapter, the author draws from more than twenty-five years of experience helping leaders manage organizational change and create climates conducive to leveraging the talents of diverse populations. It outlines four key diversity leadership skills: assume ignorance, anticipate inclusion, attain insight, and advance intelligence.

This is an updated and revised chapter on diversity leadership from the first edition by the same author, an accomplished veteran in the field of diversity management.

TABLE OF CONTENTS

CHAPTER ONE

Overview of the Field of Diversity Management

Deborah L. Plummer

THIS BOOK IS ABOUT the field of diversity management—the theory and practice of understanding human differences. Perhaps when you think of diversity you think of programs and initiatives employed in organizations, communities, agencies, and schools rather than an entire discipline of study. You may associate diversity with the principle of respect, or simply think of it as race relations. You may broadly define diversity as another name for human differences such as race, ethnicity, gender, age, sexual orientation, religion, occupational role and status, mental and physical ability, and the numbers of other ways in which humans are different. You would be partially correct with any of these thoughts. The field of diversity management is broad and is most often experienced in practice rather than studied as a discipline.

Yet, while it is a field of professional practice, it is also an area of systematic study and scientific inquiry. The field of diversity management is rooted in several disciplines—most notably the applied behavioral and social sciences, business, and education. The domain of the field focuses on multiple levels of human systems—the individual, interpersonal, organizational, and societal. For example, on the individual level, such topics as use-of-self, social group identity development, and unconscious bias are studied. Interpersonally, communicating across differences, managing resistance and conflict, and collaborative problem-solving skills are explored. On the organizational level, functions such as creating the business rationale, diversity strategic planning, recruiting and retaining diverse work populations, and measuring and analyzing diversity initiatives would be part of the portfolio. On the societal level, topics of social justice, building inclusion, eradicating isms, and creating economic parity are prominent. Thus, in order to get a grasp of the field of diversity management, one has to look through a pretty wide lens.

You may be a bit overwhelmed already by this introduction to the many areas of diversity management. Hopefully, by providing frameworks for organizing the field, this chapter will help you get a handle on the big picture. We will explore the assumptions, values, and forces that shape contemporary diversity management and its professional practice.

The objectives of this chapter are to raise your awareness of and increase your understanding of the following topics:

- ✓ history of the diversity management field
- ✓ assumptions and values of the field of diversity management
- ✓ language of diversity and its implications for professional and personal growth
- ✓ frameworks for understanding the many aspects of diversity
- ✓ levels of human systems and how systems thinking helps us to understand diversity
- ✓ exploration of social group identity development and the cultural patterns that are part of American society
- ✓ unconscious bias and its impact on recruitment, retention, and promotion of underrepresented groups
- ✓ professional practice of diversity management

Historical Perspectives of Diversity Management

Knowing the past helps us understand the present and better envision the future. The theoretical roots of diversity management lie in the disciplines of business, psychology, education, and anthropology. Heavily influenced by social processes and the spirit and zeitgeist of the times, the field of diversity management has burgeoned since its conception in the 1960s. The brief outline of the historical roots of diversity management that follows will aid in understanding the past and present perspectives. The table depicts some of the highlights of diversity management by decade.

DIVERSITY TIMELINE

1960s
- Origins in civil rights movement
- Overt segregation
- Color- and gender-blind society
- Social and moral focus
- Researchers note the psychological effects of "isms" on the victim
- Racial and gender identity development theories established
- Assimilation and acculturation are frameworks for managing differences
- Cultural-deficit models represent thinking

1970s
- Dimensions/frameworks for diversity are established
- Racial and gender differences are the primary dimensions explored
- "Quotas" influence recruitment and retention efforts
- Legal approaches are the drivers for diversity initiatives
- Emphasis on recruitment of women and people of color

1980s
- Values in the workplace begin to be studied
- Hiring/performance/retention practices are examined for diversity
- Social justice becomes the business imperative
- Culturally different models replace deficit models

- Demographic projections in *Workforce 2000* make a business impact

1990s

- Theories of difference are established
- Pluralistic models dominate thinking
- Communications structures that support inclusion are researched and practiced
- Retention issues motivate organizations to be the "employer of choice"
- Organizations incorporate value-added practices
- Learning becomes the model for progressive organizations
- Global issues influence business thought and practice
- Diversity professional organizations begin
- Diversity degree program is established and diversity certification for professionals introduced

2000s

- Shift in the meaning of work puts more emphasis on inspirational leadership and valuing people
- Management models focus on people, purpose, and process rather than structure, strategy, and systems
- Age-related cohort differences challenge the boundaries of the dimensions of diversity
- Psychographics (understanding attitudes, emotions, and values of people) in addition to demographics become business drivers

2010s

- Diversity of thought and expression are considered along with human dimensions of diversity
- Leadership-driven diversity efforts become essential to business strategy
- Diversity is tied to innovation
- Diversity is linked to employee engagement and performance
- Technology tools support building inclusive work environments
- Global reality challenges how the United States exports diversity

How does your organization's timeline align with the diversity timeline? Are you ahead or behind? What trends do you forecast for the next decade?

The Language of Diversity

Language represents our thinking and words create worlds. So it is true for the word *diversity*. The meaning and implication of diversity have evolved over the years and provide us with a window into how differences in the workplace have been perceived and managed.

The changing demographics in the United States, often cited as the catalyst for the diversity movement, greatly influenced how the nation thought about, managed, and benefited from differences in the workplace. A traditional definition of diversity took into account the historical disadvantages borne by women and racial minority groups in regard to access and success in organizations and focused on compliance and equality. This traditional understanding of diversity was sufficient for successfully navigating a diverse workforce for many decades. With the aftermath of an atypical 2016 U.S. presidential election season focused on gender, age, and race issues; the public struggle between advocates of religious liberties and advocates for LGBT equality; immigration reform's impact on the economy; movements like Black Lives Matter; pressure by millennials and Generation Z workers to align business interests with a cause; and campaigns for hiring more people with disabilities, diversity remains a critical aspect of future workplace trends.

Technological advances have allowed us to get our information from customized sources tailored to align with what we want to know, understand, and believe, making it increasingly challenging to build coalitions and advance inclusion toward the benefit of all. The gig economy, where freelancers work side by side with full-time employees, giving rise to a blended workforce, has created a different dimension of diversity to manage (Schawbel, 2016). Augmented and virtual reality challenge business health and safety policies as well as our personal privacy (Lawson, 2014).

Research by Deloitte University Leadership Center for Inclusion (2015) explored the millennial generation's influence on transforming thinking about diversity and inclusion and their embrace of cognitive diversity rather than representation or compliance. Their research found that millennials extend the concept of diversity beyond integration of demographic differences. A contemporary approach to diversity, courted by millennials and Generation Z (born 1996–2012), incorporates diversity of thought, expression, and experience that is leveraged to achieve business outcomes and drive innovation. From a social justice framework, this perspective might be considered unacceptable, as it is thought to weaken or water down the impact of the isms on certain social identity groups. Distinguishing diversity from social justice adds yet another layer to unraveling how diversity is defined.

Whether the term is conceptualized from a traditional or contemporary lens, diversity predicates change. Its meaning has evolved over the years from its roots in race and gender relations, to building inclusive environments and managing basic human differences, to being a key driver of organizational excellence and innovation. The meaning of diversity is largely dependent on its context. The following sections place diversity in context and define it from both an individual and organizational perspective.

Defining Diversity

If you were to conduct an Internet search for a definition of diversity, in less than four seconds you would have over one hundred million results to choose from. The citations would range from topic-related scholarly articles to blog posts by people of all generations and from across the globe.

Diversity encompasses the many dimensions of human differences, including thought and expression. As we work toward understanding diversity in its fullest expression, a growing body of proven methodologies has established it as part of mainstream organizational work and as essential to an organization's success (Jayne & Dipboye, 2004; Kochan et al., 2003).

In an individual or a personal context, diversity refers to the differences among people with respect to race, ethnicity, culture, gender, gender expression, age, class, mental and physical abilities, sexual orientation, religion, stature, educational level, job role and function, and personality traits. It embraces the many ways in which we are similar to and different from other human beings. As an individual, I am like some people and unlike others. I am unique, yet I am a member of the human race and share other humans' genetic and emotional constitution. That is the *paradox of diversity*. We are unique, and we are the same.

Traditional approaches to understanding differences emerged from a dominance model. This model says that, yes, we are all alike, yet some of our inherent differences are considered better than others. Males are better than females, white skin is better than dark skin, able bodies are better than disabled bodies, young is better than old, heterosexual orientation is better than gay or lesbian orientation ... and the list could go on for every existing dimension of difference.

You are perhaps reading this and thinking how illogical it sounds to think that way. Yet we tend to see differences in a hierarchical manner. That is how the brain works to be efficient and organized. It is part of our evolutionary advantage as humans. Unfortunately, this kind of thought process leads us to treat differences as independent variables—as if you could go about your day only choosing to use one aspect of your identity. For example, entering a room with only your gender or your race or your mental abilities or your age.

Current thinking treats differences from a relational perspective and takes into account the intersectionality of our differences. Holvino (2012a) cites two major forces as the impetus for changing the meaning of identity in the twenty-first century—globalization and an intellectual/political shift in how language and culture are experienced. The free flow of goods, services, capital, and information across seamless national borders challenges the notion of stable identities (Ceglowski, 2000; Lewellen, 2002). In addition, identity is now constructed through language and social practices, which makes identity more contextual, multiple, malleable, and evolving (Calas & Smircich, 2006; Hall & DuGay, 1996). Holvino's scholarship (2012b) conceptualizes race, ethnicity, gender, class, sexuality, and other human differences as simultaneous processes of individual identity, institutional/organizational practices, and social/societal practices.

Thus, we as humans are a complex intersection of the many dimensions of diversity that make us unique and yet like other people. Such thinking supports an understanding of the complex interactions of social relations and fosters the skills necessary to navigate our increasingly multicultural world. I cannot separate my gender from my race or my ethnicity, or separate my mental and physical abilities, or separate my age or sexual orientation. I am a wonderfully made, complex set of variables that makes me *uniquely me.*

WORKING DEFINITIONS

☐ **DIVERSITY:** Differences among people with respect to age, class, ethnicity, gender, gender expression, health, physical and mental ability, race, sexual orientation, religion, stature, education level, job level and function, personality traits, and other human and social differences

☐ **CULTURAL DIVERSITY:** Inclusion and acceptance of the unique worldviews, customs, norms, patterns of behavior, and traditions of many groups of people

☐ **PLURALISM:** A culture that incorporates mutual respect, acceptance, teamwork, and productivity among people who are diverse

☐ **MULTICULTURALISM:** A pluralistic culture that reflects the interests, contributions, and values of members of diverse groups

Individual Diversity

We experience diversity at an individual or a personal level through a developmental process that enables us to express some aspects of ourselves as core to our identity and others that influence and shape our core but do not fundamentally change who we are and how we understand ourselves. For example, when I was a young adult, race, gender, and religion occupied a considerable portion of my depiction of who I was and how I expressed myself in the world. As I struggled with my issues of racial identity and place in the world as a black woman, my race and gender became the looking glasses for how I interacted with the world, and religion provided a way to make sense of these issues.

Today, as I grow older, age and mental/physical abilities represent a significant portion of my visual representation of my personal diversity identity. As my racial identity and gender role have been defined and stabilized, the developmental tasks of aging have become central to my understanding of the world and my everyday experience.

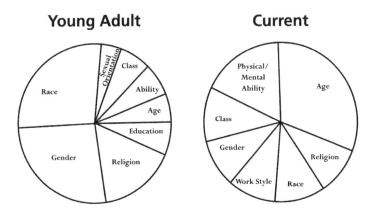

Young Adult   Current

The diagrams compare my past and present circles of diversity. Take a few minutes to think about your own circle of diversity.

Group Membership Identity

As unique as I am as an individual, I also share with others a group membership identity. Each individual, too, holds multiple identities. The expression of our identity is contextual and dependent on the human-system level at which our interactions take place. For example, for a black American woman traveling in Japan, her identity as an American might be more salient than her race or gender. For a gay man among other male executives, his sexual orientation might be more salient. A female chair of a basic science department might experience acting out her identity as an administrator when she works to implement a new policy, whereas others might give more prominence to her group identity as a woman.

Our diversity package (my specific race, gender, age, ability, sexual orientation, stature, religion, etc.) determines what level of system we engage in and the lens out of which we see our world. For example, when traveling with a white friend in a predominantly white setting, it is not unusual for another African American to say hello to me or to nod and smile. This sometimes confuses my white friend, who is baffled when she finds out that I do not personally know this individual. I explain that it is a connection of group membership identity that has prompted the greeting. Similarly, if a man finds himself in a room with all women, when another male enters there is generally an acknowledgment (often with a sigh of relief) that someone else who shares the same gender (group membership identity) is present. A physically large woman in a graduate program comments on how happy she is to see other women her size in the class. Discovering that individuals at a workshop share the same religion often brings about a sense of community for those identified members. I am sure that you can think of countless examples when you have been more aware of your group membership identity than your individual personality. You may have experienced this not only on the group level but also on the organizational or societal level. Your identity as an employee of Company X makes you different from employees of Company Y. At a meeting of Company X and Y you may be acutely aware of your differences and how similar you are to your coworker in your presentation and communication style. This may not have been in your awareness at all when you were working together at Company X. If you have ever traveled abroad you may have been much more aware of your American identity (societal level) than you ever are when you are home in America. Thus, we experience diversity interacting with system levels routinely and almost unconsciously.

Diversity in Action

Diversity cuts across all levels of human systems and intersects with the multiple identities that an individual possesses.

- **INDIVIDUAL/INTRAPSYCHIC:** Boundary is the self-system (e.g., thoughts, feelings).

- **INTERPERSONAL:** Boundary is with an individual or with a group or subgroup (e.g., connecting with spouse/partner or with a family or with the children of a family).

- **GROUP:** Boundary is a shared identity (e.g., racial identity or nation of origin or religious affiliation).

- **ORGANIZATIONAL/INSTITUTIONAL:** Boundary is a systematic set of purposes, rules, practices, and traditions (e.g., work affiliation and religious affiliation).

- **SOCIETAL:** Boundaries are many facets of culture (e.g., language, norms, values, sanctions, politics, and acculturation).

- **GLOBAL:** Boundary is worldwide (e.g., Facebook, Twitter, Instagram, World Wide Web).

(Updated from Gestalt Institute of Cleveland, class notes, 1995)

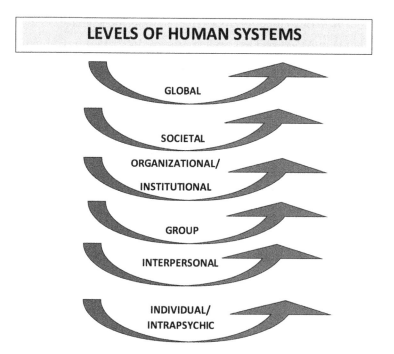

LEVELS OF HUMAN SYSTEMS

GLOBAL

SOCIETAL

ORGANIZATIONAL/
INSTITUTIONAL

GROUP

INTERPERSONAL

INDIVIDUAL/
INTRAPSYCHIC

Organizational Diversity

When organizations became aware of the changing numbers and the cultural and gender differences that would be reflected in the workforce during the twenty-first century, many organizational leaders and managers began to examine their minority representation and company policies and practices for inclusiveness. Against the backdrop of equal employment opportunity and affirmative action, the notion of fairness and doing what is right motivated many companies to increase their numbers of women and people of color. Other companies became acutely aware that unless they matched their demographics to the demographics of the consumers and constituents they wished to service, they would suffer as a business. Fully functioning organizations realized that incorporating diversity into the way they did work and including the different perspectives and thinking that human differences bring would give them a competitive advantage. Progressive companies knew that diversity not only made good business sense but that it also translated into business cents, which meant that diversity in the workplace was a foundation for innovation.

> Fair Organizations → Consumer-Oriented Organizations → Learning Organizations → Fully Functioning Organizations → Progressive Organizations

While diversity on an individual or interpersonal level focuses on respect and honoring of differences for healthy personal and professional relationships and peaceful communities, diversity on the organizational level is tied to organizational effectiveness and economic growth.

It has often been said that employees are an organization's greatest assets. Thus, it makes intellectual sense that dollars be spent to develop and support human resources. Although a great deal of research, dating back to the Elton Mayo and Hawthorne studies, reveals that the noneconomic social processes of work are an important contributor to productivity, some organizations disregard or make secondary the social factors of work. From the research on teams and group dynamics we know that heterogeneous groups often experience decreased cohesion and increased conflict, but once a shared focus is achieved, these groups evidence increased productivity and creativity (Jayne & Dipboye, 2004). Productivity and creativity are further increased if the diverse group has the skills and support systems necessary to coalesce (Kochan et al., 2003). Organizations that connect diversity to effective practices support their employees with training to help them become culturally competent and have structures that maintain a diversity-affirming environment.

Fortune (Haimerl, 2015; Zarya, 2015) reports that minority business enterprises are the fastest-growing business segment in America. African American, Hispanic, and Asian American markets represent an annual spending power of $700 billion. Seventy-five percent of consumers would buy a product from a socially responsible company or would switch retailers if cost and quality were equal. Approximately half of all business travelers are now women. The global market now compels most American companies to be more competitive in finding and retaining employees. Employees of the new generation bring different and expanded expectations to the workplace, such as a spiritual meaning and sense of making a contribution. With these facts it is easy to make the business case for managing diversity, and they demonstrate that it would simply be shortsighted not to manage diversity well (Thomas Reuter Poll, 2016).

Diversity from an organizational framework refers to utilization and leveraging of human differences toward organizational effectiveness and productive business goals. The foundations of organizational diversity are rooted in a clear understanding of the interplay between the individual and interpersonal diversity dynamics and social justice issues that are so much a part of the fabric of our society.

For example, there have been several cases where an employee's hairstyle (e.g., an African American woman with a braided style, or an American Indian man with a long ponytail) has been questioned as appropriate for the workplace, particularly in companies where profits are tied to selling to the mainstream public. Company policies have leaned toward establishing more conservative or conventional styles (typically patterned after European Americans) as the norm. The business case from this perspective is clear: if customers are impacted negatively or are even mildly curious about the hairstyle, then it will distract from the focus on the product line or service and ultimately result in the loss of a sale. The other side of this issue is equally compelling: a hairstyle is a personal preference and not a requirement for selling a product. Americans represent many different cultures, and no one cultural preference should rank over another.

What do you think about this issue? How would you handle this diversity dilemma?

Companies that are culturally competent and are characterized by learning and organizational effectiveness understand the complexity of this issue and focus on what will make the business more effective and maintain a high-performing workforce that leverages diversity. To give one side of the coin more weight than the other will lead to imbalance. Resolving this issue will mean that employees who choose to wear a culturally specific hairstyle will need to be supported with the necessary competencies to manage a possible negative reaction from a customer or even mild curiosity in ways that get the job done without offending the client. And the organization needs to further support the employee and the consumer with skills to keep the sales focused on the product or service line. Consumers also need to be educated about the value placed on diversity by an organization. Remember the majority of Americans support and expect social responsibility from companies. When cultural diversity is affirmed in a manner that makes good business sense, it is hard not to support the company's mission and vision and ultimately buy the product or use its services.

Hopefully, the interplay between individual, interpersonal, and organizational diversity stood out for you in that example. The employee exercises his/her right for a hairstyle preference (individual level), which impacts the employee/client relationship (interpersonal), which in turn may or may not affect a sale and ultimately the bottom line of the company (organizational).

Related Organizational Diversity Terms

In exploring the field of diversity management there are other frequently used terms directly related to organizational effectiveness. Knowing these terms will be useful in your understanding of organizational diversity. Progressive organizations have moved beyond equal employment opportunity requirements and matching the demographics of organizations to critical consumers or constituent groups to connecting diversity to organizational effectiveness and understanding the interplay between diversity and innovation. Here are some definitions of terms that reflect the incorporation of diversity into the organization's culture in a manner that is diversity proficient:

☐ **LEVERAGING DIVERSITY:** Enhancing organizational effectiveness and performance by making use of the different perspectives, experiences, and abilities that people bring to the workplace

☐ **CULTURAL COMPETENCE:** The capacity to function effectively with all cultures and to successfully navigate a multicultural society

☐ **ORGANIZATIONAL CULTURAL COMPETENCE:** The capacity to function effectively with all cultures and to creatively utilize a diverse workforce for meeting business goals and enhancing performance

Workplace Diversity Trends

Think about the changing demographics in the workforce—the growing racial/ethnic population, the aging population, the number of women in the workforce, the generational cohorts. How have these demographics influenced workplace trends? Can you identify what those trends might be? Compare your list to the following:

- compensation equity across race and gender
- work flexibility (how work gets done and where it gets done)
- expression of religion in the workplace
- diversity of thought tied to innovation

- thinking and acting from a global perspective
- technology and its impact on our ways of knowing
- shift in the meaning of work from "living to work" to "working to live"
- interaction of four age groups with differing values and attitudes in the workplace:
  - veterans (b. 1922–1944)
  - baby boomers (b. 1945–1964)
  - Generation X (b. 1965–1980)
  - millennials (b. 1981–1999)
  - Generation Z (b. 2000–present day)
- the "war for talent"—recruiting and retaining people with the best skills to meet business objectives and achieve the mission
- emotional intelligence, including diversity competencies necessary for workplace success

Supplier Diversity

Diverse and women-owned business enterprises are among the fastest-growing segments of the U.S. economy. Organizations realize the sourcing products and services from previously underused suppliers helps to sustain and progressively transform their supply chain. A Supplier Diversity program is a proactive business program which encourages the use of minority-owned, women owned, veteran owned, LGBT-owned, service-disabled-veteran owned, historically underutilized business, and Small Business Administration(SBA)-defined small business concerns as suppliers. As a proactive business process that seeks to provide equal access to purchasing opportunities and promote vendor participation reflective of the diverse business community, it is most effective when aligned with the organization's overall diversity plan.

The rationale for such practices is strong. The aphorism John F. Kennedy used in his 1963 speech, "a high tide lifts all boats," is often used in reference to Supplier Diversity Programs because utilizing diverse suppliers is economic empowerment for the community. Beyond a requirement for federal funding, it increases political and social capital for organizations and is simply the right thing to do.

Components of a successful Supplier Diversity Program includes tracking and measurement by analyzing the amount of money spent with diverse vendors, benchmarking utilization expenditures, using inclusive language in the RFP process, and contracting goals by categories and departments. Building relationships with community organizations that promote minority and women-owned businesses allows for efficiency in identifying qualified suppliers for advancing supplier diversity goals. Mentoring and supporting diverse vendors by sourcing and creating joint ventures and alliances with larger, established vendors, providing direction and support for certification assistance and training creates success for vendors and for the organization.

Thinking About Global Diversity

Managing diversity becomes even more challenging when organizations based in the United States try to implement domestic diversity policies and practices in cultures outside of the country. Gaining conceptual clarity on the definition of diversity and reaching consensus is an important task for any organization, whether it is a mom-and-pop operation or a corporate conglomerate. Working across geographic borders requires getting to know and understand the deep structures of that culture in order to determine what inclusive policies and practices will enhance the mission and achieve the business objectives of the organization. The bottom line is that the United States cannot export diversity; however, it can champion and promote diversity and inclusion within global organizations.

In what ways do cultural values influence business practices?

In multinational settings where cultural values are not shared, is it possible for global organizations based in the United States to achieve their business objectives and still practice diversity (e.g., gender equity and LGBT rights)?

"Big 8" Diversity Global Trends

Gleaned from the National Intelligence Council report on global trends (2017) and current thinking, here are nine conditions that underscore diversity and inclusion as a priority area of work:

- **CHANGING FACE OF AMERICA:** It's not only about race and gender but our multiple and intersecting identities and experiences across the globe.
- **CHANGING NATURE OF POWER:** How power is conceptualized and operationalized has been influenced by generational differences and technology.
- **POPULIST POLITICS:** What and who informs us and how we become media literate is a critical issue with far-reaching implications for our future.
- **INCREASED DEMAND FOR ADVANCED EDUCATION:** There is a stark realization that advanced education is necessary to compete in a post-industrial economy.
- **ADVANCEMENT OF WOMEN:** The elimination of discrimination against women and girls and their empowerment will lead to achievement of equality between women and men as partners and beneficiaries of a better global society.
- **LIFE/WORK INTEGRATION:** Quality of life and family will shape our work environments, the nature of how business gets done, and how we live in communities.
- **FAITH AND SPIRITUALITY:** Toxic leaders, greed, and global awareness have moved people to emphasize their values and life's purpose.
- **ACTIVIST CONSUMERS AND CUSTOMERS:** Buyers will continue to drive innovation and accelerate a transformation of the value chain for products and services.
- **NETWORKED ECONOMY:** The emerging economic order within the information society requires products and services to be created through global networks rather than just developed and shared locally.

Defining Inclusion

I have often made the analogy that inclusion is like being at home in someone else's home rather than just being a guest. If you're a guest in someone's home, the standard is that you will be treated respectfully. Being given an invitation to "make yourself at home" gives you a piece of the ownership. You can open the refrigerator door and get your own drink, and feel comfortable being there. Although people understand this inclusion analogy of "being at home in someone else's home," it still is a bit too subjective. To quote Benjamin Franklin, "Guests, like fish, seem to smell after three days." Inclusion extends way beyond a three-day invitation.

Inclusion is creating *conditions* that leverage differences—race, gender, gender expression, age, sexual orientation, class, religion, health, stature, educational level, physical and mental ability, job level and function, personality traits, thought and expression, and other human and social differences.

In the workplace we leverage our differences in order to drive business outcomes, spur innovation, and achieve the mission of the organization. In our communities, we leverage our differences to create peaceful environments and transform our society for the good of all. This is a very difficult and challenging process and measured not by whether or not someone *feels* that they are included. Feeling included is a by-product of an inclusive culture.

As a psychologist, I know that there are a number of variables that load into someone's feeling state and it is possible for someone not to feel included despite inclusive practices and policies. The reverse of that is also true. It is possible for someone to feel included despite discriminatory policies and inequitable practices. We evidence this phenomenon when an astounding number of women do not feel or experience sexism despite consensus that specific behaviors would be considered legal harassment, or when a number of people of color do not feel or experience any racist behaviors or practices despite reports of documented discrimination. Inclusion is more than a feeling.

Through my research with colleagues at University of Massachusetts Medical School, I've laid out eight inclusion factors:

1. **COMMON PURPOSE:** individual experiences a connection to the mission, vision, and values of the organization

2. **TRUST:** individual has confidence that the policies, practices, and procedures of the organization will allow them to bring their best and full self to work

3. **APPRECIATION OF INDIVIDUAL ATTRIBUTES:** individual is valued and can successfully navigate the organizational structure in their expressed group identities

4. **SENSE OF BELONGING:** individual experiences their social group identities being connected and accepted in the organization

5. **ACCESS TO OPPORTUNITY:** individual is able to find and utilize support for their professional development and advancement

6. **EQUITABLE REWARD AND RECOGNITION:** individual perceives the organization as having equitable compensation practices and non-financial incentives

7. **CULTURAL COMPETENCE (OF THE INSTITUTION):** individual believes the institution has the capacity to make creative use of its diverse workforce in a way that meets business goals, enhances performance, and achieves the mission

8. **RESPECT**: individual experiences a culture of civility and positive regard for diverse perspectives, ways of knowing, and expression

These factors are focused on organizational settings but can easily be applied to communities. The factors are interdependent and should be considered in aggregate. When these factors are in place, inclusion can then be defined as a set of social processes in which an individual experiences the following:

- access to information and social support
- acquisition of or influence in shaping accepted norms and behavior
- security within an identity group or in a position within the organization
- access to and ability to exercise formal and informal power (Jordan, 2009)

Full acceptance of membership in an organization depends on an individual's ability to be seen as the prototype of that organization. The prototypical member will personify the norms, behaviors, values, and even appearances seen as important to maintaining the culture of the organization and power relations within it (Dovidio & Gaertner, 2000). As a result, diversity or divergence from the prototype introduces tensions around who belongs in the organization. When understood and managed effectively, this tension can be described as a good or creative tension that produces new ideas, new products, and new processes (Thomas, 1991, 1996, 1999). Creative tensions appear and are negotiated through social dynamics that influence inclusion as it is experienced by individuals. These dynamics are the result of three factors experienced or perceived by individuals:

- **INCLUSION-EXCLUSION:** the quality, frequency, and tone of day-to-day social interactions and interpersonal experiences that move individuals toward or away from a sense of full membership
- **IDENTITY INTEGRATION:** the extent to which individuals are able to bring their social group identities (e.g., gender, race, national culture, sexual orientation) into the organization and still realize full membership
- **SOCIAL POWER:** the authority or legitimacy individuals have in exercising power within the organization or the degree to which they experience differences in how power is exercised over them compared to those who enjoy full membership (Jordan, 2009)

At the organizational level, inclusion dynamics are reinforced and embedded in an organization's culture through its:

- **MISSION, VISION, VALUES** (uses inclusive language and specifically references diversity);
- **STRATEGY, STRUCTURE, SYSTEMS** (organization is structured to allow for diverse ways of knowing, limits bureaucracy, and information and resources are accessible); and
- **POLICIES, PRACTICES, PROCEDURES** (open, transparent, and consistently applied).

Thus, inclusion can be best understood in its dynamic state. The diversity of the employee base, the inclusion dynamics they experience, and an organization's culture all influence the emergence of an inclusive work environment.

The Language of Culture

The terms *culture, ethnicity, nationality,* and *race* have often been used interchangeably in our everyday speech. Yet learning the distinct meanings of these terms and using them intentionally in our conversations can increase the effectiveness of cross-cultural and cross-racial communications. The following are some working definitions of these terms:

- ☐ **CULTURE:** a socially transmitted, shared design for living and patterns for interpreting reality on the basis of values and practices of a group of people who interact together over time

- ☐ **ETHNICITY:** a group of people related through a common racial, national, tribal, religious, linguistic, or cultural origin

- ☐ **NATIONALITY:** the status of belonging to a particular territory by origin, birth, or naturalization

- ☐ **RACE:** a pseudo-biological system of classifying people on the basis of shared genetic history or physical characteristics

Examine these definitions and see if you can determine the many cultural groups to which you belong, your ethnicity, your nationality, and your race. As a black (race) Jamaican/Panamanian (ethnicity)

American (nationality), I am aware of the many cultural groups of which I am a part (Catholic, educator, psychologist, middle class, etc.). Culture influences our thinking and behavior in ways that are most likely unconscious. These impacts are transmitted through family, the educational system, and societal practices.

The United States of America is host to over three hundred cultures that differ around such issues as control, independence, gender roles, time orientation, and risk behavior. Historically, European American culture has greatly influenced and set the standard for most American norms. Take, for example, time orientation. Researchers and anthropologists have distinguished between circular time cultures, which experience time as a circle wherein each point in time is sacred and worthy of being experienced fully in the moment, and cyclical time cultures, which experience time as being composed of the past, present, and future, with attention given to the future (Carr-Ruffino, 2013; Pant, 2016). In some cultures, time is determined by repeated cycles of activities, such as the agricultural cycle of planting, cultivating, and harvesting. From this perspective, time is only viewed in the past and present tense. Because of today's global workforce, which includes people from many different cultures, time orientation can present challenges in diverse settings.

For example, if a meeting is scheduled to start at 9:00 a.m., does that mean we begin the agenda promptly at 9:00 a.m., or do we begin to gather in the room and greet one another at 9:00 a.m.? Is the gathering as central to a successful meeting as the prompt attention to the agenda? When would someone be considered late, and what would be the consequences of such behavior?

What do you think? How would you handle time management in a meeting of culturally diverse teams?

Approaches to Managing Culture

Organizations with diverse work environments struggle to manage cultural diversity successfully. With the understanding that enabling individuals to fully express who they are maximizes creativity and productivity, organizations now consider managing diversity to be an essential component of effective strategy and institutional excellence. Managing differences evokes a bit of discomfort individually and interpersonally, and as a consequence there is discomfort at the organizational level.

Historically, most organizations and community agencies have solved the cultural dilemma by adopting one of the following approaches:

1. **CULTURAL-DEFICIENT APPROACH:** Popular in the 1960s and 1970s, cultures other than white European were considered to be lacking in cultural strengths; therefore, the best approach to dealing with those who were culturally different was to provide them with opportunities and education for cultural development. This approach is consistent with the melting pot/assimilation model, which was (and, some would argue, still is) dominant in America. Minority populations melted into or assimilated with the majority culture.

2. **CULTURAL-BLIND APPROACH:** Considered by many to be forward thinking, this approach deemphasizes cultural differences and emphasizes cultural similarity. In theory, this approach appears to be diversity-affirming, but in practice, it demonstrates a hierarchical and superior approach. In other words, to deal with differences, the idea is to pretend that the differences do not exist.

3. **CULTURAL-DENIAL APPROACH:** This approach also lays emphasis on cultural sameness, but instead of being blind to differences, the existence of differences is ignored. "We are all human beings. We are all Americans. We all put our pants on the same way. We all have red blood inside." Denial of cultural roots, the historical impact for that diversity dimension, and variance in the experience of the American Dream is prevalent in this approach.

4. **CULTURAL-TOURIST APPROACH:** This approach emphasizes the strengths of each culture and celebrates differences by sharing culture. We "visit" each other's cultures, and are welcome guests. Cultural feasts that facilitate sharing foods and traditions (usually in the form of dance and dress) are popular in organizations and educational settings. Simplistic in its orientation, this approach does not deal with the differences in expression of cultural values and norms that often lead to clashes and miscommunication.

5. **CULTURAL-TAPESTRY APPROACH:** This approach recognizes and celebrates the differences that are evident in multicultural environments. Like an exquisite tapestry that holds individual artistic impressions yet is also a unified art piece in its totality, organizations that abide by this approach incorporate the various ways of knowing and thinking and the various perspectives into the very fabric of how business is done and the mission is achieved.

What approach does your organization use? Are there more effective approaches to take to support your diversity goal?

The "Big Eight" Diversity Dimensions

Diversity management professionals and researchers have found that the following eight dimensions of human diversity are the ones most often managed for organizational effectiveness in work environments:

1. Race
2. Gender
3. Ethnicity/nationality
4. Organizational role/function
5. Age
6. Sexual orientation
7. Mental/physical ability
8. Religion

Fondly called the "Big Eight" by diversity practitioners, these dimensions and their critical issues have been the subject of intense research. The following chart summarizes these findings:

DIMENSION	CRITICAL ISSUES	INTERVENTION
Race	Communication styles, perceptions/stereotypes, unconscious bias, microinequities, microaggressions, locus of control, career mobility, competitive vs. cooperative behavior, time orientation, partisan politics, philosophical compatibility, loyalty	Diversity awareness and skill-building training, recruitment and retention of diverse employees, multicultural mentoring, group dynamics and team-building sessions, discretionary power mapping

DIMENSION	CRITICAL ISSUES	INTERVENTION
Gender	Communication styles, perceptions/stereotypes, unconscious bias, work-life balance, career mobility, competitive vs. cooperative behavior, partisan politics, loyalty, understanding and inclusion of gender expression and transgender individuals	Diversity awareness and skill training, glass-ceiling audits, cross-gender mentoring, education on transgender population
Ethnicity/ Nationality	Communication styles, assimilation vs. acculturation issues, perceptions/stereotypes, career mobility	Mentoring, diversity awareness and skill-building training
Sexual Orientation	Homophobia, sexual double standard, heterosexism, lavender glass ceiling, LGBT elder care, family, adoption	Sexual-orientation education, support and affinity groups, safe-space initiatives, Bring Your Full Self to Work training
Organizational Role/Function	Us vs. them, communication, values, partisan politics, loyalty	Diversity council / task force, deep-dive sessions, diversity dialogues, town-hall sessions
Mental/ Physical Ability	Socialization, coworker sensitivity, transportation, technical support, career mobility	ADA education, reasonable accommodations, protection from undue hardship, accessibility @ work, technology fairs
Age	Younger: work ethics, values, work-life balance, creativity meaning Older: skill obsolescence, retirement, loyalty, recognition, communication styles	Cross-generational work teams, diversity training, diversity dialogue sessions, technology fairs

DIMENSION	CRITICAL ISSUES	INTERVENTION
Religion	Religious practice during the workday, respect, prejudice, perceptions/stereotypes, religious freedoms	Diversity-awareness training, reasonable accommodations, case-by-case evaluation, interfaith ERG

Understanding Race and Sexual Orientation

Of all of the above dimensions of diversity, arguably the ones most politically and socially loaded are race and sexual orientation. Despite empirical data that support that neither of these is reflected at the genetic level, categorization of race and sexual orientation persists. Since the 1960s, scientists have adopted a "no-race" position, stating that biological variability does not conform to discrete categories labeled as "race." There is simply one race—the human race.

Similarly, though several studies have suggested a combination of biological and postnatal factors, the American Psychological Association has concluded that no findings from any scientific studies have emerged that permit scientists to conclude that sexual orientation is determined by any particular factor or factors. Simply put, we do not know what determines a person to be heterosexual or LGBT. Some researchers believe sexual orientation to be an extension of gender and part of its fluidity (Ross, Daneback, & Månsson, 2012).

Why then do racial categories and sexual orientations exist? They remain as social constructs that allow us to organize our thinking about identity and behavior as we experience them. This is why it is imperative that we remain lifelong learners when it comes to understanding people. Our brains are hardwired not to manage differences well. When we experience differences, those areas in our brains designed to analyze and interpret signals are often routed to the emotional section, where we are most susceptible to the socialization processes that lead to stereotyping, and we experience what is called an "amygdala hijack" (Goleman, 1995). Left unattended, stereotypes can lead to the perpetuation of destructive beliefs and attitudes (Page-Gould, 2010).

Let's take a moment to define and differentiate stereotypes from generalizations and cultural patterns.

- ☐ **STEREOTYPE:** a widely held belief usually oversimplified and based on limited data and perception

- ☐ **GENERALIZATION:** an inference or conclusion derived from empirical data

- ☐ **CULTURAL PATTERN:** the behaviors, attitudes, and beliefs practiced by a critical mass of a cultural group

Because these concepts are closely related, it is challenging to understand the differences when experiencing them in your everyday life. For example, a *stereotype* about Asians being conformists may have its roots in the *generalization* of a group preference over an individual one, which is linked to a *cultural pattern* of valuing harmony. Nevertheless, to attach the label of conformist to all Asians would definitely lead to cultural miscommunication and less-than-satisfactory personal and professional relationships.

Other Relevant Terms

Growing up, all of us were embedded and socialized in our cultures. As a result, most of us believe our cultural practices to be the norm for human behavior. For example, when I was a child, my mother exposed me to the Girl Scouts organization. Because I was raised Catholic and attended a predominantly white Irish Catholic school, my mother intentionally chose a troop for me that was comprised mostly of black American girls. It was within this context that I learned Negro spirituals. Consequently, I never distinguished those songs from the traditional Girl Scout songs I had learned. Because our troop leaders, too, did not make any distinction, I assumed all songs I learned in the context of Girl Scouts were "Girl Scout songs." Imagine my surprise when I found out during a county Girl Scouts summer camp that "Woke Up This Morning" and "Come By Here" were not Girl Scout songs!

Because of the human socialization process, we are all ethnocentric and culturally myopic to some extent. In addition, the human brain is designed to be reactive to the environment rather than to be proactive and take a reasoned approach. The brain specializes in quick generalizations, not subtle distinctions. We may claim to have no biases or believe that any prejudices we might have are under our control, but we all possess unconscious, hardwired processes that do not allow us to behave in egalitarian ways (Campbell, Whitehead, & Finkelstein, 2009).

We need to widen the lenses through which we see the world and remain culturally sensitive in the process. The following are other definitions useful to understanding the dynamics of cultural differences.

☐ **WORLDVIEW:** an individual's or a group's unique perspective or way of interpreting life's experiences

☐ **CULTURAL SENSITIVITY:** basic and obvious respect for and appreciation of various cultures that may differ from ours

☐ **ETHNOCENTRISM:** the tendency to use our group as a norm or standard by which to assess other groups

☐ **CULTURAL MYOPIA:** the belief that our culture is appropriate to all situations and relevant to all other individuals

☐ **PREJUDICE:** favorable or unfavorable prejudgment of people on the basis of their group membership

☐ **ISMS:** destructive attitudes or beliefs, such as racism, sexism, heterosexism, ableism, classism, ageism, and other forms of oppression based in power and prejudice about human differences

☐ **SOCIAL JUSTICE:** elimination of oppression and the isms to create a full and equal participation of all groups in a society where the distribution of resources is equitable and all members are physically and emotionally safe and secure

☐ **PRIVILEGE:** A social process whereby unearned rights, rewards, benefits, access, opportunities or advantages are received simply due to social group identity membership and without regard to achievement

☐ **UNCONSCIOUS BIAS:** our natural preference for or social categorization of people who look like us, sound like us, and share our same values and beliefs

Managing Ethnocentrism, Cultural Myopia, and Unconscious Bias

No matter how much we value diversity, successfully navigating our increasingly multiracial and multicultural society requires cultural competence. Our brains are hardwired in ways that help us to be efficient and stay safe; however, those same advantages also present challenges when we encounter differences, particularly those differences associated with negative social loadings grounded in the historical roots of inequality.

Just as we have to work to learn new skills to keep up with technological advancements, we have to do the same to be culturally competent. One of the first steps toward this is to recognize and acknowledge that we are all ethnocentric and culturally myopic in our thinking and that we have biases that shape our interactions with one another.

Acknowledging our ethnocentrism, cultural myopia, and unconscious biases extends beyond the thought process of just stating, "I own my biases!" Recall that our brains are hardwired to maintain these biases, so we have to do things actively that interrupt our natural inclination to believe that everyone who thinks and acts as we do is right and normal.

Pioneers in the Field of Diversity Management

The field of diversity management has many unsung heroes. The complete list would certainly be extensive if we included the many diversity champions. However, this section snapshots a few of the pioneers in the field for their contributions to the scholarship and practice of diversity management:

- *Taylor Cox:* As a researcher, professor, and consultant, he systematically and objectively analyzed cultural diversity in organizations, effectively blending theory and practice.
- *Elsie Y. Cross:* She inaugurated a workshop on race and men and women in the workplace in the 1970s. She coined the term *managing a diverse workforce* and then shortened it to *managing diversity.*
- *Lee Gardenswartz and Anita Rowe:* This consulting team merged diversity with management trends such as team-building in their professional resources and in practice.
- *Lewis Griggs:* His organization of videos, computer-learning products, and sponsorship of annual diversity conferences disseminated the message of diversity to millions.
- *David Jamieson and Julie O'Mara:* As consultants and authors of *Managing Workforce 2000: Gaining the Diversity Advantage,* their practice and research examined strategies for effectively recruiting and retaining employees of different skills and perspectives.
- *Judith Katz:* Through writings and research, she reframed the system of racism to educate whites on the complicity of the practice.
- *Marilyn Loden:* Through extensive research and experience, she designed models for full participation of diverse employees.

- *Frederick A. Miller:* He pioneered a methodology for strategic culture change in major corporations.
- *Lee Mun Wah:* Co-founder of Stir-Fry Productions and master trainer, he revolutionized the field of diversity through internationally acclaimed documentary films and seminars.
- *Robert Terry:* A leadership development guru, he wrote the book *For Whites Only,* a pioneering examination of racism geared toward white Americans that enlightened people of all races.
- *R. Roosevelt Thomas, Jr.:* Through his writings and research, he expanded the understanding of diversity and linked diversity management to organizational culture change.
- *Edith Whitfield Seashore and Charles Seashore:* Organizational development and change strategists, they incorporated intentional use-of-self frameworks in their practice and teaching.

Managing Diversity in Your Personal and Professional Life

I have often made the statement that despite three decades devoted to studying, teaching, and writing about the topic of diversity, the learning will never be completed. Diversity is an endless topic for exploration, and we will always be trying to make sense of it. Sometimes I hear people reduce diversity management to an issue of basic respect. It is truly that and much more. Sometimes people define diversity as simply differences. Diversity is that and much more. There are those who believe diversity is no more than a passing trend, dreamt up and kept alive by consultants to make money. Yet there is not a consultant alive who could sustain diversity's energy unless it had some reality and meaning in the lives of American workers. As our world and workforce continue to become increasingly diverse, having the skills to navigate these environments becomes a necessity.

Use of Self as a Tool for Managing Diversity

The self is a psychological term that refers to one's inner experience. We are free to share what goes on in our inner world with others or to keep the experience to ourselves. Our inner experience is constantly being impacted by what goes on in our environment. It houses all our history as well as our reactions to our world. Thus, the first place where diversity management needs to happen is within us. This is often a harder task than managing diversity for others, but learning to utilize yourself as a tool for managing personal and professional diversity issues is your greatest asset. The following is a starter list of some prescriptive behaviors for self-management of diversity issues.

Conditions for Self-Management of Diversity and Inclusion

1. Values a variety of opinions and insights
2. Recognizes the challenges and learning opportunities that new perspectives bring
3. Expectations of others are based on individual traits and qualities rather than social group identity
4. Seeks out ways to personally and professionally develop diversity competencies
5. Encourages and accepts openness in others
6. Makes people feel valued
7. When a diversity mistake is made, demonstrates emotional resilience
8. Spends time with a wide variety of people

9. Has a clear sense of self as a person of culture
10. Has a conceptual understanding of the field of
    diversity management

Effective diversity management begins with awareness and development of one's self in order to experience the positive impact of human diversity. Continued reading, engaging with diverse groups in dialogue, attendance at diversity and inclusion workshops and classes, and using social media to promote mutual understanding will further your personal understanding of diversity and enhance these professional skills in the workplace:

- collaborative learning
- creative management of differences
- conflict and collaborative problem-solving
- communicating across differences
- cultural-specific discernment skills

The Professional Practice of
Diversity Management

As you may already have gleaned from this chapter, the field of diversity management is a practitioner-based field that relies on theory and research to support the interventions that happen on multiple levels of system. In one sense, we are all diversity managers. We engage in personal and professional growth and relate to family and friends interpersonally. We manage diverse interactions presented to us in our work environments and in our society. For years, countless individuals have transferred their skills at managing human differences on many levels into professional careers. Many of these individuals have developed models and frameworks. Some have written articles, books, book chapters, essays, and lectures to capture their thinking and share that learning with others. These factors, along with the changing demographics in America and the shift to a global perspective, have set the stage for the science of diversity management to emerge. By the 1990s, it was clear that the field of diversity management warranted being considered a field of independent study. Characteristic of an independent field, professional organizations have emerged and training in the field has become more structured and systematic. For example, in 1997 the first master's degree in diversity management was offered at Cleveland State University. I had the privilege and honor of being its founding director for ten years. The Diversity Management Program remains an innovative professional development program of education and training in diversity theory, research, and practice. Since 1997 a number of other educational programs and professional organizations have become available to support people's understanding of the complexity of managing human differences in the workplace and in our communities. Active programs of research that further the scholarship in the field keeps the field alive and well.

As a field well past its infancy, diversity management still struggles with defining its parameters. Paramount in this struggle is the continuous dialogue about how much of oppression and social justice theory "belongs" in the field. Social justice and diversity are two sides of the same coin. In many ways the field is one of social action and advocacy, and in many ways it is a field of scientific inquiry on the management of human differences. The focus of the chapters of this handbook is on diversity management.

Likewise, because diversity management remains a burgeoning area of interest to many professionals in corporations, nonprofits, social services, faith-based organizations, and government agencies, the discussion of credentials and certification becomes necessary. What kind of training should a professional diversity practitioner have, and how intense should it be? As the work grows in complexity, individuals who enter this field to do professional work need to be supported by a deep understanding of the scholarship as well as experience in its practice.

As a field that is defined by the interplay of human differences in interpersonal, organizational, community, and societal settings, it is not surprising that the boundaries may appear a bit fuzzy. However, despite ongoing discussions of theoretical boundaries and certification (among other topics), diversity management is a vibrant field of study that enhances the presence and positive impact of human diversity in organizations and communities.

Conclusion

This chapter is intended to support your journey of understanding the field of diversity management and to heighten your awareness of your own identity as a member of this diverse society. Understanding diversity and your multiple social identities is key to developing your skills for personal and professional growth. No matter where you are on your journey toward understanding diversity—just getting started or well down the road—hopefully you have been enlightened by this overview and will be enriched by the topics to be presented in the following chapters. As our world becomes increasingly diverse, may you find this book a useful navigator for managing diversity and advancing inclusion.

REFERENCES

Calas, M.B., & Smircich, L. (2006). From the "women's point of view" ten years later: Toward a feminist organization studies. In S. Clegg, C. Hardy, T. B. Lawrence, & W. L. Nord (Eds.), *The sage handbook of organization studies.* Thousand Oaks, CA: Sage.

Campbell, A., Whitehead, J., & Finkelstein, S. (2009). Why good leaders make bad decisions. *Harvard Business Review, 87*(2), 60-66.

Carr-Ruffino, N. (2013). *Managing diversity: People skills for a multicultural workforce* (9th Edition). San Francisco, CA: Thomson Executive Press.

Ceglowski, J. (2000). Has globalization created a borderless world. In P. O'Meara, H. Mehlinger, & M. Krain (Eds.), *Globalization and the challenges of a new century* (pp. 101-111). Bloomington, IN: Indiana University Press.

Dovidio, J. F., & Gaertner, S.L. (2000). Aversive racism and selection decisions: 1989 and 1999. *Psychological Science,* 11(4), 315-319.

Goleman, D. (1995). *Emotional intelligence.* New York: Bantam Books.

Hall, S., & DuGay, P. (Eds.). (1996). *Questions of cultural identity.* London: Sage.

Haimerl, A. (2015, June 29). The fastest-growing group of
    entrepreneurs in America. *Fortune*. Retrieved from http://
    fortune.com/2015/06/29/black-women-entrepreneurs/

Holvino, E. (2012a). The "simultaneity" of identities: Models and
    skills for the twenty-first century. In C. L. Wijeyesinghe & B.W.
    Jackson (Eds.), *New perspectives on racial identity development*:
    Integrating emerging frameworks (pp. 164-191). New York: New
    York University Press.

Holvino, E. (2012b). Time, space and social justice in the age of
    globalization: Research and applications of the simultaneity
    of differences. *Practicing Social Change, 5*. Arlington, VA: NTL
    Institute.

Jayne, M. E., & Dipboye, R. L. (2004). Leveraging diversity to
    improve business performance: Research findings and
    recommendations for organizations. *Human Resource
    Management, 43*(4), 409-424.

Jordan, C.G. (2009). Rethinking inclusion: Case studies of identity,
    integration, and power in professional knowledge work
    organizations [dissertation]. Cleveland, Ohio: Case Western
    Reserve University.

Kochan, T., Bezrukova, K., Ely, R., Jackson, S., Joshi, A., Jehn, K.,
    & Thomas, D. (2003). The effects of diversity on business
    performance: Report of the diversity research network. *Human
    Resource Management, 42*(1), 3-21.

Lawson, B. D. (2014). Motion sickness symptomatology and origins. In K. S. Hale & K. M. Stanney (Eds.), *Handbook of virtual environments: Design, implementation, and applications* (pp. 531-599).

Lewellen, T.C. (2002). *The anthropology of globalization: Cultural anthropology enters the 21st century.* Westport, CT: Begin and Garvey.

National Intelligence Council (2017, January). *Paradox of progress.* Retrieved from https://www.dni.gov/index.php/global-trends/letter-nic-chairman

Pant, B. (2016, May 23). Different cultures see deadlines differently. *Harvard Business Review.* Retrieved from https://hbr.org/2016/05/different-cultures-see-deadlines-differently

Page-Gould, E. (2010). The unhealthy racist. In J. Marsh, R. Mendoza-Denton, & J. A. Smith (Eds.), *Are we born racist? New insights from neuroscience and positive psychology.* Boston: Beacon Press.

Ross, M. W., Daneback, K., & Månsson, S. A. (2012). Fluid versus fixed: A new perspective on bisexuality as a fluid sexual orientation beyond gender. *Journal of Bisexuality, 12*(4), 449-460.

Schawbel, D. (2016, November 1). 10 workplace trends you will see in 2017. *Forbes* [Blog post]. Retrieved from https://www.forbes.com/sites/danschawbel/2016/11/01/workplace-trends-2017

Smith, M.C., & Turner, S. (2015). *The radical transformation of diversity and inclusion: The millennial influence.* Retrieved from Deloitte University Leadership Center for Inclusion & Community Impact: https://www2.deloitte.com/us/en/pages/about-deloitte/articles/radical-transformation-of-diversity-and-inclusion.html

Thomson Reuters Poll (2016). *Making the business case for diversity.* Retrieved from https://blogs.thomsonreuters.com/answerson/business-case-for-diversity/

Thomas, Jr., R. R. (1991). *Beyond race and gender: Unleashing the power of your total work force by managing diversity.* New York: AMACOM.

Thomas, Jr., R. R. (1996). *Redefining diversity.* New York: AMACOM.

Thomas, Jr., R. R. (1999). *Building a house for diversity.* New York: AMACOM.

Zarya, V. (2015, August 21). The fastest-growing group of entrepreneurs in the U.S.? Minority women. *Fortune.* Retrieved from http://fortune.com/2015/08/21/women-small-business-diverse/

CHAPTER TWO

Moving to Strategic Diversity Management: A Necessary Shift

Melanie Harrington and April Thomas

JANE, THE NEWLY HIRED chief diversity officer (CDO) for ABC Company, starts her job meeting with her team, peers, and senior leaders. With each meeting, she is confronted with a host of different expectations, requests, and sometimes doubts about the ability of the organization to address its diversity management issues. Her boss has placed a great deal of confidence in her and strongly suggested she produce some early wins to build support and credibility for her work and the position. She has a variety of tactics and techniques that she has learned over the years and is anxious to get started. However, the organization has been down this road before with new CDOs, new strategies, and a laundry list of initiatives and training courses. Despite these efforts, the organization's demographic representation is lower than the industry average, workforce engagement survey results suggest a lower than desired level of employee engagement, and in the few days that Jane has been with the organization, she has listened to more grievances than ideas on how to advance diversity management goals. As Jane begins to build her strategy, she focuses on these key questions: How can she help her organization exit a frustrating cycle of diversity management efforts? What is at the crux of the organization's inability to operate effectively in the midst of differences and similarities? Where does she begin?

In the face of expectations coming from the highest and lowest levels of the organization, Jane may feel pressure to act quickly and turn to her arsenal of best practices. However, the practices selected may not be best for the organization. Moreover, because of the need to deliver an early win, she may resort to tactics that are more easily implemented and face the least amount of resistance; but these tactics are not yet woven into a broader strategy or built on a foundation that is designed to achieve sustainable results. Jane and the organization may not even be clear about the desired results. Jane may execute work that tackles the proverbial trees but misses the forest and the broader strategic opportunities altogether. The outcome may be a never-ending cycle of activities that do not yield sustainable results and an environment that is fatigued and increasingly resistant to supporting additional tactics.

The pressure to produce a quick fix places considerable constraints on the diversity practitioner's ability to develop and implement sustainable strategic approaches (Thomas, 2010). It causes some to default to tactics or rely on band-aid methods or legal mandates (like affirmative action) that often provide a temporary redress for the historic or present-day vestiges of exclusionary, unfair, or disparate treatment. But in the end, such tactics or mandates are not sustainable beyond the tenure of the leader who enacted them.

Thomas (2006) further noted that affirmative action was created principally because America's institutions weren't ready for diversity. Although progress has been made, nearly forty years later, society remains overly reliant on band-aid tactics like affirmative action, which has allowed society to ignore its inability to address diversity effectively. Thomas further predicted that society must look beyond tactics and regulatory mandates to create workable organizations and communities for diversity, or face another forty years of limited progress.

It should be noted that Thomas's use of the term affirmative action was intended to capture a variety of globally used tactics that are designed to affect diversity representation, including regulatory or compliance measures that offer temporary remedies for past wrongs and redress issues of underrepresentation and unequal treatment of certain legally protected groups. His premise was that a tactical method like affirmative action, albeit a critical and often necessary stopgap measure, has not required the users of the method to develop a capability for managing diversity (Thomas, 2010). It was this concern that prompted Thomas to develop the concept of strategic diversity management (SDM).

Strategic Diversity Management Core Concepts

SDM is a cognitive, learnable craft for enhancing the way people make quality decisions in situations where there are critical differences, similarities, tensions, and complexities (Thomas, 2006). By developing SDM, Thomas was seeking to change the way organizations, communities, and societies view diversity management—from just something that they do to something that they learn and master as a capability.

This chapter will focus on the need for making a shift away from compliance-driven approaches to SDM. Organizations benefit greatly when they expand their efforts from just doing diversity to building a diversity management capability that will create sustainable changes that achieve best results. The first critical step in this process is to expand the way individuals and organizations think about diversity.

To that end, the chapter will begin with an introduction to SDM by examining the 4-Quadrants ModelSM, a core framework of SDM that identifies four strategic approaches to diversity management. The chapter will also introduce the Personal Diversity ParadigmSM model (PDP), which identifies four dominant paradigms that individuals and organizations can hold about diversity. It then explores six common methods used today to address diversity challenges and their corresponding placement within the 4-Quadrants and PDP models. There is also an examination of this placement to determine whether an organization is stuck in a specific approach or advancing to additional approaches and therefore developing diversity management capabilities. Finally, the chapter will examine the idea and work of making the shift to SDM by examining the influence of undergirding paradigms or mindsets and their potential impact on an organization's approach to diversity management.

Strategic Diversity Management and Conceptual Clarity

A foundational concept of SDM is the premise that diversity management is integral to achieving the overall mission, vision, and objectives of an organization or community; it is not an end in and of itself (Thomas, 2010). SDM is a capability that is used to achieve organizational goals.

In mastering any craft, unless you are gifted with innate capabilities, you must learn the elements of the craft. Each element builds on the concepts, terminologies, frameworks, and methods that make up the components of the craft. A craft is the collected concepts and skills that are fundamental to success in an area of achievement (Connelly & Rianoshek, 2002). SDM refers to the mastery of a collective set of terms, concepts, frameworks, and methods as well. And like other crafts, understanding each element and concept of the craft is essential to building diversity management capability. Studying and practicing the craft develops what Thomas termed strategic diversity management capability, or the ability to make quality decisions in the face of a wide array of diversity challenges. SDM is not about the work or the diversity management tactics. It is about learning how to do the work, building capability, and achieving master-level success with the capability (Brotherton, 2011; Thomas, 2010).

The Foundation

The terms and definitions that follow are the building blocks that form the foundation of strategic diversity management. Some of these concepts will be used or referred to throughout the chapter and will aid in the reader's understanding of SDM.

Complexity is that which makes something difficult to explain or manage.

Diversity is any collective mixture of differences and similarities, and their related tensions and complexities. The elements of the mixture are defined by the environment or the context in which the mixture exists. For example, is the mixture in the context of the workforce, customers, vendors, organizational functions, or employees of a merger or acquisition? The elements are the characteristics of the collective mixture, and upon close examination of a mixture, there can be a significant, overwhelming number of dimensions of diversity.

Diversity-Challenged is the difficulty that an individual or institution has making quality decisions when differences, similarities, tensions, and complexities exist. Recognition and awareness of the concept of being diversity-challenged is critical to developing mastery in the SDM craft. To acknowledge that you are diversity-challenged does not necessarily indicate a character flaw, a motivation, or a mindset. It simply means that, relative to the existing collective mixture, the individual or group is unable to make quality decisions.

Diversity Management is the ability to make quality decisions in the midst of any set of differences and similarities and their related tensions and complexities.

Diversity Maturity is being able to understand and act upon diversity management concepts with wisdom, experience, and good judgment.

Diversity Skills are the abilities that help a person recognize critical mixtures, determine whether action is needed, and select the appropriate action or set of actions.

Diversity Tension is the tension that results from the dynamics of the differences and similarities in the elements of the mixture.

Paradigm is a mindset (Thomas, 2010). More specifically, paradigms are the written or unwritten rules that establish the boundaries by which one's behavior is guided. Personal paradigms about diversity are often taken-for-granted assumptions about what diversity means and the appropriate actions needed to foster it (Barker, 1993).

Quality Decisions are choices and actions that move an individual or organization toward individual and/or organizational objectives.

Requirements, in the context of strategic diversity management, are those factors that are necessary to accomplish the individual's or the organization's mission, vision, and strategy. Requirements are not traditions (doing things the way they have always been done), preferences (doing things the way I would like them to be done), or conveniences (doing things the way that is easiest).

Tension is the feeling of pressure or tautness that a person experiences when faced with a challenging situation. It is neither inherently good nor bad. It is more an indicator that something is not the status quo. It may come in the form of anxiety, stress, or excitement, depending on the situation. The key is how a person responds to it (Thomas, 2006; , 2010).

To place these definitions in context, consider Jane, our fictional CDO referenced at the beginning of this chapter. As Jane kicks off her first set of meetings in ABC Company offices around the globe, she is likely to encounter a wide variety of expectations. People's current paradigms about diversity will inform those expectations. As a student of strategic diversity management, Jane begins her work by providing the entire organization with a set of terms and definitions, establishing a commonly understood language and foundation for her strategy and work. In doing so, she is giving the organization's employees tools they need to communicate across teams, departments, and countries about diversity management. Jane works with ABC Company's leadership and diversity councils to ensure the full commitment of the organization to the terms and definitions. In Jane's communication strategy and whirlwind visits, she promotes, teaches, and uses the language, reaffirming for some and introducing to others a diversity management language that serves as the foundation for the organization's ongoing diversity management efforts.

It is also important to understand Thomas's use of the term "managing" or "management" in the context of diversity management. Thomas defines "managing diversity" as the process of creating and maintaining an environment that naturally enables *all* participants to contribute to their full potential in pursuit of organizational objectives (Thomas, 2010). A critical premise of this view is that everyone has a responsibility to manage diversity. Managers, from the frontline manager to the human resources and diversity manager, have a responsibility to engage and enable their people and resources in a manner that furthers their ability to contribute to the pursuit of organizational objectives. All individuals, regardless of their level in the organization, have a responsibility to push themselves and encourage others and the organization to improve continually in managing diversity. Thomas's use of the term "management" speaks to the process of enablement and empowerment of elements in the mixture—not exercising control over them.

As we continue to expound upon Thomas's work in our respective practices, we have found utility and flexibility in the use of the term "management" in diversity management. Incorporated in the term are a broad spectrum of options and approaches, like the array of work many diversity practitioners are doing under the heading of "inclusion."

The 4-Quadrants Model

Thomas captured in his 4-Quadrants Model what he believed to be the core approaches to managing differences and similarities and their related tensions and complexities. The model is an organizing framework that categorizes the work of diversity management into four quadrants, or buckets, to group various tactics and approaches. (See fig. 1.) The model does not prescribe a path through the quadrants, nor does it place more or less importance on a particular approach. It does, however, capture the approaches or directions that the work can take. The model does not suggest that one approach must be taken to the exclusion of other approaches, but rather provides an illustrative view of the breadth of approaches that an organization will need to consider and ultimately pursue over time to achieve organizational mastery in SDM (Thomas, 2010).

Figure 1: The 4-Quadrants

Quadrant 1 (Q1)—Managing Representation

The critical questions for Q1 are who or what should be included in the mixture and how do organizations ensure necessary representation. While mixtures can be comprised of any dimension (people, places, or things), most organizations tend to limit their work in Q1 to increasing the demographic representation of people groups that are not represented in the organization as desired. Most organizations seem to begin their diversity management efforts in Q1 and often get stuck there as they launch various representation initiatives, such as adherence to compliance mandates, as well as recruiting, hiring, and professional development programs (such as mentoring or coaching) that seek to increase representation throughout all levels of the organization.

Returning to Jane, our CDO, she could develop a series of campaigns designed to hire and promote ethnic minorities. However, if she fails to expand the organization's diversity management efforts beyond this work of adding numbers to its workplace mixture, the gains the organization achieves will not be sustainable. And she'll find herself implementing similar campaigns down the road.

By working with ABC Company's diversity council, Jane could expand the representation discussion to examine the degree to which current employees of different backgrounds are represented throughout the organization, not just in the hiring process. Such a conversation would begin to explore the degree to which employees of all backgrounds are represented in the range of everyday aspects of organizational life, such as giving input or being consistently considered and tapped as participants in any activity (like team formation or special projects or assignments that provide exposure, challenge, and growth). Such conversations would enable Jane to extend the representation discussion beyond just the numbers coming in the door, to ensuring appropriate representation for all participants in all aspects of organizational life.

Q1 efforts are often critical components of an organization's diversity management work, but they are not a complete strategy. If Jane fails to expand her diversity management efforts beyond Q1, the representation gains she makes will not be sustainable. She will find herself repeating tactics, expending resources, and achieving few, if any, net gains, as people enter and exit the organization because the environment did not enable them to contribute fully to organizational objectives.

Quadrant 2 (Q2)—Managing Differences

The focus of methods in Q2 addresses the question of how organizations work through differences to achieve organizational objectives. How do organizations embrace the differences or reduce the tension that may arise from the differences? Just as Q1 mixtures can be comprised of people, places, or things, the differences organizations need to manage can span the same dimensions. Organizations doing work in this quadrant focus on managing workforce relationships to build harmony in the workplace by accepting, understanding, and valuing differences and similarities.

Continuing our example from our Q1 discussion, let's assume that Jane's campaigns to increase the number of underrepresented racial groups have been successful. One aspect of her work in Q2 could be to develop education and learning strategies that help increase awareness of biases, bridge the gap in understanding different cultures and communities, and ultimately foster relationships across differences. The hope is that understanding differences and learning to value them will minimize tension in the workplace and foster a climate conducive to optimal productivity.

Jane could build upon this existing Q2 work of addressing ethnic differences by exploring other strategic differences across the spectrum of people, places, and things. What differences might prevent the finance and marketing departments from working together effectively? Why is critical information not shared between field and office teams? Such a company-wide conversation could examine which differences truly matter and which do not, given the specific tasks at hand. By extending the practice of understanding differences and building relationships from people differences to geographic, functional, occupational, or other dimensions, Jane will be building the diversity capability of her organization.

Quadrant 3 (Q3)—Managing Organizational Culture

Q3 approaches address the organization's systems, policies, practices, and behaviors to determine if they allow everyone to contribute fully toward organizational objectives. For example, does an employee's tenure, position, department, or location determine whether she or he is promoted? Does the company have a system in place to accept input from all contributors? Are career pathways enabling all workers to contribute their best work? These are all dynamics that impact every employee, regardless of the person's identity group. Q3 encompasses the methods an organization may use and the actions it may pursue to access the full potential of its talent and motivate employees to contribute one hundred percent of their skills and abilities.

A major focus of Q3 is organizational culture change, meaning a change in the organizational values communicated through norms and artifacts and observed in behavioral patterns (Homburg & Pflesser, 2000; Schein, 1992). These values act as social principles that guide behaviors and set a broad framework for organizational routines and practices (Hogan & Coote, 2013). Organizational culture is comprised of the fundamental assumptions that drive the organization and the manifestations that flow from those assumptions (Thomas, 2010). These values, assumptions, and manifestations can either hinder the diversity management work of an organization or facilitate it. Addressing hindering assumptions and building on facilitating assumptions and values are critical to Q3 efforts.

In our experience, we have found that the work in Q3, particularly culture change work, is sometimes overlooked as a necessary component in diversity management. Organizations pursuing approaches in Q1 and Q2 may find that the effects of their work lead them to pursue Q3 approaches, although an organization can begin its diversity management efforts in Q3.

Another objective of Q3 is to develop the manager's capability to engage and empower demographically and behaviorally diverse talent pools. To manage an organization at an SDM master level, managers must be proficient in managing both people and diversity (Thomas, 2010). Moreover, the ability to effectively engage and enable a diverse pool of talent cannot be the province of a few human resources functions and the chief diversity officer in an organization. An organization operating at an SDM master level also holds all organizational contributors responsible for developing their own diversity management capability. It is the combined diversity management capability of both the managers and the contributors that is the focus of Q3.

Returning to Jane, to expand her work beyond counting the different groups that are represented in the organization and building relationships across differences, in Q3 Jane can work with her colleagues to examine and develop managers' employee-engagement capabilities. Additionally, she can examine the systems, policies, practices, and behaviors that may be affecting recruitment, hiring, placement, evaluation, development, and promotion decisions. For Q3 Jane may ask, Is the pathway to advancement clear, articulated, and executed equitably throughout the organization? Is the organization driven by its true requirements, as opposed to its organizational traditions, preferences, and conveniences?

An exercise developed to sort out requirements from traditions, preferences, and conveniences is the Cultural Dig Exercise, a process for excavating the culture of an organization (Plummer, 2000). Every culture has indicators whose symbolic meanings convey messages— whether intentionally or unintentionally—about the culture's beliefs, values, and norms. Cultural indicators include artifacts/objects, stories, myths, rituals, rites of passage, and relationships that reflect the organization's culture. One way to learn more about an organization's culture—its beliefs, values, and norms—is to gather artifacts and objects that represent these indicators. Participants in the exercise are asked to choose two artifacts or objects that they believe represent their experience of the organization. One object would represent what they experience as the best aspects of the organizational culture, and the other would represent some aspect of the organization's culture that does not serve it well or that is not aligned with the organization's mission and values. These artifacts can then be sorted into which ones represent requirements, which are traditions, which are simply preferences developed over time, and which are simply conveniences.

The task for the participants is to determine which of the requirements should be focused on to deepen and enhance how organizational members engage with each other and how the mission and business objectives can be achieved. Participants can decide if there are any traditions that need to be placed in the archives and resurrected for anniversary celebrations, and if there are preferences or conveniences that have seeped into requirements and need to be unraveled. Policies and procedures can then be reviewed to determine if preferences and conveniences have been labeled as requirements.

These Q3 considerations show that organizational culture change is complex work that takes time, expertise, and leadership support. However, the efforts of Q3 work are what help shift the organization from one that is simply doing diversity to one that is operationalizing the capability of pursuing organizational objectives in the midst of differences and similarities and their tensions and complexities—in other words, building diversity management capability.

Quadrant 4 (Q4)—Managing All Strategic Mixtures

When an organization can identify and assess all types of mixtures through the lens of diversity management, the organization has advanced to the Q4 approach. The focus of this quadrant is on shifting the work from merely doing diversity to mastering a capability to apply diversity management concepts and skills to any strategic mixture. Thomas (2010) referred to this quadrant as a "focus on SDM, that is, focusing on the proverbial forest, as opposed to different types of diversity, the trees."

The work of Q4 requires organizations to hone their diversity management skills and build their diversity maturity through practice. It requires the ability to recognize strategic mixtures (for example, people differences, product differences, functional or departmental differences, customer differences, etc.) and select those mixtures that (1) the organization can influence and (2) can affect the organization's pursuit of its objectives. Once the strategic mixtures are identified and prioritized, the organization can begin to determine how to approach these mixtures: managing the representation of the strategic mixtures, per Q1; managing the relationships among the strategic mixtures, per Q2; and managing the engagement or collective potential of the strategic mixtures, per Q3 (Thomas, 2010).

As Jane continues to assess her organization, she observes that ABC Company's growth strategy is to acquire new organizations to grow market share and increase product offerings. However, the benefits of the acquisitions are slow to materialize because the integration of the acquired organizations is not effective and too slow. Jane realizes that ABC Company's acquisition strategy is struggling with a diversity management challenge: effectively incorporating a different organizational culture into the existing one. Jane shares her observations with the leadership. As a result of her ability to identify acquired organizations as a strategic mixture (Q4), Jane's office could become part of the mergers and acquisitions team, helping to assess culture and organize comprehensive Q1, Q2, and Q3 approaches that are incorporated into business acquisition strategies. This would move her organization to a sustainable level of diversity-management mastery that is required by Q4—managing all strategic mixtures.

The Paradigms That Influence Organizations' Approaches to Diversity

Before an organization embarks on work in a specific quadrant and mobilizes the necessary resources, there is a mindset, or an undergirding paradigm, that has influenced the selection of the approach and type of resources that are committed to the effort. For each quadrant of the 4-Quadrants Model, Thomas provided a corresponding paradigm.

Figure 2: The Personal Diversity Paradigm Model

The quadrants and their corresponding paradigms are captured in chart 1. The chart describes four mindsets individuals and organizations can hold about diversity. The paradigm that resonates most with an individual is a person's "dominant paradigm." An organization's dominant paradigm is subsequently based on the collective dominant paradigm of its leaders and workers. A clear understanding of the organization's underlying dominant paradigm—as well as an awareness of the other paradigms that may not be widely held—is a necessary component of mastering the craft of SDM.

An organization's approach to diversity management is influenced by the dominant paradigm of its leaders and workers. The organization's dominant paradigm typically reflects its primary assumptions about diversity and affects the organization's expectations of and approaches to diversity management efforts. The paradigm can channel an organization's thinking in powerful ways. It can be a limiting factor or a facilitating factor depending on the alignment of the paradigm to the organization's goals and the leadership's vision of the purpose of a diverse workforce (Thomas & Ely, 1996). The paradigm will also influence the investment the organization is willing to commit to the learning that will be needed to address the underlying assumptions of the paradigm.

Chart 1: Personal Diversity Paradigm Model (PDP) Driving Questions and Paradigms Undergirding Each Quadrant

Q	Quadrant Title	Key Questions	P	Related Paradigm	Motivation	Emphasis
1	Managing Representation	Who's in the mix? Who needs to be at this table?	1	Make Amends for Past Wrongs	Social Justice / Civil Rights	To create a representative workforce and mainstream the disadvantaged
2	Managing Differences	How well can we work through our differences?	2	Apply the Golden Rule (Treat others as you would want to be treated)	Social Justice / Civil Rights / Harmony	Pursuit of harmony required for quality work relationships

Q	Quadrant Title	Key Questions	P	Related Paradigm	Motivation	Emphasis
3	Managing Organizational Culture	Do our systems, policies, practices, and behaviors allow us to fully access everyone's ideas and talent?	3	Maximize Individual Engagement	Business / Organizational Viability	To make quality decisions in the midst of workforce differences, similarities, and related tensions
4	Managing All Strategic Mixtures	What additional mixtures (e.g., functional, customer, product, or other differences) are impacting our organization?	4	Maximize Stakeholder Engagement	Business / Competitive Advantage / Viability	To develop a universal organizational, managerial, and individual capability for addressing strategic diversity of any kind

In the PDP chart, four main paradigms that individuals have about diversity are identified.

Paradigm 1 (P1)—Make Amends for Past Wrongs

This paradigm focuses primarily on diversity as the representation of groups that have been historically oppressed and underrepresented in the workplace. Those who hold this paradigm see making amends for former laws and practices that have disadvantaged certain groups as a moral imperative for organizations and society. Therefore, they expect and/or advocate for organizations to focus on achieving the appropriate distribution of demographic representation at all levels of the organization.

Paradigm 2 (P2)—Apply the Golden Rule

This paradigm defines diversity as focusing on both demographic representation and establishing harmony. The Golden Rule—"Treat others as you would want to be treated"—underpins this paradigm and focuses on expanding, understanding, and accepting differences of all kinds. Advocates of the Golden Rule support efforts that foster the sharing and celebrating of differences. While there are many who now adhere to the "Platinum Rule"—"Treat others as they would want to be treated"—instead of the Golden Rule, Thomas's hesitancy to replace the Golden Rule was born out of his skepticism that people have developed the ability to act on the Platinum Rule.

Does Thomas's perspective still hold true today? While we are not yet prepared to change the model, it is SDMS 360's belief that individuals need to be able to recognize and appreciate the value of both rules. However, we do believe that the Golden Rule has to be in place and maintained before the Platinum Rule can be effectively applied. The Golden Rule establishes a basic principle for the humane treatment of others. As that universal principle is accepted, people can expand their awareness and behavior to pursue the understanding, inquiry, and relationship-building that are the next steps in seeking to treat people as *they* would like to be treated. An increasing number of people and organizations are discovering the value of treating people as prescribed by the Platinum Rule. The news is replete with examples of organizations attempting to provide benefits such as flexible schedules, relaxed dress-code requirements, fun and open workspaces, and more flexible paternity benefits, all in an attempt to treat their employees like they would like to be treated.

We note that in our respective consulting and advisory practices, we have found that constructing initiatives and organizational systems that are consistent with both the Golden and Platinum Rules require (a) an understanding of requirements as defined above and (b) the ability to differentiate between true requirements versus preferences, traditions, or conveniences. Adherents of both Golden and Platinum Rules must be willing to hold each other accountable for honoring those practices and policies that are necessary requirements while being flexible in the areas of preferences, traditions, and conveniences (or non-requirements).

Paradigm 3 (P3)—Maximize Individual Engagement

This paradigm addresses the engagement of a demographically and behaviorally diverse environment where there is a diversity of thought, perspective, approaches to solving problems, and life experiences.

All relevant types of workforce/workplace diversity are important because they represent the range of talent from which an organization can choose. Creating or expecting a supportive, encouraging environment is critical to holders of this paradigm, which focuses on an environment designed to utilize fully all the available ideas, solutions, skills, and talents a person can contribute.

Paradigm 4 (P4)—Maximize Stakeholder Engagement

This paradigm views diversity as differences and similarities of all kinds. Those who hold this paradigm see all workplace challenges as having diversity (or mixtures) at their core. They seek to apply a universal approach to address any diversity management challenge they may encounter. A key focus of this paradigm is learning to make decisions in the midst of differences, similarities, and related tensions and complexities—decisions that are based on true requirements versus personal preferences, traditions, or conveniences. In order for Jane, our fictional CDO, and her colleagues to view the challenge of managing the integration of newly acquired businesses as a diversity management challenge, the organization's undergirding assumptions about diversity would need to be broader than a limited set of demographic groups, and the organization would need to possess the capability to identify and focus on diversity mixtures (as diversity is defined in the SDM model) that can further or hinder organizational objectives.

For example, Jane and our fictional ABC Company realize that different businesses and business functions make up a diversity mixture. Additionally, they understand that the effective integration of business functions, markets, and resources—including the human resources—in a manner that best serves organizational goals is a diversity management opportunity to which the 4-Quadrants Model can be applied. ABC Company's ability to recognize these other mixtures and the broader utility of strategic diversity management will be a facilitating factor in developing the diversity management capability of the organization and increasing the value and sustainability of this work to the business.

Unpacking Paradigms

The process of identifying and examining people's paradigms reveals a person's deep-seated beliefs and provides insight into an individual's way of thinking about diversity. It also assesses the degree to which the beliefs about diversity held by the workplace correspond to the approaches the organization uses or does not use to manage diversity. In the consulting practice of SDMS 360, we ask clients to complete a ten-question online assessment. The assessment takes approximately fifteen minutes to complete. The assessment is taken anonymously to encourage transparency without fear of repercussions. Upon completion, users will receive a score in each of the four paradigms. The paradigm with the highest score represents the user's dominant paradigm. Some users may have two dominant paradigms (identical high scores in two paradigms). Users are also able to download a PDF workbook to further their understanding and practice application of the concepts of the PDP in their everyday work environments.

It is important to note that the results of the assessment tool indicate that respondents have dominant paradigms and non-dominant paradigms. They do not hold one paradigm at the exclusion of the others, but are influenced by a dominant paradigm and to a lesser extent non-dominant paradigms as well.

One key lesson in discovering the dominant paradigm for both individuals and organizations is that all four paradigms have validity and no one paradigm is "better" than the others. They just are. Understanding and awareness of all four paradigms is necessary to achieve SDM mastery. In fact, not considering and factoring in all four paradigms during the process of developing an organization's strategy can limit stakeholder buy-in and thus the effectiveness of their efforts. If the organization's diversity management actions are not a reflection of what the organization's stakeholders recognize as addressing their version of diversity, they may conclude that the organization is not "doing" diversity.

Approaches, Paradigms, and the Frustrating Diversity Cycle

Thomas observed that a great deal of diversity management work hovered in quadrants 1 and 2 of the model (Thomas, 2006). Our contention is that the inability of organizations to move beyond quadrants 1 and 2, and move more of the work into areas that affect organizational norms, cultures, and behaviors, can cause organizations to get stuck in a frustrating cycle of work that is not sustainable. (See fig. 3.)

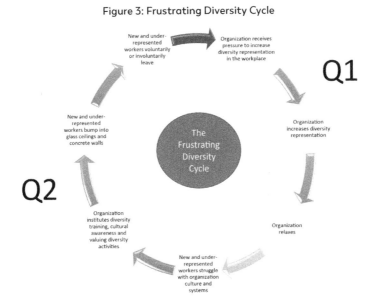

Figure 3: Frustrating Diversity Cycle

The work done in Q1 and Q2 plays a critical role in mounting a comprehensive diversity management strategy. However, such work can have limited results and, in some instances, be harmful to the overall organizational goals if it is implemented as isolated methods and tactics. It is the equivalent of tackling the trees without a view of the forest. Below is an examination of six common methods of addressing diversity that we have observed contribute to the frustrating cycle. They are categorized by their relevant quadrants and paradigms.

Method 1: Diversity Representation (Intervention, Compliance, Affirmative Action)
Quadrant ID: Q1   **Paradigm ID: P1**

In contrast to the broad definition of diversity used in SDM, many organizations limit their definitions of diversity to people or workforce dimensions. Some organizations still include a finite list of demographic groups in their definitions of diversity. The goal of this representational focus is to ensure that identified and selected underrepresented groups are represented in the workplace in proportion to their availability to do the work.

Though affirmative action was instituted in the U.S. in 1961, organizations today still struggle to establish and maintain the representational environment that proponents of the policy hoped it would create. While more people from underrepresented demographic groups are in the workforce today, organizations still suffer from the perpetual "revolving door" syndrome. Those who stay with their organizations often remain underrepresented in the C-suites and boardrooms of companies. This is not news to the organizations or the diversity practitioners who service them. The diversity representation tactics are often interventions driven by external regulatory pressures or internal actors whose efforts may be supported by some but are not an integral part of the organizational culture or practices. Thus, once the laws change or support within the organization disappears, the representational gains are lost and the diversity representation efforts start all over again (Sabharwal, 2014; Thomas, 2010). The goal of increasing diversity representation may be critical for the organization. However, if it is the sole method or is disconnected from a broader Q1-Q4 approach, it is a limited strategy that may get stuck in the frustrating cycle.

Method 2: Valuing Differences
Quadrant ID: Q2   ***Paradigm ID: P2***
With a number of barriers to entry to the workplace removed due to antidiscrimination laws and regulatory measures that have provided a redress for past wrongs, previously underrepresented groups have entered the workforce in greater numbers. But where these new groups and their majority counterparts have not previously worked alongside each other in the workforce, the tensions caused by their differences have not been as easily surmountable as anticipated. To address this challenge, organizations have turned to valuing differences, an approach that seeks to create harmonious relationships by increasing cultural awareness (Thomas, 2006).

As diversity practitioners, we have observed more organizations choosing to value and celebrate cultural differences and identities rather than suppress them. As the types of mixtures that society recognizes grows, more organizations have placed greater emphasis on training and other tactics that build awareness and cultural competency, reduce bias and micro-aggressions, and increase environmental harmony and mutual respect. But is the work of valuing differences enough to create environments where all participants are able to contribute fully? Despite the progress made through valuing differences, it has not staved off the revolving door of talent from these demographic groups (Sabharwal, 2014; Thomas, 2010).

Method 3: Diversity Training
Quadrant ID   Q1, Q2   Paradigm ID: P1, P2

Diversity training and education can have the effect of clarifying and affirming an organization's diversity message and strategic approach. Educational approaches are critical components of an overall strategic diversity management approach. As diversity practitioners, we use educational strategies to aid Q1, Q2, and Q3 efforts and build awareness and capability. As noted earlier in this chapter, establishing a foundation, a common language, and definitions are critical to bringing the organization together around a diversity management strategy.

However, diversity training to date has largely centered around sensitivity, awareness, and organizational harmony (Anand & Winters, 2008). Such training can alienate certain groups if based on a "shame and blame" platform. This approach can cause people to disengage from training or diversity efforts or make them resistant to the idea that they are to blame for past discrimination or unwilling to be shamed into conformity (Dobbin & Kalev, 2015). Such disengagement can result in resistance to the very change that the training efforts are designed to generate.

Method 4: Dos and Don'ts Diversity Training
Quadrant ID: Q2　　　Paradigm ID:　P2

Some diversity training has led to a "legislation of tactics." Just as policy makers have legislated employment rules, so, too, have practitioners created "how-tos" or rules that instruct people on how to respond to specific diversity challenges—in essence, a list of dos and don'ts. Examples of such training include sexual harassment and EEO trainings (which ensure legal compliance), as well as training about cultural competency and micro-aggressions.

The limitation of dos and don'ts training is that, while awareness and legal compliance are necessary and a list of possible responses is helpful, there's little room for people to think critically and discover and draw upon a wider array of alternative actions that address their diversity challenges. They have static lists for very dynamic life situations. This type of training, rather than develop people's capability to manage diversity, teaches them to follow instructions. This does not provide the knowledge and skills necessary for individuals to make quality decisions when business is predictably unpredictable. Instead, the training offers a prescriptive set of dos and don'ts and does not increase the person's ability to think through options.

Method 5: Shamming of Diversity
Quadrant ID: Q1, Q2　　Paradigm ID:　P1, P2

Another approach organizations have taken, though often unconsciously, is the "shamming of diversity" (Thomas, 2013). Shamming occurs when practitioners and organizations present content and strategies using labels that suggest they are doing work across the quadrants but in actuality are doing Q1 tactics that are not connected to a broader Q1-Q4 strategy. The consequence of this practice can be confusion when terms are co-opted and used in ways that misrepresent the actual work being done. This practice creates the risk of discrediting or making meaningless terms that represent new, different, and comprehensive approaches. Moreover, it provides ammunition for opponents of diversity management who believe that any new efforts are merely more of the same, subjecting new and different efforts to hindering paradigms.

Method 6: Bully or Shame Approach
Quadrant ID: Q2   Paradigm ID: P2

Another approach is the "bully or shame" approach. When someone offends the collective sense of right and wrong, the public demands the individual be fired or publicly shamed or bullied, many times via social media. There is no opportunity for learning or understanding. The shaming and bullying objective does not appear to generate collective awareness or empathy but to instill fear and exact retribution. The result is a tendency for the offending individuals to retreat to safe spaces with those who share the same views.

In our consulting and advisory roles, we do not view these tactics as managing differences and similarities and related tensions and complexities. Instead, they have the effect of social policing by mob rule.

Bully or shame reactions often generate resentment and resistance or cause people to shut down. It is not clear that these reactions create the change in thinking and behaviors that results in organizations that are more diverse and more effective at managing differences, similarities, tensions, or complexities. Robin Ely (2006) noted that assaults, whether the person is the offended party or the offender who becomes the recipient of a counter-assault, produce "identity abrasions" that cause both parties to burrow down into their own camps, only listening to feedback that confirms their positions and demonizes the other side. If organizational objectives require that people work together across differences and draw upon their best ideas and techniques to develop solutions, organizations will need to develop the capability to respond to offenses in ways other than a reciprocating escalation of counter-offenses. Bullying or shaming does not build diversity management capability or engage more people in the diversity management work.

Method Summary

Traditional diversity training has expanded beyond managing representation (Q1) to include managing differences (Q2). But both Q1 and Q2 are rooted in the paradigms of social justice and harmony. In this context, Q1 and Q2 methods do not tackle the factors of managing organizational culture (Q3), which would help address not only the high attrition rate of underrepresented groups but also the environmental factors that limit the ability of all members to contribute fully to organizational objectives. They also do not encourage the development of mastery by applying the principles of diversity management to major organizational challenges, such as mergers and acquisitions (Q4).

Also, while training has expanded to include Q2 dynamics, most companies need help fully maximizing the mixture dynamics of Q1 and Q2. Those organizations that are firmly grounded in the social justice paradigm have difficulty exploring not only "who is in the organization's mixture" but also "what is in the mix" (e.g., organizational function differences, product differences, customer and market differences, union versus management differences, as well as individual identity groups) (Thomas, 2010).

Perhaps the proliferation of unconscious bias training indicates an awareness that bias is part of the human condition. Consequently, the practice of leaning on regulations and other compliance mandates like affirmative action will remain important tools in addressing diversity. But without supporting these regulations and policies with broader, overarching approaches such as SDM, the innovative and creative potential of a diverse organization will not be fully realized (Thomas, 2006).

Making the Shift

An approach limited to only a portion of the 4-Quadrants Model will impact the effectiveness of the diversity management effort. Moreover, it is likely to thrust an organization into the perpetual frustrating diversity cycle. How does one make the shift from the frustrating cycle to strategic diversity management?

As stated earlier, an organization's dominant diversity paradigm (determined by the dominant paradigms of the individuals in the workplace) greatly influences the actions that the organization will consider in developing and executing a diversity management strategy. The underlying assumptions of the paradigms determine the behaviors that are identified as appropriate to achieve the goals. If the mindset (paradigm) influences action (Q), a shift in action must first start with a shift in mindset.

Therefore, a further review of the Personal Diversity Paradigm framework (chart 1) and an understanding of the four diversity paradigms are the first necessary steps in mastering a diversity management capability. Each paradigm provides a useful perspective about diversity that can add value to a diversity management effort. It is important to note that each paradigm carries its own advantages and limitations. Therefore, it is beneficial to be able to flex in and out of dominant paradigms and to explore the assumptions, goals, actions, and benefits associated with them. Education that highlights these paradigms and develops this flexibility helps ensure that all diversity management efforts are coordinated and able to complement each other.

The process of developing a greater awareness of one's personal paradigms and the organization's collective dominate paradigm has three primary purposes:

1. **INCREASE SELF-AWARENESS:** Responsibility for diversity starts with the individual. Thus, it is important to be aware of one's own diversity paradigm.

2. **EXPAND ONE'S THINKING AROUND DIVERSITY:** Through exposure to the PDP model, the individual and the organization will understand that other alternative perspectives about diversity exist. They will also understand that others' views and definitions of diversity may be different.

3. **INCREASE ONE'S UNDERSTANDING OF OTHERS:** In becoming aware of additional diversity paradigms, individuals and organizations will discover that others may not think as they do about diversity, and learn that these perspectives are each valid and necessary for a successful diversity management strategy.

Changing individual paradigms is not a purpose of the PDP model. Paradigms are established over an individual's lifetime and are not easily modified. Education and communication can create and increase awareness that might make people more open to considering other perspectives, but changing individual perspectives is not a goal. However, the increased awareness is designed to foster greater mindfulness about the motivations driving the organization's approach. Clarity about the driving motivations offers organizations an ability to choose with greater understanding and ultimately skill from a broader array of diversity management approaches that align with strategic objectives (Thomas, 2010).

Additionally, becoming aware of the existence of multiple diversity paradigms encourages individuals to accept the existence of different paradigms. However, acknowledging the other dominant paradigms does not negate or invalidate each learner's own dominant paradigm. Nor are learners expected to abandon their perspective for a different perspective. This requires the skill of maintaining one's own perspective while simultaneously acknowledging additional perspectives and points of view.

Holding Multiple Points of View

In the context of Thomas's PDP model, the notion of holding multiple points of view means:

- standing firm in a person's own paradigm while simultaneously considering additional paradigms and perspectives;
- not feeling threatened by the existence of contrary paradigms; and
- not feeling the need to disprove or discount them.

This means that an individual can evaluate his or her dominant paradigm in the midst of other paradigms and explore what aspect of each is necessary for the organization to achieve its objectives (Strategic Diversity Management Solutions 360, 2017). Being able to hold multiple points of view also helps develop contextual knowledge—an awareness of the various components of a mixture and how these components fit together. Exploration of the four paradigms cultivates an ability to identify different points of view and how they relate to the desired organizational objectives. Continued practice in understanding both one's own paradigm and those of others, as well as exploring how those paradigms affect everyday interactions, helps develop an individual's diversity maturity and aids in the quality of the diversity management decision-making process.

The practice of becoming aware of the existence of multiple diversity paradigms encourages individuals to accept the existence of different paradigms without negating or invalidating each learner's own dominant paradigm or requiring the learner to abandon his or her paradigm for a different paradigm. However, the practice does build diversity maturity and aids the individual and the organization in making the shift to SDM.

Methods like affirmative action, diversity recruitment initiatives, or cultural competency training are narrow in scope and target specific issues. Without clarity about the range of approaches and the undergirding paradigm that drives each approach, diversity challenges will be addressed with methods that are constrained by limited awareness and dominant (and perhaps unconscious) paradigms, whereas greater awareness builds diversity management capability, which is a transferable skill that can have broad applicability with continuous practice and mastery. Whether the diversity challenge is among internal groups (colleagues, supervisors, direct reports, or partnering business units) or among external stakeholders (clients, regulatory agencies, or competitors), diversity management capability equips learners with the ability to make quality decisions in the midst of a broad array of simple and complex diversity challenges.

This chapter has presented the 4-Quadrants Model and PDP as a starting point for developing a diversity management capability for both the individual and the organization. Additionally, the 4-Quadrants Model and PDP provide a framework for leadership to assess where it is currently engaged, in what quadrants, and whether the organization is advancing in its diversity management efforts.

Conclusion

Organizations are facing never-before-seen levels of global competition, and rapid technological disruptions are causing industries to rethink organization models and human capital plans. Will the approaches organizations have used in the past work in this ever-changing environment? History has shown that even when the organizational environment was not changing as quickly as it is now, the demographic-based approaches of Q1 and Q2 have not provided the necessary sustained change. If this historical pattern continues to hold true, there is no reason to think the effectiveness of these approaches will improve in the immediate future, especially in such a fast-changing environment. Repeatedly retracing its steps in the frustrating cycle of Q1 and Q2 is not a luxury any organization can afford.

With their investment in human capital being the largest investment most organizations make, organizations need an approach to diversity management that attracts the best talent, retains that talent, and makes room for that talent to contribute fully to accomplishing organizational objectives. To do this, organizations must shift to strategic diversity management—or a similar framework—and expand the scope of diversity management to:

1) include Q3 and Q4 approaches, and
2) push beyond the demographic-focused approaches in Q1 and Q2.

As a result, the gains made in Q1 and Q2 can be sustained and organizations can access the full potential of both the individual talents and the organizational units they comprise.

Let's return to Jane, our fictional CDO of ABC Company. How does she create and sustain a diversity management learning culture in her organization?

A key first step for Jane is to determine what ABC Company's starting point is. An organization may have high hopes for where it wants to end up, but it first needs to be clear about where it is starting. We would recommend a two-pronged call to action to assist in making this determination:

Step 1: Assess what the organization thinks about diversity management.

By conducting the Personal Diversity Paradigm assessment or similar exercise to determine individual members'—and ultimately the organization's—dominant diversity paradigms, Jane can determine the undergirding drivers that will need to be addressed to build organizational diversity management capability at ABC Company.

Step 2: Assess what the organization does in diversity management.

Jane can conduct a gap analysis using the 4-Quadrants Model to determine in which quadrants the activities of the current organizational strategy fall. This will allow stakeholders to determine which quadrants the organization's current activities fall. It will also make it easier to identify areas of opportunity and improvement in the organization's current strategy.

Combining the information from these two steps will provide Jane with critical data to answer critical questions. Does the organization's dominant paradigm align with the quadrant in which it takes the most actions? Do these actions help ABC Company reach its desired destination? Or do they keep the organization in a frustrating cycle? And while the organization has a dominant paradigm, how can it make room for the non-dominant paradigms held by its members, to gain organization-wide support for ABC Company's diversity management strategy? Answers to these questions will help an organization take its next steps while also making the shift to SDM.

REFERENCES

Anand, R., & Winters, M. (2008). A retrospective view of corporate diversity training from 1996 o the present. *Academy of Management Learning & Education, 7*(3), 356–372. doi:10.565/amle.2008.3251673

Barker, J. A. (1993). *Paradigms: The business of discovering the future.* New York, NY: Harper Business.

Brotherton, P. (2011, May 19). Interview with R. Roosevelt Thomas, Jr. *TD Magazine*. Retrieved January 23, 2018, from https://www. td.org/magazines/td-magazine/r-roosevelt-thomas-jr

Connelly, M., & Rianoshek, R. (2002). *The communication catalyst: The fast (but not stupid) track to value for customers, investors, and employees.* New York, NY: Kaplan Publishing.

Dobbin, F., Schrage, D., & Kalev, A. (2015). Rage against the Iron Cage. *American Sociological Review, 80*(5), 1014–1044. doi:10.1177/0003122415596416

Ely, R. J. (2006, September). Rethinking political correctness. *Harvard Business Review, OnPoint.*

Hogan, S. J., & Coote, L. V. (2013). Organizational culture, innovation, and performance: A test of Schein's model. *Journal of Business Research. Retrieved from http://dx.doi.org/10.1016/j. jbusres.2013.09.007*

Homburg, C., & Pflesser, C. (2000). A multiple-layer model of market-oriented organizational culture: Measurement issues and performance outcomes. *Journal of Marketing Research, 37*, 9–62.

Plummer, D. (2000). Cultural dig exercise. Available for use with permission from www.dlplummer.com

Sabharwal, M. (2014). Is diversity management sufficient? Organizational inclusion to further performance. *Public Personnel Management*. doi:10.1177/009102601522202

Schein, E. H. (1992). *Organizational culture and leadership*. San Francisco, CA: Jossey-Bass.

Strategic Diversity Management Solutions 360. (2017). *Personal Diversity Paradigm: A Tool for Exploring Your Orientation to Diversity: Individual Action Workbook* [Pamphlet]. Atlanta, GA: Strategic Diversity Management Solutions 360.

Thomas, D. A., & Ely, R. J. (1996, September–October). Making differences matter: A new paradigm for managing diversity. *Harvard Business Review*. Retrieved January 23, 2018, from https://hbr.org/1996/09/making-differences-matter-a-new-paradigm-for-managing-diversity

Thomas, R. R., Jr. (2006). *Building on the promise of diversity: How we can move to the next level in our workplaces, our communities and our society*. New York, NY: AMACOM.

Thomas, R. R., Jr. (2010). *World class diversity management: A strategic approach*. San Francisco, CA: Berrett-Koehler.

Thomas, R. R., Jr. (2013, August 12). The shamming of diversity. *TD Magazine*. Retrieved January 23, 2018, from https://talentmgt.com/2013/08/12/stop-using-diversity-as-a-sham__trashed/

CHAPTER THREE

Creating Inclusion for Oneself: Knowing, Accepting, and Expressing One's Whole Self at Work

Bernardo M. Ferdman and Laura Morgan Roberts

IN AN ELOQUENT *New York Times* OP-ED, K'naan (2012)—a singer and poet born in Somalia, raised in Canada, and now based in New York, whose song "Wavin' Flag" became one of the anthems for the 2010 FIFA World Cup—describes the pressures he felt from the American music industry to, as he put it, "change the walk of my songs" (p. SR7). Before he completed his third album, executives of his music label explained to K'naan how songs that are less anguished, more fun, and less focused on difficult subjects than his first two albums tend to get more radio air play, sell more, and be more successful in the United States. Without being told exactly what to do, K'naan nevertheless felt pressure—which he attributes mostly to himself—to conform for the sake of success and to, as his inner voice rationalized, "reach more people" (p. SR7).

In comparing his earlier and later work, he writes, "The first felt to me like a soul with a paintbrush; the other a body with no soul at all" (p. SR7), and he concludes by poetically explaining that one cannot successfully hide out as he temporarily tried to do: "while one can dumb down his lyrics, what one cannot do without being found out is hide his historical baggage. His sense of self. His walk. ... I come with all the baggage of Somalia—of my grandfather's poetry, of pounding rhythms, of the war, of being an immigrant, of being an artist, of needing to explain a few things. Even in the friendliest of melodies, something in my voice stirs up a well of history ..." (p. SR7). After using self-censorship to try to fit in and "walk like a prophet" (his metaphor for trying to be what others expected), K'naan found that his true strength came from his roots and his own walk. K'naan, like many others, discovered the dangers of suppressing key aspects of himself and the benefits of being authentic, of being fully himself, in his work. In the process, he first learned who he was and what was important to him; he then accepted these as things he did not want to give up, and found ways to express those identities and their associated values through his work, so as to strengthen both his output and himself.

Similar—albeit more ordinary—examples abound. One of us recalls a newly hired academic colleague who was afraid to tell her department chair that she was pregnant for fear of being seen as a less-than-serious assistant professor, and who suffered greatly as a result, both because she was not able to properly take care of her health throughout the pregnancy, and because she was constantly worried about being discovered; interestingly, her research focused, in part, on risk prevention. Participants in our workshops talk about wanting to feel like they really belong in their organizations and work groups, while at the same time struggling with dilemmas about how much to share with coworkers about various aspects of themselves, such as their culturally grounded experiences, their religious identities, or their families. Colleagues, relatives, or friends whose names are hard to pronounce for English speakers struggle with whether to adopt nicknames that are easier for coworkers to say or even with whether to change their names. Gay and lesbian people in organizations make choices daily about when and how, and whether, to come out to coworkers; even when their sexual orientation is known to their heterosexual coworkers, gay and lesbian individuals must continually make choices about how much information to share about their daily lives outside work. And many others, by trying to fit in or assimilate to their workplace in a range of ways, use up energy that could be spent more productively or lose valuable opportunities to draw on unique experiences or connections that could lead to innovation or creativity and otherwise add value to the organization and to their work groups.

Inclusive practices create environments in which a broader range of people can feel safe, accepted, valued, and able to contribute their talents and perspectives for the benefit of the collective. Much of the emphasis in diversity and inclusion work is on how organizations can effectively incorporate differences of various sorts, as well as on how individuals can better engage with dissimilar others without seeking to eliminate the differences. Given this, in discussing inclusion, the focus is typically on what organizations must do to be inclusive and how each of us can be more inclusive of others. Yet inclusion starts with oneself (Ferdman, 2007): knowing, accepting, and expressing one's whole self creates a platform for welcoming inclusion within one's organization. We believe that the ways in which we as individuals combine, manage, and express our multiple identities—in short, how we show up and express our full selves at work—are a key part of the dynamic process of inclusion.

Thus the focus of this chapter is on the practice of self-inclusion, bringing one's whole self to work, as a fundamental component of inclusion overall.

Embracing Our Multiple Identities: The Foundation of Inclusion

Inclusion starts with our selves—recognizing and honoring the various components, characteristics, and identities that combine in each of us to make a whole person. To include others effectively and wholeheartedly, we first have to include ourselves; when we acknowledge the diversity of experiences, interests, and values that exists within ourselves, we are better equipped to notice and recognize the diversity around us in a more generative manner. Specifically, to be able to understand, engage, and value diversity at work and to effectively create inclusion for themselves and others, both leaders and employees must understand and appreciate all of their selves, without being required to compromise, hide, or give up any key part of what makes them who they are. Indeed, one could argue that being effective at work often involves a responsibility to be oneself, rather than using energy and resources trying to be someone different. Bell (2010), for example, in providing advice for women on including themselves and moving up in the corporate world, writes that "in order to succeed you have to bring your whole self to the table. ... The higher you ascend, the more important it is to be authentic and comfortable with yourself. The finest, most accomplished, most effective leaders don't hide who they really are. In fact, the best leaders generally have a great deal of self-awareness and have learned from the ... experiences that shaped their lives and enabled them to move ahead" (p. xiii).

Appreciating and using diversity for collective advantage involves recognizing, valuing, and leveraging the range of identities, perspectives, and approaches to work and life that are represented in any particular group or organization. In the same way, knowing about and engaging with one's full self (and its various components) is vital both to tapping into all of one's potential as well as to maximizing one's contributions in diverse groups and organizations.

Inclusion is deeper and more powerful than understanding or working successfully across multiple differences. At the individual level, it involves being able to connect to and integrate the various components of our identities so as to experience ourselves more fully, as well as helping to create the conditions that can help others do this (Ferdman, 2007). Only when we are able to access and appreciate our full selves can we wholly experience inclusion, which means feeling that we are "safe, trusted, accepted, respected, supported, valued, fulfilled, engaged, and authentic in our working environment, both as individuals and as members of particular identity groups" (Ferdman, Barrera, Allen, & Vuong, 2009, p. 6). This *experience of inclusion* (Davidson & Ferdman, 2002; Ferdman & Davidson, 2002; Ferdman et al., 2009; Ferdman, Avigdor, Braun, Konkin, & Kuzmycz, 2010)—the psychological sense that we (and others who are like us) matter and that our voices and contributions are important—should be a fundamental goal of inclusion initiatives. The experience of inclusion helps us draw on our full resources and make our maximum contributions. Moreover, it provides a secure base and a model for how to respect the differences that others bring into the workplace.

To permit and encourage others to be fully themselves, we first need to be able to do that for ourselves. How can individuals do that? What are some approaches for being able to draw on more of our full selves at work and in our work in ways that foster integration, authenticity, engagement, and empowerment and that allow us to make our best contributions to our groups and organizations? In this chapter we address these questions, together with the following:

- What do we mean by *whole self*, and how does it connect to diversity and inclusion?
- How do multiple identities relate to inclusion?
- How can people access and use more of their relevant selves at work? What can people do to include themselves more (or to include more of themselves) and to feel and be more authentic at work?
- What is the responsibility of individuals to create inclusion for themselves and others?

Much of the literature on workplace diversity focuses on how people perceive and treat each other, on intergroup relations, and on structural aspects of organizations and society (Ferdman & Sagiv, 2012). These are core aspects of diversity and inclusion. Yet much of that literature does not directly address the internal phenomenology of inclusion—how people experience it psychologically—or the responsibilities of individuals with regard to including themselves. That is our focus here. We do want to highlight, however, that we do not see these as mutually exclusive issues, and our focus on the work of individuals is not intended to negate or minimize the critical importance of combating oppression, discrimination, and structural impediments to inclusion.

Views of the "Self"

The notion of *one's whole self* is at once simple and complex. Most individuals, when asked, "Who are you?" or when they ask themselves, "Who am I?"—depending on the context—can answer quickly and without much reflection. They may, for example, describe their occupation, their values and beliefs, or their name and the names of their parents. They might focus on family roles (for example, "parent," "daughter") or their gender and hometown (for example, "I'm from New York," or "I'm a country girl"), or they might mention something about their typical behavior ("I like to play tennis") or personality ("I'm organized and persistent"). Yet our notions of "self" can also be quite layered and complex and are colored by culture and context (Ferdman, 1995, 2000, 2003).

The Self Incorporates Our Multiple Identities

A focal subject of much of psychology, the *self* is not static or fixed; rather, it is quite dynamic and develops over time, and incorporates not only descriptions but also thoughts, feelings, intentions, and various other facets. In other words, when we speak of our whole self, we include and highlight our various identities—the labels and categories that situate us in a social world through the construction of defining characteristics and relationships with other entities—as well as the associated thoughts, feelings, and intentions (Roberts & Creary, 2012).

Identities are multifaceted; they encompass meanings that evolve from a range of sources, including group categories and memberships (for example, "Latino," "man," "Princetonian"), social roles ("mother,"

"customer," "neighbor"), self-narratives ("I persist in the face of difficulty," "I'm a reliable and dedicated friend"), reflected appraisals and
interpersonal encounters ("My boss acknowledges that I'm a hard
worker," "She understands how important my family is to me"), social
structures ("rich," "poor," "citizen," "undocumented"), individuating
traits and characteristics ("extroverted," "tall"), and values ("democ-
racy," "hard work") (for a review, see Roberts & Creary, 2012). They
also include our views and beliefs about the groups we are part of
and the cultural characteristics of those groups (Ferdman, 1990, 1995;
Roberts & Creary, 2012). And each of us has particular accounts of
how or why we came to be who we are (Ferdman, 2000) and how the
various identities relate to each other.

For example, as management and leadership scholars, both of us
(Bernardo and Laura) study and write about diversity in organizations from a psychological perspective. We both participate actively
in the Academy of Management meetings. We are both parents and
spouses. We both engage in religious practices, but we are from different faith traditions. We enjoy teaching, consulting, mentoring, and
researching. One of us lives on the U.S. West Coast; the other lives in
the mid-Atlantic United States. And these are just a few of our many
identities and characteristics.

Additionally, we each have particular ways to describe what it
means to be part of each of these groups, and what cultural features
tend to characterize them. Indeed, each of us has a different description even for identities that we share (such as "scholar"). These cultural identities—our views of the cultural features characterizing the
groups we belong to, our feelings about those cultural features, and
the degree of overlap we see between ourselves and "typical" members
of these groups—can range from being quite idiosyncratic to being

quite similar to those of others (Ferdman, 1995; Ferdman & Gallegos, 2001). Finally, each of us integrates our multiple identities in an individualized way and gives meaning to the intersections and relationships among the identities in the context of our particular life path and social history (Ferdman, 1995, 2000; Roberts & Creary, 2012).

The self, then, is indeed complex!

Divided Versus Integrated Selves

Later in the chapter, we discuss in additional detail some of the ways that even how we construct the notion of the "self" is very much culturally grounded. At this point, we highlight that individuals vary in the degree to which they view people's multiple identities as distinct and separable, or as part of an inseparable whole. For example, from some perspectives, it may be seen as wholly reasonable that a person could be primarily (or completely) a "corporate executive" from eight in the morning until six in the evening, and then "mother" and "spouse" from six p.m. until eight a.m., with the two identities not having much to do with each other. Other perspectives would see the two identities as inseparable, with both present and important to the individual at all times, albeit with differential salience. (By the way, were you surprised, even a bit, when you learned that the corporate executive is also a mother? To the degree that this reaction is typical, it highlights one of the problems that both lead to and are exacerbated by the splitting of such identities.)

Individuals who have identities that are stigmatized in some way and believe that these should be hidden may be particularly likely to keep their public, or "self-at-work," and their private, or "self-at-home," separate and even divided (Sedlovskaya et al., 2013). In a recent series of fascinating studies, Sedlovskaya et al. (2013) showed that, among people who have such stigmatized identities (for example, gay men and religious students at a secular university), those who actively hid those identities in public—compared to those who did not—made larger distinctions between their public and private selves. And, on average, those with greater public-private distinction experienced more psychological distress (such as depression-type symptoms). There was a cost associated with maintaining a divided self.

Boogaard and Roggeband (2010) studied processes of inequality in the Dutch police force on the basis of gender, ethnicity, and organizational identity. They found that particular ways of splitting off identities—for example, emphasizing one's higher rank in the system rather than one's gender—could have the paradoxical effect of perpetuating gender-based inequality. This is because gender and rank were intertwined in the Dutch police force, as they are in many organizations around the world. Their findings can also be interpreted to suggest that there are more positive effects both for the individual and for the organization—in terms of highlighting and addressing inequality—to the extent that people claim more integrated and holistic identities.

In sum, then, I may experience more dilemmas regarding when and how it is permissible, advisable, or helpful to bring the various parts of my identity to my work role, and I may experience more pressure to split off parts of myself, to the degree that I hold or that my cultural environment holds the more fragmented view of the self—a view that is relatively common in North America, Western Europe, and similar cultural contexts—or to the degree that some or many of my identities may be seen negatively by others at work.

Whether or not we (or the people around us) believe that our various identities can be separated from each other in some way, these identities nevertheless coexist within the same person. Scholars who focus on identity have begun to refer to the interconnections among identities—especially those that are in some way stigmatized or treated unequally in society—as *intersectionality* (for example, Cole, 2009; Holvino, 2010). This perspective (see also Ferdman, 1995, 2003) emphasizes the interweaving of each person's various identities in cultural, societal, and organizational contexts that privilege or give power to some groups over others (Gallegos & Ferdman, 2012). Learning more about how the various parts of our identities connect with and interact with each other in an integrated and holistic way to make us who we are, as well as understanding more about the relative privilege or power (or lack thereof) associated with our various identities (Davidson, Wishik, Ewing, & Washington, 2012; Ely, 1995), can help support development of a more integrated and whole sense of self that spans one's multiple identities. It can also contribute to processes leading to less inequality and greater inclusion in our work groups and organizations.

Bringing One's Whole Self to Work: What Do We Mean and Why Does It Matter?

In this section, we discuss the key aspects of inclusion in organizations that are communicated by the phrase *bringing one's whole self to work*, together with some of their applied implications. Our argument comprises four central assertions: (1) each of us has different degrees of awareness regarding our multiple identities and makes choices about how to express those identities in different situations, including at work (Roberts, 2005); (2) each of us, as well as our organizations, will derive important benefits when we can be more authentic, by connecting with and expressing more of our multiple identities at work; (3) doing this is challenging and demands a great deal of presence and attention, together with discretion and flexibility; and (4) our social and organizational contexts play an important role in either hindering or facilitating the likelihood that we will connect with and express the various facets of our selves at work. Although our choices are affected by our social environment, our values, and our beliefs, we believe that ultimately, when we can be authentic and draw on our full range of identities in an integrated and holistic way, we will be better off—and so will our work groups and organizations.

For example, based in part on the assumption that having to hide one's sexual orientation was damaging both to service members and to the military more generally, the United States recently repealed its "Don't Ask, Don't Tell" policy that had barred people who are openly gay, lesbian, or bisexual from serving in the U.S. armed forces. Sedlovskaya et al. (2013) cite a range of evidence showing that hiding one's identities can be associated with less psychological well-being. Bowen and Blackmon (2003) describe how individuals who believe that they can freely disclose their various identities at work—including those that may be less visible—in the context of a supportive climate are more likely to express their views on important organizational issues and to "engage in organizational voice" (p. 1408). One of us (Bernardo), in conducting workshops on this topic, often asks participants what benefits they anticipate for their organization when they bring more of their full selves to work; responses typically include a sense of feeling heard and connected, increased engagement and retention, higher morale, stronger connection to and desire to be at work, more loyalty to the company, more creativity and innovation, and more productivity. Both intuitively and based on theory, research, and social practice, self-inclusion can reduce negative outcomes and increase positive ones, in ways that are beneficial both for individuals and for organizations.

We Each Make Choices About
How Much to Know and Be

So what meaning is carried by the concept of *bringing one's whole self to work?* First, the action word *bringing* indicates the notion of individual agency—the person's power to act in and on the world, including the power to choose who and how to be. We believe that individuals routinely make conscious and unconscious choices about how fully to embody and express the various facets of their identities in specific contexts and interactions. In particular, they consider how much to display or make salient certain components of their identity in particular situations (Bell & Nkomo, 2001; Bowen & Blackmon, 2003; Creed & Scully, 2000; Hewlin, 2003; Meyerson & Scully, 1995; Ragins, 2008; Roberts & Roberts, 2007; Stone-Romero, Stone, & Lukaszewski, 2006). For example, in the case of the pregnant woman mentioned earlier, she made a choice not to tell others at work about her pregnancy. Someone else may choose to be quite open about his religious beliefs, sexual orientation, and/or preferred sports teams, among many possible identities that he could highlight.

This type of choice may involve either specifically mentioning a particular aspect of one's identity to others or providing signals or cues regarding a particular identity (such as wearing a necklace with a religious symbol, putting a bumper sticker on one's car, or displaying a photograph of one's family in one's workspace). Note that this presumption of agency (or choice) and selective disclosure and expression of identities is grounded in a Western cultural context; in other cultural contexts, there may be less choice and/or less separation among identities. The presumption of agency also applies to emotional and attitudinal displays: bringing one's whole self correspondingly involves being honest and transparent about one's feelings and one's opinions, rather than keeping them hidden. (Later in the chapter, we acknowledge the necessity of wisdom, discretion, and respect for others when bringing more of one's identities, emotions, and beliefs into the workplace.)

These choices about *bringing one's whole self* should preferably emerge from self-awareness of our multifaceted identities and critical reflection on our own actions. How we think about and experience ourselves shapes whether or not we explicitly mention or highlight those identities to others. When we psychologically activate certain identities in our organizations, in the sense that we become consciously aware of them, we pay more attention to how (and whether) we might wish to draw on aspects of those identities—including associated experiences and perspectives— in work activities and interactions (Rothbard & Ramarajan, 2009). In other words, even before making choices regarding what to disclose to others about ourselves, the first step involves being clearer about the many identities that make us who we are, so that we can feel more whole and more empowered, including when we are at work—rather than split off from valued parts of ourselves.

For example, a former Olympic athlete, now working in an unrelated industry, may choose—consciously or unconsciously—not to note, mention, or even think about her athleticism or accomplishment while at work because it seems irrelevant in that context. Likewise, a manager in an organization who has extensive experience in a different domain outside of work—an amateur musician, for example—may not think about or make any connections between those activities and his role as a manager. Yet the creative talents associated with his musicianship and the leadership experience involved in heading a band may lend insight into how best to coordinate the work efforts of his team. Thus his team might benefit were he to bring more of his musician identity to his managerial work and identity.

Being inclusive of one's whole self, by attending to one's own multifaceted identities and related experiences and "bringing" them to work, can provide avenues for greater creative insight into one's work and can also foster a greater range of interpersonal relationships in diverse organizations (Dutton, Roberts, & Bednar, 2010). Thus we advocate being intentional in developing such self-awareness.

There is another benefit of self-awareness of one's multiple identities. People often prefer to think of themselves in individual terms rather than see themselves in terms of their membership in social collectives (such as those based on gender, race, nationality, ethnicity, or religion); this is especially true for those who are part of the dominant or more powerful groups in society (Ferdman, 2007). By becoming aware of not only these particular dominant-group identities, but also one's full set of important identities, it becomes easier to both acknowledge our connections to these larger groups and at the same time continue to see ourselves as unique individuals. This is because each of us has a particular configuration of identities that, in large part, makes us who we are (Ferdman, 1995). So we can experience ourselves as unique individuals and at the same time also be more aware of how that individuality is grounded in a set of social identities.

In figure 3.1, we illustrate an exercise that one of us (Bernardo) typically uses in workshops designed to encourage individuals to learn more about their multiple identities and the expressions or implications of these identities in the workplace (see also Ferdman, 2003; Hannum, McFeeters, & Booysen, 2010). In this exercise, participants are asked to list their multiple social identities and to reflect on them in various ways. This activity typically results in a greater sense of wholeness and new insights about oneself and about identity more generally. It also helps participants set the stage for exploring the possible relevance of these identities to their work, even when they previously had not seen or considered such connections.

More Wholeness and Authenticity Are Better

Our second assertion focuses on the whole self: individuals and organizations benefit from authentically including a wider (rather than narrower) range of multifaceted experiences, thoughts, perspectives, and attitudes at work. Why is this important? Inclusion, from this vantage point, is valuable because it brings a number of benefits, not just for groups and organizations but also for individuals who experience it. By experiencing inclusion, in the sense that they can access and contribute more of themselves, individuals are more likely to develop and grow in healthy ways that build on their strengths and to become more self-actualizing (Roberts, Dutton, Spreitzer, Heaphy, & Quinn, 2005). As we discussed earlier, they are also clearer about who they are and what matters to them and do not need to use energy to maintain a divided self.

Figure 3.1: Exploring the Sources of Our Identity

Some Sources of Our (Social) Identity

Ethinicity   Job Type   Academic/
Religion/Spirituality   Professional Affiliation
Health   Division, Function in
                              the Organization
Education   Nationality
Physical/Menal Abilities   Gender
Geographic Factors   Family
Politics   Sexual Orientation
Phenotype/Genetics   Race
Birth Order   Professional Identity
Language(s)   Class/Economic Status
                              Age/Cohort
Life Experiences   Ability/Disability

What are the Sources of Your Identity?
List as many of your social (group based) identities as you can

Exploring Our Identities at Work

Which of your identities and characteristics are the most obvious and/or important to others at work?

Which of your identities and characteristics, especially those that are important to you, are either relatively hidden or less known at work?

What identities do you see yourself acquiring, developing, or highlighting in the future? How/why are these identities important to you? How do they or can they make a difference for you and others at work?

How comfortable and/or uncomfortable are you in sharing more of yourself at work? Why? What conditions have helped or would help you share more?

When you think about being fully included and engaged at work, what does that look like for you? What behaviors from others and from yourself help you experience more inclusion? What behaviors do you believe help others around you experience more inclusion?

Copyright 2013 by Bernardo M. Ferdman. Reprinted with permission. Note: The first image is adapted from Ferdman, 2003. Copyright 2003 by Bernardo M. Ferdman.

Developing Our Best Selves

People continue to mature throughout their life span. For this reason, we take a developmental view of the whole self, rather than a static one, in which each individual takes a unique developmental path. Individuals who experience more inclusion—in the sense of experiencing more internal breadth and integration—will be more likely to develop in ways that can help them realize their potential, and in that way move toward becoming their reflected best selves (Roberts, Dutton, et al., 2005). This is because such individuals are more likely to follow their own developmental path rather than one imposed externally or modeled on others who are very different.

The Reflected Best Self Exercise (RBSE)™, developed by researchers at the Center for Positive Organizational Scholarship (Ross School of Business, University of Michigan, Ann Arbor), is a valuable tool for helping people develop in ways that promote inclusion. The RBSE exercise involves soliciting examples of strengths-in-action from key constituents, such as family, friends, and/or coworkers, and then identifying the common patterns and themes that define one's reflected best self. (For detailed instructions, see http://positiveorgs.bus.umich. edu/cpo-tools/reflected-best-self-exercise-2nd-edition/.) One of us (Laura) has facilitated this exercise with thousands of emerging and accomplished leaders across the globe. People are initially very resistant to the idea of focusing on their strengths as a platform for development; they would rather focus on and seek feedback about their weaknesses, to avoid being perceived as arrogant and to address what they deem to be their most urgent developmental challenges (Roberts, Spreitzer, et al., 2005). However, after experiencing this intense immersion in their own best-self moments, people begin to develop a clearer, more elaborate, and more refined understanding of their own potential to contribute to their workplaces, communities, and families in unique and valuable ways.

From an inclusion point of view, this emphasis on developing into one's reflected best self helps people to understand the critical connections between their strengths and weaknesses. It also reveals core themes in life that have surfaced during their best-self moments, creating a deeper sense of coherence between their past, present, and anticipated future. The intense exploration into one's reflected best self also requires examining various life experiences within and outside of the workplace; people are surprised to discover the consistency in how their friends, family, and coworkers perceive their contributions. Thus the fragmentation between the work and non-work self is reduced as people realize that their best self is more consistent across contexts than they may have originally believed. To develop into one's best self, inclusion involves examining one's strengths and contributions across the span of one's life, both inside and outside the workplace.

This self-understanding also allows for learning the critical distinctions between one's best self, typical self, and worst self, given the acknowledgment that one's best self is an authentic, but not a constant, state of being. Identifying with one's best self also builds confidence, providing a secure base from which to confront the moments and situations in which we are less than our best selves (Roberts, 2007) and to develop concrete action plans to be at our best more often and to make our best selves even better (Roberts, 2013).

Committing to develop into our best self requires the courage to deviate from our own typical self, as well as from social expectations for who one should be or become. At our best, we actively engage our strengths and values in ways that enhance our own vitality and that also create value for the social systems in which we are embedded (Roberts, Dutton, et al., 2005). Often, these best-self moments call for positive deviance—standing out from the crowd and departing from the norm in honorable ways (Roberts, 2013). When I experience my environment as welcoming all of me, just as I am, then paradoxically, I may be more able to grow and change in healthier ways; the key is that I work to become my best self, grounded in who I am now, who I have been in the past, and my own aspirations and hopes, rather than trying to become someone else. Even when we are most likely to focus on fitting in and proving our legitimacy in our work roles and organizational memberships, we benefit from incorporating a broader range of our identities into our work. For example, Cable, Gino, and Staats (2013) found that incorporating best-self development into organizational socialization processes resulted in higher retention and performance outcomes; specifically, inviting organizational newcomers to describe their best selves and how they might engage their best selves to contribute to their employing organizations was more effective for promoting inclusion than was emphasizing the organization's identity or other typical socialization tactics that involve diminishing individuality for the sake of organizational conformity.

Role-Modeling and Leadership for Inclusion

Individuals with more access to themselves and their own identities and experience are also more likely to develop richer and deeper relationships with others (see, for example, Avolio & Gardner, 2005; Bushe, 2009; Shamir & Eilam, 2005). They are less likely to be stressed and more likely to experience psychological well-being (Sedlovskaya et al., 2013). They are more likely to be content with their work as well as to be effective and powerful in their roles. Finally, in being grounded in their own values, goals, and convictions, they are more likely to show courage and determination in the face of challenges and to be better able to support development of a more inclusive and better environment for others (Avolio & Gardner, 2005; Ferdman, 2007; George, 2003; Goffee & Jones, 2006). By serving as role models of integration and self-inclusion, such individuals can help create the kind of world that will be better for themselves and for others.

As Mahatma Gandhi wrote, "if we desire that change, we must first change ourselves" (Gandhi, 1999, Vol. 24, p. 22), and, "We but mirror the world. All the tendencies present in the outer world are to be found in the world of our body. If we could change ourselves, the tendencies in the world would also change. As a man changes his own nature, so does the attitude of the world change towards him. ... We need not wait to see what others do" (Gandhi, 1999, Vol. 13, p. 241). In other words, it is unlikely that we can accept and value others unless we can first accept and value ourselves—including both our similarities to and differences from those around us.

Experiencing and Manifesting Authenticity

Ultimately, embodying Gandhi's charge requires authenticity. Authenticity is about being genuine, honest, centered, and consistent with one's values. Essentially, it is about being true to oneself by committing to a never-ending process of actively knowing and sharing one's experience. Bushe (2009), in his work on what he calls *clear leadership,* argues that a key to effective leadership is being able to access one's thoughts, feelings, and wants, as well as one's observations, and being able to share those with others when relevant.

While building on Bushe and others (Avolio & Gardner, 2005; Erikson, 1995; George, 2003; Goffee & Jones, 2006) in this chapter, we see authenticity as being broader than individual expression of personal beliefs, feelings, and experiences. Authenticity, as it relates to the practice of inclusion, also involves being clear about and true to the full range of who we are, not only as individuals but also as members of various social and cultural groups. In this sense, it can be helpful to recognize that we are shaped by our social identities and cultural backgrounds, and that for many of us, these are meaningful both symbolically and substantively (Ferdman, 1995, 1997). Once we do that, we then can begin to shape our own account of what it means to be part of these groups. Because there is great diversity within every social and cultural group, recognizing our cultural connections and social identities need not mean that we are stereotyping ourselves or advocating that we be seen simply or only in group terms. Indeed, each of us has a particular perspective on what it means to be a member of particular cultural groups and of a particular set of groups (Ferdman, 1995) and therefore has an individualized story to tell. At the same time, it is difficult to be fully authentic in a multicultural group, organization, or society without including these group-based identities in the picture in some way.

Beyond this, authenticity recognizes the inconsistencies in one's own behavior, takes responsibility for self-imposed failures, and embraces a holistic view of personal strengths and limitations that complement or undermine each other. For example, during the 2012 U.S. presidential election, President Barack Obama publicly acknowledged to the news media and general public (sometimes seriously, other times jokingly) that he was not at his best during his first televised debate against opponent Mitt Romney. Obama framed this debate performance as "having a bad night"; in so doing, he took responsibility for his own "failure," but he continued to maintain that this event did not define his capability or undermine his track record.

Authenticity also encompasses a commitment to share cultural experiences and cultural perspectives, which are associated with dimensions of difference related to social identities (Roberts, 2005). During the same 2012 campaign season, one of us (Laura) was teaching a leadership executive education course in Denmark on the U.S. election day, and she actively engaged these Danish leaders in a discussion of the social and political dynamics that influenced the election of the first African American president in the United States, as well as of the factors that influenced perceptions of his performance. In so doing, Laura brought her expertise as a diversity scholar, as well as her experience as an African American, female citizen of the United States to give her Danish students a different perspective on the U.S. presidential campaign. Laura followed this discussion with a lecture and case analysis of cross-cultural leadership and gender dynamics in European organizations. Thus authentic engagement was a theme for the entire day's discussions of global leadership. Authenticity involves giving voice to underrepresented perspectives and voices, shining light on marginalized groups, and making sense of teammates' competing commitments to different cultural traditions.

Authenticity Is Challenging and Requires Presence and Attention

Our third assertion is that bringing one's whole self is an effortful process that requires attention, discretion, and flexibility (Roberts, Cha, Hewlin, & Settles, 2009). We argued earlier that integration—experiencing oneself as a whole person with multiple identities, interests, and roles—has particular benefits; here we also suggest that there may be limits to the authentic expression of all the details and nuances of our identities, in the sense that we do not advocate necessarily or automatically being completely open to others at all times about all the facets of one's self. At the same time, this need to be thoughtful and attentive should not preclude us from developing a more integrated sense of self.

For some people, accessing certain identities or values in a context where these are not accepted or where they may even be disdained can be jarring and problematic, at best, and in some cases even dangerous.

In other cases, it can be inappropriate. We do not mean to suggest that one should always or even sometimes express the totality of one's thoughts and feelings at work.

"Bringing one's whole self" does not constitute the freedom to behave impulsively at work in ways that will be detrimental to other people in that environment—and likely harmful to oneself as well (Roberts et al., 2009). Rather, we advocate for a more strategic approach to self-inclusion, in which individuals increase alignment between internal experiences and external expressions of the most valued and valuable aspects of their identities at work (Roberts, 2007).

The challenge is that for many people the bias has been toward hiding and splitting off identities rather than toward integration. In many organizations, and for many people, there seems to be an assumption that one's non-work identities are somehow not relevant or important at work. To support positive exploration of unexplored connections between one's work role and one's identities previously hidden or less salient at work, and particularly to explore how these and similar identities can be positively integrated with one's work identity, one of us (Bernardo) typically asks workshop participants to conduct appreciative interviews with one another in which the listener asks the speaker to describe a specific work situation in which she or he felt fully integrated and authentic and was also able to be particularly effective (see exhibit 3.1). This activity is usually quite powerful for participants and can quickly fill a room with a great deal of excitement and energy. Beyond providing an opportunity to engage more deeply in challenging participants' prior assumptions about what belongs "inside" and "outside" the workplace, the activity also allows them to tell their own stories from their own perspective while receiving unconditional regard and interest from a work colleague or fellow participant.

Exhibit 3.1. Sharing Experiences of Inclusion and Success

Exercise: Exploring Our Best and Whole Selves at Work

Objective: To explore in depth an example of inclusion in your own experience, and to draw out implications for creating more inclusion for yourself and others.

Instructions to listener: Listen, be curious, and "bring out" the interviewee, on his/her own terms, rather than yours. Do not compare your experience with his/hers; rather, support your interviewee in exploring his/her identities through his/her own perspectives. If desired, jot down a few key quotes, themes, and examples from the "stories."

Questions:

1. What are one or two of your identities or parts of yourself that are very important to you yet not often particularly "up" for you or visible at work? Why is that part of yourself important to you?

2. Now, describe a time, either at your current organization or in another work setting, when you felt particularly engaged with your work and with yourself. You felt and experienced yourself to be effective, powerful, valuable, successful, authentic, energized, complete, proud, and fully ALIVE. You and others valued your work, you contributed fully to your group/organization, AND you could be your "best" and "whole" self. What happened? What made you your "best self" in that situation? Who was involved? What did you feel? How did the parts of yourself that you mentioned before show up and support you and your work? How did they integrate with the other parts of your identity?

3. Explore what it was that helped you to feel included:

   a. What did you do? How did it feel?

   b. What did others do? How did it feel?

Exercise: Exploring Our Best and Whole Selves at Work

Debriefing questions (for group): What was the experience like? Where was
the energy? What was the feeling of releasing or disclosing? What are some
insights/implications/learning/hopes?

Questions for further dialogue and/or reflection:

- What dilemmas have you experienced with regard to being more
  personally and culturally authentic at work? How have you handled
  these dilemmas?

- How can/should our cultural identities show up at work? Why?

- How will brining more of our full selves and our culture to work help us,
  our colleagues and our organizations?

- What stories can you share about any of these topics?

Source: Copyright 2013 by Bernardo M. Ferdman. Used with permission.

Exhibit 3.1. Sharing Experiences of Inclusion and Success

When we consider authenticity and self-expression in light of cultural
and social identities, personal expressions, and critical reflection on
one's own behavior, we bring to light some of the dilemmas and even
paradoxes raised by the desire and imperative to bring all of one's self
to work. Specifically, in finding effective and appropriate ways to be
authentic, we need to figure out and decide when and how to address
our individual connections to cultural and group-based experiences
as well as when it may make sense to hold back. For example, for
some men, part of their group experience may have been telling sexist
jokes. We would not advocate telling those jokes at work as a way to
bring all of one's self and to create more authentic self-expression. In
a different example, someone's identity outside of work may involve
being a religious missionary; that person need not keep this missionary involvement a secret, yet it would be inappropriate to condemn
coworkers' religious beliefs while on the job in a secular organization.

In yet another example, a mid-level manager, who often finds herself disagreeing with her new boss's strategic plans, may struggle with determining when and how to express her concerns with his plans. In this circumstance, the need for diplomacy is clear; we advocate not undermining one's boss by gossiping about or sabotaging his plans, but rather being clear, specific, and direct in communicating how the specific concerns expressed are related to specific outcomes within one's own purview.

Being true to one's core values is the primary standard we advocate; other questions of inclusion can be considered based on their consistency with or contradiction of such values. These dilemmas are even more pointed for leaders, who have responsibility not only to include themselves but also to help make room for diversity and inclusion across the organization (Wasserman, Gallegos, & Ferdman, 2008). In this role, they must regularly make tactical and strategic choices about self-presentation that will enhance their own authenticity while creating an inclusive environment for others. For example, should I, as a manager, express my anxiety over tomorrow's executive staff meeting to members of my team? Should I raise my voice in anger with my boss (or even mention the feeling) for his (perceived) failure to support me in a cross-departmental meeting? Should I ask my administrative assistant how she and her children are dealing with their recent divorce? Should I invite my teammate to attend Bible study with me during lunch hour? Should I bring my same-sex significant other to the family picnic next weekend? Should I wear my favorite beer-can tie to work on dress-down day? Should I avoid telling my sales team the joke I just heard about a celebrity's sexual indiscretion?

Of course, sometimes core values can compete with each other; for example, I value having as much time with family as possible, but I also care about my job security, so I may not go home as early as I would like because it may put my job in jeopardy. By being clearer about my various identities and the commitments and values that each represents, I can then be more able to sort out what approach might make the most sense for me (and for others I care about). Moreover, I can be more discerning about the impact of my enacted values upon those around me when I choose to bring more of myself to work. And I may be better able to see how my choices are not always solely individual choices but may be grounded in one or more of my social identities. For example, some Latino leaders tell us that they find it relatively challenging to "toot their own horn"—to self-promote at work; for many of them, this is not simply an individual idiosyncrasy but reflects values grounded in cultural identity.

For us, then, a key part of authenticity involves learning how to manage one's effects on others and being able to engage effectively with the diversity present in one's environment, including one's work group. Each individual is responsible to learn that not everyone is like him or her. In this sense, then, part of including myself also involves being aware of my effect on others.

Work and Social Contexts Matter

Our fourth assertion addresses how the work context influences employees' experiences of inclusion: if certain aspects of identity are deemed less relevant or less valuable by an organization, industry, or profession, workers may be less likely—cognitively and behaviorally—to bring these aspects of their identity to work. For instance, even though I may be clear that I am a parent, former athlete, or musician, the conditions of my work environment may make those aspects of my identity more or less salient in my own mind while I am at work.

Such messages are not always explicit. They can be communicated in a variety of ways, including by the way work gets done, by the types of interactions and processes that are typical or normative, and by the symbols and artifacts that are typically displayed in the workplace. In some organizations, for example, it may be quite normal and appropriate for a mother to nurse her newborn infant at her desk, while in others this would be unheard of and even grounds for dismissal. In some organizations, meetings may be scheduled for any time of the day or week, including during hours that are presumably "off," or employees may be sent on long-distance assignments from one day to the next without being asked first. In other organizations this would be considered inappropriate or extremely unusual, since it would be normative to check with the relevant individuals first.

To understand the dynamics of bringing (or not bringing) ourselves to work, we need to consider the systems of control, boundaries, containment, and prediction that often lead us to express only what we believe is normative, welcomed, or relevant in the work context. How much we reveal about ourselves and even how much we think about the different facets of our selves at work can depend, for example, on what we think the spoken and unspoken rules are for what is considered appropriate in that context. Being aware of these dynamics is important for all who wish to create more inclusion for themselves and others, and particularly so for leaders. Individually and with coworkers, creating inclusion for self and others involves ongoing reflection on the following questions: How can we move to give each other and ourselves more permission and support for authenticity? How do we co-create contexts that engage more of ourselves at work? Without such reflection, the process can at times be quite daunting; to the extent that we can create opportunities to collaborate on the processes of self-inclusion, the likelihood that it can occur and lead to benefits will be enhanced.

Earlier, we alluded to the cultural framing of the "self;" here, we elaborate on this and place the concept in a cultural context. Sampson (1988) described the distinction between the *ensembled* or *relational self*—more common in collectivistic cultures such as those found in China, Africa, and Latin America—and the *autonomous self*, which is more common in individualistic cultures such as those found in North America and Western Europe. Autonomous or self-contained views of the person construct the boundary between the self and others as firm, consider control over behavior and experience to reside solely in the person, and typically define self and non-self as mutually exclusive (Sampson, 1988). In contrast, ensembled views of the self construct the boundaries between self and non-self as more fluid, even overlapping, and consider that power and control over one's behavior does not fully reside in the individual but rather in the relationship between the individual and his or her environment (which includes important others).

The question of inclusion depends, then, on how we think of our "self" and how it is constituted—as ensembled or as autonomous. The dominant cultural assumption in the United States is that the self is autonomous and self-contained, and that we can therefore split ourselves up—for example, in different situations. From this perspective, one could be a parent in the evening and a professor by day, and the two do not have to have anything to do with each other. Many people in the United States conceive of the self as multiple, fragmented components that can be selectively featured, prioritized, or concealed and forgotten. In contrast, a notion of the ensembled self views our identities as very much connected to the groups and other people in our lives. From that perspective, our identities are constituted in relationship to others and in our various roles. In that view, being a parent and a professor cannot really be separated, even though the two roles are each in the foreground at different times. For those who hold an ensembled view of self, there is no choice in bringing the whole self, as there is no way to separate its various and interrelated components. And when such an individual works in an environment that seems to demand such splitting, it can be particularly stressful.

In both types of cultures, particularly in those settings that require more specialization, we see that people are more likely to split themselves up, as it were, and, when they go to work, to forget about aspects of themselves when they do not see those identities as quite relevant to the situation. For example, I may be a parent at home, but my role as a parent may never come up at work, or it may be experienced as being in conflict with my role as professor or consultant (rather than an integral part of the role). This fragmentation can create dilemmas regarding whether, when, and how to bring my whole self—professor, consultant, *and* parent—to work. It can also make it more difficult for someone with that view of self to call upon parts of herself that could be important or helpful at work in some way yet do not seem immediately pertinent.

Given these dynamics, we believe that leaders and organizations have a responsibility to help create the conditions within which individuals can more fully include themselves. The study by Cable et al. (2013) that we referenced earlier provides specific examples of how leaders can help to create inclusion during socialization—the initial period of organizational membership—by inviting people to think about and discuss their personal identities and best selves. At the same time, each individual has a responsibility to take up the challenge of self-inclusion and to help create conditions that will allow others to be fully themselves as well. We often operate based on our assumptions about whether our whole self will be welcomed in a situation or an interaction. Yet our concerns about being rejected may lead us to miss the subtle cues or invitations that sharing more of ourselves can promote our own growth or can help to promote someone else's growth. In our workshops on authenticity, one of us (Laura) asks participants to discuss circumstances in which they wear "masks" at work, and their rationale for so doing. People respond that they wear masks because they often fear the presumed consequences of authenticity, assuming that people from different backgrounds will not understand their own perspectives, experiences, or interests. We discuss experiences in which these assumptions have proven false. We also discuss how people can respond to moments in which others (for example, dominant group members and/or bosses) disclose aspects of their own personal identities, in a way that creates a deeper authentic connection, without feeling forced to share more than what they feel comfortable sharing. It is our individual responsibility to be observant, take initiative, and be prepared to share different parts of ourselves when the opportunities present themselves. It is also our responsibility to respect others' decisions to disclose more or less than we choose to disclose in our workplaces. To the extent that more of us take personal responsibility to start on the path of becoming more integrated and whole and to also behave accordingly, it is more likely that the collective—those around us—will become similarly integrated and whole.

Toward Integration: Dilemmas and Challenges

Throughout this chapter, we have argued that it is helpful to be more integrated—first for ourselves, then for others. This leads to more open expression of thoughts, feelings, and intentions, and the ability to draw on more resources. What constitutes strategic and appropriate self-presentation and access? How do we move toward integration? As we have pointed out, we do not see bringing the whole self to work as being about "letting it all hang out" or sharing all aspects of oneself with others. Rather, this process involves sustaining commitment to understanding the complexity within ourselves and in others.

The Responsibility to Define and Express Ourselves

Bringing one's whole self to work is a process of self-definition. A key part of this involves our individual responsibility to understand our own cultural identity—in other words, to learn how our connections to rituals, practices, and perspectives are products of our cultural experience as well as our individual history (Ferdman, 1995). To what degree am I aware of how much my taken-for-granted assumptions about what is appropriate and normal are culturally grounded? And to what extent and in what ways am I able to express this awareness and these cultural connections? For example, I may have certain beliefs about privacy and individual expression—whether inside or outside of work—that come from the norms, values, and practices common in my identity groups. Or I may have views about the appropriateness of discussing one's dating partners at work—or about the need to do so. Similarly, groups can differ on what is considered safe and appropriate to share. If I can develop an awareness of what is going on inside me and why, and a willingness and skill to express and communicate it appropriately, I can be more likely to create a space not only in which I can more fully include myself, but also one in which others can do so for themselves. The key to this is developing skills and practices to be able to share with others my needs, drivers, and perspectives—both as an individual and as a member of multiple identity groups.

Bringing one's whole self to work requires individuals to be accountable for their authenticity. Difficult choices of intrapersonal inclusion can confront us when we want to express, at work, certain aspects of ourselves that we value but that are not typical or are even looked down on by others. That is, although a person may consider a particular aspect of identity to be critical to her self-definition, other people in the organization—its leaders, for example—may view it as insignificant, irrelevant, or even damaging to the dominant cultural practices. Choosing to express a non-dominant aspect of identity at work will likely result in some degree of questioning and resistance by those who are less comfortable with that aspect of one's identity (Roberts et al., 2009). At the same time, doing so can make more visible the reality of diversity in that context and can serve at least to initiate a process of questioning and, hopefully, dialogue and learning. Choosing not to suppress but rather to "come out" with regard to such identities can ultimately strengthen individuals' capacity to contribute to the organization (Bowen & Blackmon, 2003). For example, one of us was recently approached at a workshop by a participant who explained that she was very uncomfortable with the expectation that she join in certain social events at work, because she believed that doing so was contrary to her religious convictions, and she also felt uncomfortable explaining her feelings and their bases to her colleagues and supervisor. Paradoxically, these events were designed with the goal of allowing coworkers to get to know each other better.

In this type of situation, it may be more useful to the individual and to the group to take the risk of being more open.

Just as organizations that welcome inclusion should develop systems and strategies to manage resistance, individuals should do so as well. When we choose to bring more of our whole self to work, we are more likely to participate critically in life; as we do this, we learn to consider others' expectations and interpretations of who we are, but to reject these expectations and interpretations when they do not resonate with our own experiences (Heidegger, 1962; Shamir & Eilam, 2005). In this sense, when we decide how to display the most valued and valuable aspects of our identities at work, we also gain clarity about our own boundaries. We become clearer about our preferences for permeability, integration, or segmentation among the different facets of our life; we make this abstract conceptualization of boundaries more concrete through our choices of self-expression.

Being Our Imperfect Selves: Embracing Diversity, Inconsistency, and Humility

Inclusion can be uncomfortable when we have to coexist with differences that are unsettling. This is especially uncomfortable when we acknowledge the inconsistencies and differences among our own roles, identities, commitments, words, and deeds. To put forth our best self, we must recognize our multiple parts, including the imperfect parts of our complex selves. While some people may produce cutting-edge, innovative concepts for new product development, they may also lack sensitivity to deadlines and budget constraints. Others have a keen eye toward details, but may be frustrated by loosely defined visions that lack plans for implementation. Some of us may embrace change but have difficulty following through on long-term commitments. Others may thrive in front of audiences but crave the spotlight so voraciously that they consistently overshadow (or intentionally demean) others' equally valuable contributions. Bringing one's whole self to work involves being honest about these combinations of strengths and limitations, while recognizing that each of us is constantly developing and learning. This honesty enables diverse teams to complement one another's strengths, address limitations, and discover unique paths to thrive collectively.

Bringing one's whole self to work also means recognizing inconsistencies between our own espoused values and actions. Perhaps we consistently state that we value all of the members of our team, but we disproportionately allocate resources toward those who consistently support our own visions, at the expense of those who push back on our (seemingly brilliant) ideas. We must be honest about our ego-defensive routines so as to bring our vulnerability and awareness of insecurities into our work; this honesty is critical to override biases against those who differ from us (Ely, Meyerson, & Davidson, 2006). Recognizing these inconsistencies within ourselves can also help us show more grace toward ourselves and others when we notice that intentions and impact may contradict each other. In sum, we would like to avoid an overly glossy view of the whole self and how it promotes inclusion for groups, organizations, and societies. Bringing one's whole self should be motivated by the desire to become one's best self, and this involves the whole-hearted embrace of a multifaceted, imperfect, and yet valuable self.

Finally, bringing one's whole self to work requires humility. A key aspect of humility is that, at the same time that I claim my identities, I do not claim full ownership or definition of the groups those represent. For example, I may have a particular take on what it means to be

Jewish, and can be proud and authentic about that, while recognizing that another Jew may have a different take on the same social identity. That way, I can be myself, grounded in my social identities, without placing myself and others in some kind of stereotypical bind.

In conclusion, the process and practice of inclusion begin with ourselves: identifying and affirming the multifaceted nature of our own self-concept and being strategic about how to engage various parts of ourselves to strengthen ourselves, our relationships, and our organizations. In this vein, inclusion requires concentrated effort and critical self-awareness; yet it is more rewarding and empowering to be ourselves than to expend our energy in trying to fragment and hide different parts of our identities when we fear they will not be embraced. In bringing our whole selves to work, we are able to focus our energy on fulfilling our potential and becoming our best selves.

REFERENCES

Avolio, B. J., & Gardner, W. L. (2005). Authentic leadership development: Getting to the root of positive forms of leadership. *The Leadership Quarterly*, 16, 315–338.

Bell, E. L. J. E. (2010). *Career GPS: Strategies for women navigating the new corporate landscape*. New York: HarperCollins.

Bell, E. L. J. E., & Nkomo, S. M. (2001). *Our separate ways: Black and White women and the struggle for professional identity*. Boston, MA: Harvard Business School Press.

Boogaard, B., & Roggeband, C. (2010). Paradoxes of intersectionality: Theorizing inequality in the Dutch police force through structure and agency. *Organization, 17,* 53–75. doi:10.1177/1350508409350042

Bowen, F., & Blackmon, K. (2003). Spirals of silence: The dynamic effects of diversity on organizational voice. *Journal of Management Studies, 40,* 1393–1417.

Bushe, G. R. (2009). *Clear leadership: Sustaining real collaboration and partnership at work.* Boston, MA: Davies-Black.

Cable, D. M., Gino, F., & Staats, B. R. (2013). Breaking them in or eliciting their best? Reframing socialization around newcomers' authentic self-expression. *Administrative Science Quarterly, 58,* 1–36.

Cole, E. R. (2009). Intersectionality and research in psychology. *American Psychologist, 64*(3), 170–180.

Creed, W. E. D., & Scully, M. A. (2000). Songs of ourselves: Employees' deployment of social identity in workplace encounters. *Journal of Management Inquiry, 9,* 391–412.

Davidson, M. N., & Ferdman, B. M. (2002, August). The experience of inclusion. In B. Parker, B. M. Ferdman, & P. Dass (Chairs), *Inclusive and effective networks: Linking diversity theory and practice.* All-Academy symposium presented at the 62nd Annual Meeting of the Academy of Management, Denver.

Davidson, M. N., Wishik, H., Ewing, T., & Washington, S. B. (2012, August). *Social identity dominance: How we all live privileged identities (and what to do about it).* Workshop presented at the 72nd Annual Meeting of the Academy of Management, Boston.

Dutton, J. E., Roberts, L. M., & Bednar, J. (2010). Pathways for positive identity construction at work: Four types of positive identity and the building of social resources. *Academy of Management Review, 35,* 265–293.

Ely, R. J. (1995). The role of dominant identity and experience in organizational work on diversity. In S. E. Jackson & M. N. Ruderman (Eds.), *Diversity in work teams: Research paradigms for a changing workplace* (pp. 161–186). Washington, DC: American Psychological Association.

Ely, R. J., Meyerson, D. E., & Davidson, M. N. (2006). Rethinking political correctness. *Harvard Business Review, 84*(9), 79–87.

Erikson, R. (1995). The importance of authenticity for self and society. *Symbolic Interaction, 18*(2), 121–144.

Ferdman, B. M. (1990). Literacy and cultural identity. *Harvard Educational Review, 60,* 181–205.

Ferdman, B. M. (1995). Cultural identity and diversity in organizations: Bridging the gap between group differences and individual uniqueness. In M. M. Chemers, S. Oskamp, & M. A. Costanzo (Eds.), *Diversity in organizations: New perspectives for a changing workplace* (pp. 37–61). Thousand Oaks, CA: Sage.

Ferdman, B. M. (1997). Values about fairness in the ethnically diverse workplace. [Special Issue: Managing in a global context: Diversity and cross-cultural challenges]. *Business and the Contemporary World: An International Journal of Business, Economics, and Social Policy, 9*, 191–208.

Ferdman, B. M. (2000). "Why am I who I am?" Constructing the cultural self in multicultural perspective. *Human Development, 43*, 19–23.

Ferdman, B. M. (2003). Learning about our and others' selves: Multiple identities and their sources. In N. Boyacigiller, R. Goodman, & M. Phillips (Eds.), *Crossing cultures: Insights from master teachers* (pp. 49–61). London: Routledge.

Ferdman, B. M. (2007). Inclusion starts with knowing yourself. *San Diego Psychologist, 22*(4), 1, 5–6.

Ferdman, B. M., Avigdor, A., Braun, D., Konkin, J., & Kuzmycz, D. (2010). Collective experience of inclusion, diversity, and performance in work groups. *Revista de Administração Mackenzie, 11*(3), 6–26. doi:10.1590/S1678 -69712010000300003

Ferdman, B. M., Barrera, V., Allen, A., & Vuong, V. (2009, August 11). Inclusive behavior and the experience of inclusion. In B. G. Chung (Chair), *Inclusion in organizations: Measures, HR practices, and climate.* Symposium presented at the 69th Annual Meeting of the Academy of Management, Chicago.

Ferdman, B. M., & Davidson, M. N. (2002). A matter of difference—Inclusion: What can I and my organization do about it? *The Industrial-Organizational Psychologist, 39*(4), 80–85.

Ferdman, B. M., & Gallegos, P. I. (2001). Latinos and racial identity development. In C. L. Wijeyesinghe & B. W. Jackson III (Eds.), *New Perspectives on racial identity development: A theoretical and practical anthology* (pp. 32–66). New York: New York University Press.

Ferdman, B. M., & Sagiv, L. (2012). Diversity in organizations and cross- cultural work psychology: What if they were more connected? (Focal article). *Industrial and Organizational Psychology: Perspectives on Science and Practice, 5*(3), 323–345. doi:10.1111/j.1754-9434.2012.01455.x

Gallegos, P. V., & Ferdman, B. M. (2012). Latino and Latina ethnoracial identity orientations: A dynamic and developmental perspective. In C. L. Wijeyesinghe & B. W. Jackson III (Eds.), *New perspectives on racial identity development: Integrating emerging frameworks* (2nd ed., pp. 51–80). New York: New York University Press.

Gandhi, M. K. (1999). *The collected works of Mahatma Gandhi* (Electronic Book, 98 volumes). New Delhi: Publications Division Government of India. Available at www.gandhiserve.org

George, B. (2003). *Authentic leadership: Rediscovering the secrets to creating lasting value.* San Francisco: Jossey-Bass.

Goffee, R., & Jones, G. (2006). *Why should anyone be led by you? What it takes to be an authentic leader.* Boston, MA: Harvard Business School Press.

Hannum, K. M., McFeeters, B. B., & Booysen, L. (2010). Mapping your social identities. In K. M. Hannum, B. B., McFeeters, & L. Booysen (Eds.), *Leading across differences: Cases and perspectives* (pp. 183–192). San Francisco: Pfeiffer.

Heidegger, M. (1962). *Being and time* (J. MacQuarrie and E. Robinson, Trans.). London: SCM Press.

Hewlin, P. F. (2003). And the award for best actor goes to . . . : Facades of conformity in organizational settings. *Academy of Management Review, 28,* 633–656.

Holvino, E. (2010). Intersections: The simultaneity of race, gender and class in organization studies. *Gender, Work & Organization, 17*(3), 248–277. doi:10.1111/j.1468–0432.2008.00400.x

K'naan. (2012, December 9). Censoring myself for success. *New York Times,* p. SR7.

Meyerson, D., & Scully, M. (1995). Tempered radicalism and the politics of ambivalence and change. *Organization Science, 6*(5), 585–600.

Ragins, B. R. (2008). Disclosure disconnects: Antecedents and consequences of disclosing invisible stigmas across life domains. *Academy of Management Review, 33,* 194–215.

Roberts, L. M. (2005). Changing faces: Professional image construction in diverse organizational settings. *Academy of Management Review, 30,* 685–711

Roberts, L. M. (2007). Bringing your whole self to work: Lessons in authentic engagement from women leaders. In B. Kellerman & D. L. Rhode (Eds.), *Women and leadership: The state of play and strategies for change* (pp. 329–360). San Francisco: Jossey-Bass.

Roberts, L. M. (2013). Reflected best self-engagement at work: Positive identity, alignment and the pursuit of vitality and value creation. In I. Boniwell & S. David (Eds.), *The Oxford handbook of happiness* (pp. 767–782). New York: Oxford University Press.

Roberts, L. M., Cha, S. E., Hewlin, P. F., & Settles, I. H. (2009). Bringing the inside out: Enhancing authenticity and positive identity in organizations. In L. M. Roberts & J. E. Dutton (Eds.), *Exploring positive identities and organizations: Building a theoretical and research foundation* (pp. 149–169). New York: Routledge.

Roberts, L. M., & Creary, S. J. (2012). Positive identity construction: Insights from classical and contemporary theoretical perspectives. In K. Cameron & G. Spreitzer (Eds.), *The Oxford handbook of positive organizational scholarship* (pp. 70–83). New York: Oxford University Press.

Roberts, L. M., Dutton, J. E., Spreitzer, G. M., Heaphy, E. D., & Quinn, R. E. (2005). Composing the reflected best-self-portrait: Building pathways for becoming extraordinary in work organizations. *Academy of Management Review, 30*, 712–736.

Roberts, L. M., & Roberts, D. D. (2007). Testing the limits of antidiscrimination law: The business, legal, and ethical ramifications of cultural profiling at work. *Duke Journal of Gender Law & Policy, 14*, 369–405.

Roberts, L. M., Spreitzer, G., Dutton, J., Quinn, R., Heaphy, E., & Barker, B. (2005). How to play to your strengths. *Harvard Business Review, 83*(1), 75–80.

Rothbard, N., & Ramarajan, L. (2009). Checking your identities at the door? Positive relationships between nonwork and work identities. In L. M. Roberts & J. E. Dutton (Eds.), *Exploring positive identities and organizations: Building a theoretical and research foundation* (pp. 125–148). New York: Routledge.

Sampson, E. E. (1988). The debate on individualism: Indigenous psychologies of the individual and their role in personal and societal functioning. *American Psychologist, 43*, 15–22. doi:10.1037/0003– 066X.43.1.15

Sedlovskaya, A., Purdie-Vaughns, V., Eibach, R. P., LaFrance, M., Romero- Canyas, R., & Camp, N. P. (2013). Internalizing the closet: Concealment heightens the cognitive distinction between public and private selves. *Journal of Personality and Social Psychology.* doi:10.1037/ a0031179

Shamir, B., & Eilam, G. (2005). "What's your story?" A life-stories approach to authentic leadership development. *The Leadership Quarterly, 16*, 395–417.

Stone-Romero, E., Stone, D., & Lukaszewski, K. (2006). The influence of disability on role-taking in organizations. In A. Konrad, P. Prasad, & J. Pringle (Eds.), *Handbook of workplace diversity* (pp. 401–430). Thousand Oaks, CA: Sage.

Wasserman, I. C., Gallegos, P. V., & Ferdman, B. M. (2008). Dancing with resistance: Leadership challenges in fostering a culture of inclusion. In K. M. Thomas (Ed.), *Diversity resistance in organizations* (pp. 175–200). Mahwah, NJ: Erlbaum

CHAPTER FOUR

Global Inclusion: The Mandate for Successful Organizations

Herb Stevenson

THE INCREASING COMPLEXITY of our world has been compounded by the immediacy of access to various forms of media such as television, movies, and the internet (Twitter, email, Instagram, etc.). Google has the capacity not only to provide directions to any location but to render a street view of the actual location. Geopolitical boundaries are blurred in the minds of those who created and/or continue to identify with such boundaries. This blurred perception continues to permeate the observations of the leaders of many organizations and countries throughout the world, leading to quasi civil wars during presidential elections, internal rebellions over immigration such as Brexit, and the rise of ISIS. As part of a diverse, complex world, we are frustrated with the inability to acknowledge, understand, embrace, and integrate the differences within each person, organization, culture, and country.

In this chapter, we will explore diversity within organizations. The focus will be to examine diversity as presently practiced, often unsuccessfully, within the United States as well as attempts to export diversity globally. To increase our understanding, a global (and cultural) perspective of authenticity will be presented to indicate that unconscious and/or unexamined core values and assumptions cross-culturally can lead to unintended consequences that create a perception of authentic irresponsibility. Authentic irresponsibility occurs when people are not true to the embedded values that are part of their larger societal contracts. Their behavior is not consistent with the expectations that are part of this implicit agreement, either at their work or in their own moral codes. Confusing this issue are the multiple levels that societal contracts imply (Wassenaar, Dillon, and Manz, 2015, p. 133). When applied to the larger organization or a much larger system such as the United States of America, an analysis may reveal unintended consequences—for example, how the lack of attention by the Democratic Party to the white working class led to the controversial win by Donald Trump in the 2016 presidential election. The exclusion of white working class Americans in the racial-disparity conversation led to distrust between a diverse workforce and the Democratic leadership. The chapter closes with a call to create transcultural leaders and employees. "Transcultural competence involves being able to adapt to various sociocultural settings anywhere in the world, with or without prior knowledge of the cultural orientations of those people and societies they are encountering" (Glover and Friedman, 2015, p. 8). Until transcultural competency is created, the perception of authentic irresponsibility will continue and trust will not evolve within organizations.

Diversity in Organizations

In the United States, diversity in basic terms has been defined as the effort to understand and value differences for the intended good of advancing the mission and business objectives of an organization. Diversity policies have sought to eliminate inequitable treatment toward various groups by developing more formal methods of determining who receives recognition and rewards. Nonetheless, micro-inequities permeate much behavior, though often unconsciously. More specifically, "discriminatory micro-inequities are tiny, damaging characteristics of an environment, as these characteristics affect a person not indigenous to that environment. They are distinguished by the fact that for all practical purposes one cannot do anything about them; one cannot take them to court or file a grievance. They are actions which, reasonable people would agree, are unjust toward individuals, when the particular treatment of the individual occurs only because of a group characteristic unrelated to creativity and work performance (for example, sex, race, religion, age, or country of origin)" (Rowe, 1990, pp. 4-5). The impact to the receiving individual is exponentially increased when we add cross-cultural values and assumptions that unconsciously clash. The impact is experienced as an existential attack on the person.

In organizations, conclusions about the perceived or assumed competencies of individuals have often been based on embedded biases related to group identity such as race, culture, gender, national origin, religion, and sexual orientation. An example would be that Mexicans are weak or lazy because they take siestas during the heat of the day. Moreover, not delving deeper into the root causes of these biases leads many policies to have unintended consequences. For example, research by Dover, Major, and Kaiser (2016, p. 2) revealed that diversity policies rarely make companies fairer for people of color or women and frequently are experienced as threatening to white men. The research indicated that "even when there is clear evidence of discrimination at a company, the presence of a diversity policy leads people to discount claims of unfair treatment" (Dover, Major, and Kaiser, 2016, p. 3). This belief was found to be especially true for members of the majority culture and those that tend to believe the system is generally fair. When these fairness beliefs are challenged, the majority culture can feel threatened, as if one's talent and effort are being dismissed (Burrell, 2016, p. 3). If sufficiently threatened, the individual often counters with accusations of reverse discrimination in response to any efforts to rebalance the situation. Moreover, the intensity of the individual's response is often directly related to a sense of being morally attacked. If the individual's self-perception is one of being a "non-prejudiced person," consistent with the organization's diversity policy and successful within the merit system for performance, it is experienced as a personal character attack (Castilla and Benard, 2010, p. 7). The experience of the attack sets up a perceptual tension within the person between possible unearned rewards (or privileged treatment) and the publicly recognized high performance via accolades, performance reviews, and/or bonuses. The tension creates dissonance—the person may or may not be as good as he or she believes—which the person perceives as an existential attack on character, competence, and/or performance. Therefore, when inequities are described as privileges for certain groups or unfair barriers and disadvantages for others, it triggers a potential angst in the person's self-image of not truly having earned what has been given or attained, and an emotionally charged reaction occurs. Returning to the 2016 presidential election, while Democrats were focused on the continued success of civil rights, including women's and LGBTQ rights, they ignored the fact that white working class Americans were feeling pummeled for being white while "factories were closing, incomes were dragging and white-Christian identity [was] a transfiguration of all evil and the butt of every joke" (Flood, 2016, p. 3). The social agenda of the Democratic Party became classism, a subject more sensitive than most all other isms.

Emilio Castilla and Stephen Benard (2010) named this the "paradox of meritocracy." They indicated that when leaders proclaim a commitment to fairness in their organizations, stereotypes can cause them to evaluate and treat equal performers differently. These stereotypes are reinforced through policies and the intent-impact gaps that ensue through daily behaviors. Hence, their public commitment to fairness clashes with their unconscious biases. For example, people of color and/or women, due to stereotypes, are unconsciously perceived and treated differently than white males.

Creating much of the unconscious reactions that result from the "paradox of meritocracy" are core beliefs about what is fair and what is just. For example, if those in power think the world is basically fair and just, they will tend not to recognize and therefore not focus on systemic unfairness (Burrell, 2016, p. 4). Therefore, how we frame our perceptions through our immediate (and unconscious) point of reference determines what to focus on and from what to make meaning. This framing process is exemplified by the 2011 United States Supreme Court ruling in a class action case against Walmart. The Court ruled that the presence of the company's antidiscrimination policy was sufficient defense against allegations of gender discrimination. If we return to the often-accepted perception that the world is generally fair, and add to that assumption that the intent of an organization is measured by the existence of a policy and not its impact, we begin to get a sense of why the United States often struggles with diversity (and why there is deep frustration for the affected groups). In other words, the intention of an organization under these legal beliefs will always override the impact that it has on its members.

Diversity Matters

It is simplistic to state that diversity does not matter. It does. Ongoing research by McKinsey & Company reveals a significant connection between diversity and the financial performance of organizations in the United Kingdom, Canada, the United States, and Latin America. Companies in the top quartile for gender diversity were 15 percent more likely to exceed the financial performance of their national industry median, and companies in the top quartile for racial/ethnic diversity were 35 percent more likely to exceed the financial performance of their national industry median. The research does not indicate a clear causal connection between diversity and greater profitability. Rather, "it indicates that companies that commit to diverse leadership are more successful" (Hunt, Layton, and Prince, 2015, p. 3).

With such evidence that diversity has its benefits, it is challenging to understand why more effort is not paid to supporting diverse groups so that they can work effectively together. A partial explanation for this lack of support is that it is hard work to establish the root cause of why diversity has not been universally adopted or more successfully integrated within organizations and to more clearly focus on the hidden values and unconscious biases that determine organizational strategies. Being successful cross-culturally instead of forcing the majority culture's approach onto others requires a deep self-examination of the majority culture's assumptions and core values. In other words, it requires delving deeply into cultural differences, commonly hidden in biases and stereotypes, to find how to successfully engage each other.

Global Diversity

Diversity is any dimension that can be used to differentiate groups and people from one another. It is about acknowledging and embracing differences such that people can respectfully understand and include each other in conversation, work, and life.

When we expand our lens to global diversity, we add another layer of complexity. As U.S. companies became multinational, the original business model was to place U.S.-born-and-raised managers in leadership positions for all their affiliate countries. This strategy was purely based on stereotypes, such as "the U.S. approach is best," that were commonly derived from deeply embedded cultural values and historical success. "These embedded values guide perceptions of the typical U.S. manager, even though he or she knows that [other] countries are separate entities with distinctively different cultural values" (Bloom, 2002, p. 48). In a one-size-fits-all unconscious assumption, the common behavior is to ignore cultural differences beyond trying to bend and shape behavior consistent with the U.S. policies; i.e., clone the operation in the foreign location. Rarely has this been successful. At a minimum, the local culture, now led by foreign nationals in the form of U.S. professional administrators, medical doctors, and support staff, can experience a sense of disrespect and, in some cases, feel oppressed when values collide. For example, a Pacific island hotel, known for excellent service and cuisine, experienced a significant drop in service after installing a digital order-taking system. Even though the waiters were proficient in the use of the system, speed of service declined. The U.S. manager was angered and made frequent derogatory statements that further demoralized the workers. A consultant revealed that the cooks could not read, and therefore, after inputting the orders on the digital tablets, the waiters walked to the kitchen to orally deliver the order. This added time to every order and frustration for the customers. It did not occur to the U.S. manager to determine whether everyone could read before installing automation, nor that the waiters would not reveal the inability of the cooks to read for fear of the cooks getting fired (Glover, Rainwater, Jones, and Friedman, Winter 2002, pp. 27-28). The same logic applies to diversity programs—just because the diversity program works in the U.S. does not ensure that it will work exactly the same in other countries.

Whereas the assumption might be that the U.S. is an accumulation of immigrants strewn over fifty states that is accustomed to a working diversity program, Europe is an unwieldy agglomeration of countries. U.S. organizations espouse diversity values in principle. In practice, they establish policies and practices as if the U.S. were a homogeneous country—one size fits all. In U.S. multinational organizations with business holdings in Europe, they often have exported this philosophy of a homogeneous country. However, from a European perspective, diversity is defined by its national cultures and languages—a reality Europeans have lived with for centuries (Bloom, 2002, p. 48).

Global diversity is the understanding and application of global differences and cultural perspectives. These differences and commonalities include, but are not limited to, ethnicity, religion, age, gender, culture, cognitive ability, life experiences, family situations, and sexual orientation. It requires considering very different cultures, histories, languages, and social and economic systems and how they apply to an organization. This means a deep understanding of each nation and its long traditions of how to behave to thrive in the world. Therefore, the task for diversity professionals is to dig deeper and begin to shift the focus to inclusion. Inclusion is not only about the obvious differences such as race, gender, and ethnicity, it is also about different styles of working, sexual orientation, core values, and dress. It includes different life stresses such as self-image in comparison to other countries and family care responsibilities. It includes understanding the core assumptions, beliefs, and values that drive the behavior for each culture. As such, inclusion is a set of social processes, which influence an individual's

- access to information and social support;
- acquisition of or influence in shaping accepted norms and behaviors;
- security within an identity group or in a position within the organization;
- access to and ability to exercise formal and informal power. (Jordan, 2009).

Dimensions of Culture: Dilution or Diffusion

As the world becomes ever more diffuse, we find that more national cultures are being overlaid digitally as well as through the massive immigration movement of the last decade. Thus, some nations are repelling immigrants as if they were an invasion while others struggle to understand how providing safe havens for refugees can become so painfully difficult. In the passages that follow, we will lay the foundation for understanding that whether through immigration or absorption of refugees, the inflow of different cultures both diffuses and dilutes the home cultures, creating a sense of unease and in many cases outrage. As immigration creates a diffuse and diluted culture within countries, organizations within those countries are therefore commonly comprised of workers of multiple nationalities. As will be seen, understanding cultural dimensions is imperative to global diversity and therefore to global inclusion within nationalities as well as all organizations, global and domestic.

Culture: The Invisible Way of Knowing What to Do

Culture is the method through which human beings—and the nations and organizations they create—organize their perception (make meaning), and we begin to realize that this perceptual process is complex and fraught with hidden traps leading to misunderstanding. Generally, as indicated by Trompenaars, Hampden-Turner, and Hofstede, national cultures tend to involve these characteristics:

1. Culture is the accumulation of practices and traditions that a group of people employs to solve problems, reconcile dilemmas, and make meaning in their day-to-day lives. Previously solved problems disappear from consciousness and become unconscious basic assumptions that drive beliefs, meaning-making, and therefore action. For example, in the U.S. it is common to be more stoic and less expressive, whereas in Israel emotional expressiveness is considered sincere and respectful.

2. Culture occurs in a variety of layers that have been learned and imprinted over the course of one's life. It is often referred to as the way we do things without further reflection on its applicability to the present situation. For example, in the

U.S., punctuality is considered proper behavior. In Japan, Argentina, and Mexico, punctuality is not a driving factor for meetings.

3. An individual who participates in his or her parent culture can never thoroughly understand other cultures until he moves into or at a minimum fully embraces another culture. Therefore, the assertion that there is one best way to manage a business is untrue unless we specify under what condition and within what culture we are making the assertion, because managing a business is culturally based. For example, in the Middle East, getting to know one another during dinner and many social encounters is considered the best way to do business. It is believed that it is important to establish character and competency before engaging in business discussions. In the U.S., there is often no desire to get to know one another beyond the immediate negotiations. Both approaches are successful in their own countries, but not necessarily in the other's country.

4. Every culture experiences authority, bureaucracy, creativity, good fellowship, verification, and accountability in radically different ways. Therefore, similar business organizations from two cultures are experienced and therefore perceived differently. For example, in Japan, the leader is responsible for the success of every employee, while in Canada, success is based on individual achievement.

5. How cultures come to understand and perceive reality has a different interpretation depending on the culture. For example, different products mean different things to people in different cultures; McDonald's is junk food in Boise but ostentatious gourmet fare in Minsk.

6. We become transcultural by learning to acknowledge, understand, appreciate, and include the embedded cultures of others. For example, several fast food giants failed miserably in foreign countries by assuming the U.S. menu would be accepted without changes to reconcile it with local culinary beliefs. After learning local food preferences, however, success began to evolve.

Cultural Dimensions

Fons Trompenaars and Charles Hampden-Turner partnered to create and test the Model of National Culture Differences. This involved a large-scale survey of 8,841 organization managers and employees from forty-three countries. It is a framework for cross-cultural communication applied to general business and management that indicates the cultural differences between nations. The model has seven dimensions: five orientations covering the ways in which human beings deal with each other, one that concerns how people deal with time, and one that concerns how people relate to the environment. These orientations combine to create the under-girth of the countries' unique culture for making meaning and interrelating with people, time, and the environment.

Universalism vs. Particularism
(Rules vs. Relationships)

Universalism is the belief that ideas and practices can be applied everywhere without modification, while particularism is the belief that circumstances dictate how ideas and practices should be applied. It asks the question, What is more important, rules or relationships? Cultures with high universalism see one reality and focus on formal rules. Business meetings are characterized by rational, professional arguments with a "get down to business" attitude. Trompenaars's research found there is high universalism in countries like the United States, Canada, the United Kingdom, Australia, Germany, and Sweden. Cultures with high particularism see reality as more subjective and place a greater emphasis on relationships. It is important to get to know the people one is doing business with during meetings in a particularist environment. Someone from a universalist culture would be wise not to dismiss personal meanderings as irrelevancies or mere small talk during such business meetings. Countries that have high particularism include Venezuela, Indonesia, China, South Korea, and Russia.

Table 1: Universalism vs. Particularism
(Rules vs. Relationships)

Cultural Dimension	Cultural Characteristics	Strategies for Building Culturally Common Ground (and Trust)
Universalism	A highly held importance on guiding principles in the form of laws, rules, values, and obligations. They try to deal fairly with people based on these rules. The guiding principles rule over relationships. Common universalist cultures include the U.S., Canada, the U.K., the Netherlands, Germany, Scandinavia, New Zealand, Australia, and Switzerland.	Support understanding how their work ties into their values and beliefs. Provide clear instructions, processes, and procedures, including culturally implicit expectations. Keep promises and be consistent. Words are important. Understand how time is used to make meaning and to make decisions, then provide accordingly. Use an objective and explicit process to make decisions, and explain your decisions if others are involved.
Particularism	The circumstances and relationships of the situation dictate the deciding rules they live by. Their response to a situation may change based on what's happening in the moment and who's involved. Common particularist cultures include Russia, Latin America, and China.	Provide expectations and/or desired results, then give them the autonomy to make their own decisions. Understand and respect others' needs when you make decisions. Allow how you make decisions to breathe in others' perspectives. Be flexible. Build relationships and get to know people so that you can better understand their needs. Highlight important rules and policies that need to be followed.

An Example

As a biracial Native American, I find myself stuck between the rules-based culture of modern America and the associative, relationship-based culture of Native Americans. This played out in my first job as a banker. I was trained to be a lending officer. I understood the policies and procedures for making lending decisions, and I was blind to my own personal bias of knowing people. One day, a locally prominent individual came into the bank and requested a loan. I looked at his financial statements and knew him to be honest and honorable. I approved and closed the loan. A few days later, I was called into the main office for violating multiple bank practices, including approving loans beyond my official lending authority. I was dumbfounded to see how these rules were rigid and unbending. Moreover, I was relieved not to be fired, as was threatened. Over time, I realized, if I wanted to stay employed, I needed to understand the immutable rules of the organization, including the unwritten rules of succeeding and surviving. This was my first conscious understanding of cultural differences.

Individualism vs. Communitarianism

Individualism refers to people regarding themselves as individuals, while communitarianism (or collectivism) refers to people regarding themselves as part of a group. Trompenaars's research yielded some interesting results and suggests that cultures may change more quickly than many people realize. It may not be surprising to see a country like the United States with high individualism, but Mexico and the former communist countries of Czechoslovakia and Russia were also found to be individualist. In Mexico, the shift away from a previously communitarian culture could be explained by its membership in NAFTA and involvement in the global economy. (This

contrasts with Hofstede's earlier research, which found these countries to be collectivist, and shows the dynamic and complex nature
of culture.)

Table 2: Individualism vs. Communitarianism
(The Individual vs. the Group)

Cultural Dimension	Cultural Characteristics	Strategies for Building Culturally Common Ground (and Trust)
Individualism	Personal freedom and achievement are core beliefs. They believe that you make your own decisions, and that you are responsible for taking care of yourself. Common individualist cultures include the U.S., Canada, the U.K., Scandinavia, New Zealand, Australia, and Switzerland.	Recognize and reward individual performance. Provide the autonomy to make their own decisions within their purview of work and to use their initiative to get work done. Culturally bridge people's needs with those of the group or organization. Allow people to be creative and to learn from their mistakes.
Communitarianism	The group is more important than the individual. The group provides help and safety in exchange for loyalty. The group always comes before the individual, including making sacrifices for the group. Common communitarian cultures include countries in Latin America, Africa, Germany, China, France, Japan, and Singapore.	Recognize and reward group performance often. Individual recognition should be in private. Support involving others in decision-making, even if it requires more time. Avoid showing favoritism. Avoid any form of public embarrassment.

An Example

A Japanese corporation purchased an American global energy corporation as part of a new strategic initiative to reinvent itself. Seeking to acquire a large market share and massive economies of scale (efficiencies), the Japanese corporation acquired several more complementary organizations. In a relatively short period, it became clear that the strategic plan had been implemented too quickly and without adequate due diligence (determination of quality and value). In short order, it was realized that the new strategy did not sufficiently determine the quality of the purchases, and it was revealed that a multibillion-dollar write-down was required under generally accepted accounting practices. This led to a decision to reduce all one hundred thousand employees' compensation by 20 percent, even though the energy division responsible for the losses involved only eight thousand employees, mostly in the U.S.

Japanese culture is collectivist, so the Japanese corporation believed that all employees should share in the solution to reduce costs and save the organization. Counter-culturally, the U.S. employees were dumbfounded, as individual responsibility is the norm and the decisions to acquire other organizations were made in Japan. Therefore, dissent rose quickly and several high-performance individuals left the organization. Both the Japanese and their U.S. counterparts were in deep cultural dissonance, unable to reconcile their perceptual and core-value differences.

Neutral vs. Emotional

A neutral culture is a culture in which emotions are held in check, whereas an emotional culture is a culture in which emotions are expressed openly and naturally. Neutral cultures that come rapidly to mind are those of the Netherlands, Japanese and British. Some examples of high emotional cultures are Mexico, Italy, Israel, and Spain. In emotional cultures, people often smile, talk loudly when excited, and greet each other with enthusiasm. So, when people from a neutral culture are doing business in an emotional culture, they should be ready for a potentially animated and boisterous meeting and should try to respond warmly. As for those from an emotional culture doing business in a neutral culture, they should not be put off by a lack of emotion.

Table 3: Neutral vs. Emotional
(How People Express Emotions)

Cultural Dimension	Cultural Characteristics	Strategies for Building Culturally Common Ground (and Trust)
Neutral	Control of their emotions is imperative. Reason influences their actions far more than their feelings. People don't reveal what they're thinking or how they're feeling. Common neutral cultures include the U.K., Sweden, the Netherlands, Finland, and Germany.	Develop emotional intelligence to manage your emotions effectively. Ensure your body language doesn't convey negative emotions. "Stay on task" and "stick to the point" in meetings and interactions. Learn to observe people's reactions carefully, such as body language, as they may be reluctant to outwardly show their emotions.

Cultural Dimension	Cultural Characteristics	Strategies for Building Culturally Common Ground (and Trust)
Emotional	Expressing emotions at work, even spontaneously, is a natural part of one's being. In these cultures, it's welcome and accepted to show emotion.\n\nCommon emotional cultures include Italy, France, Spain, and countries in Latin America.	Express enough of your convictions and beliefs to build trust and rapport.\n\nUse emotion to comfortably communicate your objectives.\n\nLearn to manage conflict effectively, before it becomes personal.\n\nUse body language to effectively communicate, positively and negatively.\n\nEnjoin a positive attitude with a clear message; i.e., this is not sugarcoating.

Specific vs. Diffuse

A specific culture is one in which individuals have a large public space they readily share with others and a small private space they guard closely and share with only close friends and associates. A diffuse culture is one in which the public and private spaces are similar in size and individuals guard their public spaces carefully, because entry into the public space affords entry into the private space as well. These dimensions describe how separate a culture keeps their personal and public lives. Fred Luthans and Jonathan Doh (2014, p. 132) give the following example:

An example of these specific and diffuse cultural dimensions is provided by the United States and Germany. A U.S. professor, such as Robert Smith, PhD, generally would be called "Doctor Smith" by students when at his U.S. university. When shopping, however, he might be referred to by the store clerk as "Bob," and he might even ask the clerk's advice regarding some of his intended purchases. When golfing, Bob might just be one of the guys, even to a golf partner who happens to be a graduate student in his department. The reason for these changes in status is that, with the specific U.S. cultural values, people have large public spaces and often conduct themselves differently depending on their public role. At the same time, however, Bob has private space that is off-limits to the students who must call him "Doctor Smith" in class. In high diffuse cultures, on the other hand, a person's public life and private life often are similar. Therefore, in Germany, Herr Professor Doctor Schmidt would be referred to that way at the university, local market, and bowling alley— and even his wife might address him formally in public. A great deal of formality is maintained, often giving the impression that Germans are stuffy or aloof.

Table 4: Specific vs. Diffuse
(How Far People Get Involved)

Cultural Dimension	Cultural Characteristics	Strategies for Building Culturally Common Ground (and Trust)
Specific	Work and personal lives are strictly separated. It is strongly believed that relationships don't impact work objectives, and, although good relationships are important, they believe that people can respectfully work together without having a good relationship. Common specific cultures include the U.S., the U.K., Switzerland, Germany, Scandinavia, and the Netherlands.	Be direct and to the point. More detail creates less confusion. Focus on objectives as you slowly build the trust to focus on strengthening relationships. Provide clear instructions, processes, and procedures. Understand and reveal your (culturally implicit) expectations. Allow people to keep their work and home lives separate until they decide to bridge it.
Diffuse	Work and personal lives are intertwined. It is believed that good relationships are vital to meeting business objectives. Moreover, it is believed their relationships with others will be the same at work or when meeting socially. Social time outside work hours with colleagues and clients is considered normal. Common diffuse cultures include Argentina, Spain, Russia, India, and China.	Lean into building a good relationship before you focus on business objectives, even if it feels frustrating. Work will go faster if relationships are built. Find out as much as you can about the people you work with and the organizations you do business with. Personal information is as critical as business skills. Examine any personal/cultural inclination to focus on work only before engaging—"get to know before get to work." Be prepared to discuss business on social occasions, and to have personal discussions at work. Try to avoid turning down invitations to social functions, while graciously expressing regrets when declining.

An Example

A business executive from the United States was working in a Middle Eastern nation to build a Western-style hospital. It was part of a community-development effort initiated by a local government. The executive went to a meeting with an Arab official to finalize the plans to open the hospital. During that meeting, he intended to obtain a permit from the official that would signify the government's approval to open the hospital. After arriving at the official's office, the executive appeared rushed and almost impatient with the official's insistence on making small talk. He wanted to get to the point and appeared to anger the Arab official when he immediately asked for the permit to be signed. The American also was uncomfortable with the Arab official's multitasking activities, as the official answered his phone while speaking with the executive, was interrupted several times by his assistant, and was apparently not ready to discuss the permit until later in the meeting. The meeting ended without the permit being given to open the hospital. The executive was frustrated that the official had not shared his urgency to open the hospital and expressed concern about how many people might not receive medical treatment due to this delay. But the official had found the outsider to be rude and disrespectful of how things were done in that country. He was heard to say that his people had survived many years without this hospital, and they could survive a little longer (Glover and Friedman, 2016, pp. 273-283).

Achievement vs. Ascription

In an achievement culture, people are accorded status based on how well they perform their functions. In an ascription culture, status is based on who or what a person is. Does one have to prove himself to receive status or is it given to him? Achievement cultures include the U.S., Austria, Israel, Switzerland, and the U.K. Some ascription cultures are Venezuela, Indonesia, and China. When people from an achievement culture do business in an ascription culture, it is important to have older, senior members with formal titles, and respect should be shown to their counterparts. However, for an ascription culture doing business in an achievement culture, it is important to bring knowledgeable members who can prove themselves proficient to the other group, and respect should be shown for the knowledge and information of their counterparts.

Table 5: Achievement vs. Ascription
(How People View Status)

Cultural Dimension	Cultural Characteristics	Strategies for Building Culturally Common Ground (and Trust)
Achievement	You are what you do, and individual worth is based on your capacity to do your job and get work done. These cultures value performance, no matter who you are. Common achievement cultures include the U.S., Canada, Australia, and Scandinavia.	Reward and recognize performance appropriately. Indicate awareness of low as well as high performance. Avoid favoritism at all costs, even though high performers might seek it. Develop low performers and new people within the cultural expectations of the organization. Use formality and titles only when relevant. Model critical behaviors and competencies.

Cultural Dimension	Cultural Characteristics	Strategies for Building Culturally Common Ground (and Trust)
Ascription	You should be valued for who you are. Power, title, and position matter in these cultures, and these roles define expected behavior (from and toward). Common ascription cultures include France, Italy, Japan, and Saudi Arabia.	Use formalities and titles, especially when these clarify people's status in an organization. Show respect to people in authority, especially when challenging decisions. Don't embarrass people in authority (by indicating incorrectness or ignorance). Don't let your authority prevent you from performing well in your role. (Honor closely aligns the person with title in many cases.)

Time: Sequential vs. Synchronous

Aside from the five relationship orientations, another major cultural difference is the way in which people deal with the concept of time. Trompenaars has identified two different approaches: sequential and synchronous. In cultures where sequential approaches are prevalent, people tend to do only one activity at a time, keep appointments strictly, and show a strong preference for following plans as they are laid out and not deviating from them. In cultures where synchronous approaches are common, people tend to do more than one activity at a time, appointments are approximate and may be changed at a moment's notice, and schedules generally are subordinate to relationships. People in synchronous-time cultures often will stop what they are doing to meet and greet individuals coming into their office.

Table 6: Sequential Time vs. Synchronous Time
(How People Manage Time)

Cultural Dimension	Cultural Characteristics	Strategies for Building Culturally Common Ground (and Trust)
Sequential Time	They can be misperceived as "fussy" or "starched," as they like events to happen in order. There is a strongly held value on punctuality, planning (and sticking to your plans), and staying on schedule. In this culture, there are certain held truths such as "time is money." They can see the world as mechanical and therefore don't value when their schedule is thrown off. Common sequential-time cultures include Germany, the U.K., and the U.S.	Focus on one activity or project at a time. If the setting is cross-cultural, put breathing space between projects, and use stand-up breaks to create awareness of differences. Be punctual and call ahead when late. Keep to deadlines, within reason, in multicultural settings. Set clear deadlines and clarify when changes can and will occur. Highlight course corrections in detail to support people in reconfiguring their plans.
Synchronous Time	Perceptually, the past, present, and future are interwoven periods. They can seem dissociative and unfocused, as they often work on several projects at once, and view plans and commitments as flexible. Common synchronous-time cultures include Japan, Argentina, and Mexico.	Take the time to understand how time is culturally viewed. Remember that so long as the work gets completed, how time is managed is less important. Be flexible in how you approach work. Allow people to be flexible on tasks and projects where possible. Highlight the importance of punctuality and deadlines if these are key to meeting objectives. Highlight unintended consequences of missing deadlines—e.g., if they impact others.

Environment: Internal vs. External Control

Trompenaars also examined the ways in which people deal with their environment. Specific attention should be given to whether they believe in controlling outcomes (inner-directed) or letting things take their own course (outer-directed). One of the things he asked managers to do was choose between the following statements:

- What happens to me is my own doing.
- Sometimes I feel that I do not have enough control over the directions my life is taking.

Managers who believe in controlling their own environment would opt for the first choice; those who believe they are controlled by their environment and cannot do much about it would opt for the second. For example, the following countries believe that what happens to them is their own doing (in order of strength of belief—highest to lowest): the United States, Switzerland, Australia, Belgium, Indonesia, Hong Kong, Greece, Singapore, Japan, and China.

In the United States, managers feel strongly that they are masters of their own fate. This helps account for their dominant attitude (sometimes bordering on aggressiveness) toward the environment and their discomfort when things seem to get out of control. Many Asian cultures do not share these views. They believe that things move in waves or natural shifts and one must "go with the flow," so a flexible attitude, characterized by a willingness to compromise and maintain harmony with nature, is important.

Table 7: Internal Direction vs. External Direction
(How People Relate to Their Environment)

Cultural Dimension	Cultural Characteristics	Strategies for Building Culturally Common Ground (and Trust)
Internal Direction (also known as internal locus of control)	The innate, often immutable belief that they can control nature or their environment to achieve goals. This includes how they work with teams and within organizations. Common internal-direction cultures include Israel, the U.S., Australia, New Zealand, and the U.K.	Support development of their skills and responsibility for taking control of their learning, including cross-cultural learning. Set clear objectives that people agree with. Be open about conflict and disagreement, and allow people to engage in constructive conflict. Highlight importance of team if it begins to feel like herding cats. Highlight cultural differences if they are impacting team performance.
External Direction (also known as external locus of control)	Strongly held belief that nature, or their environment, controls them; they must work with their environment to achieve goals. The innate focus of their actions is on others, and they avoid conflict where possible. People often need reassurance that they're doing a good job. Common outer-direction cultures include China, Russia, and Saudi Arabia.	Take the time to understand the local culture. Provide people with the needed resources to do their jobs effectively. Provide direction and regular feedback so they know how their actions are affecting their environment, including other people. Constantly inform people they're doing a good job to support their confidence. Manage conflict quickly and quietly. Encourage people to take responsibility for their work.

Recognition, Respect, Reconciliation, and Realization

Trompenaars concludes that for cultural competency to develop, a transcultural process must take place (Glover and Friedman, 2015, pp. 120-134). This process involves the following:

- **RECOGNITION:** How competent is a person to recognize cultural differences around him or her?

- **RESPECT:** How respectful is a person about those differences?

- **RECONCILIATION:** How competent is a person to reconcile cultural differences?

- **REALIZATION:** How competent is a person to realize the actions necessary to implement the reconciliation of cultural differences?

These four steps will be further elaborated later in the chapter.

Authenticity

Cultural and transcultural implications become clearer when we apply them to authenticity. A major paradox in global diversity is how to be authentic. In basic terms, it is common to describe authenticity as the ability to be genuine, as in your true self, maintaining strict coherence between what you feel and what you say or do, and making choices consistent with your core values (Ibarra, 2015, p. 4). It becomes a paradox when we add "according to whom." For example, what is authentic when a Malaysian executive in a manufacturing company, where people value a clear chain of command and make decisions by consensus, suddenly takes on a different meaning when the company is purchased by a Dutch multinational with a matrix structure. The Malaysian executive is now working with peers who see decision-making as a competitive contest for the best-debated ideas. Within the executive's cultural norms, aggressive competition does not come easily to him, and it would contradict everything he has learned growing up about humility and treating people with respect. In a performance meeting, he would be instructed by his boss to sell his ideas and accomplishments more aggressively. Faced with an internal paradox, he must choose between failing in his job within the new organization and being disrespectful and mean.

Authenticity, therefore, is as much about perception as it is about actual behavior (Goffee and Jones, 2005, pp. 2-3). In basic terms, an individual must have an awareness that words and actual behaviors must be cross-culturally congruent or mixed messages could result. To ensure this congruency, the individual needs to find common ground with the people in the organization, especially where the individuals are multicultural, multinational, multiethnic, etc.

Authentic Responsible Behavior

As I have observed this disconnect between different nationalities and ethnicities in many clients, it reminds me of the quote by Ralph Waldo Emerson: "What you do speaks so loudly I cannot hear what you say." The actions and behaviors by individuals and organizations cross-culturally are often experienced as confusing, frustrating, demeaning, and paradoxical. Embedded deep in our own unconscious, culturally created meaning-making, there seems to be no frame of reference for being both authentic and responsible.

Charles Manz, Christina Wassenaar, and Pamela Dillon coined the term *authentic irresponsibility* (2015, p. 130) to capture this cultural paradox. At first glance, the term creates dissonance around what is commonly perceived as authentic and responsible. Our embedded assumptions are that one would be responsible if they were authentic.[1] However, in global diversity, being responsible and authentic are not so easy to accomplish.

Authentic Responsibility

Responsible behavior arises from a sense of obligation to do something that reflects a certain level of care and concern for others while taking into consideration the impact of decisions on others, both inside and outside the organization (Waldman and Galvin, 2008, p. 328). Within organizations, responsible behavior requires absolute clarity about the depth and breadth of all the roles implied in the various positions as well as the people who fill those roles. When applied to trust, employees attempt over time to establish if the organization is responsible by determining if it (1) is caring and motivated to act in employees' interests rather than acting opportunistically for itself (benevolence and servant leadership); (2) is making good-faith agreements, telling the truth, and fulfilling promises (integrity and social contracts); (3) has the ability or power to do what an employee needs done (competence, capability, and capacity); and (4) takes actions (good

---

1 It reminds me of the impact that occurred when Barbara Kellerman noted the innate bias of leadership when she wrote the book *Bad Leadership*. Until that time, very little had been written to reveal that there is as much "bad" leadership as there is "good" leadership. This led to an in-depth assessment of what is bad leadership, instead of relying on the oft-used phrase, "I know it when I see it."

or bad) that are consistent enough to be forecasted in each situation (predictability across all roles) (McKnight and Chervany, 2001, p. 36).

Organizations that take responsible actions can be trusted because they are influenced by a sense of accountability toward others, revealing an "in service to others" orientation as a central value and a general sense of an implicit responsibility that functions like a social contract across all roles and levels of the organization (Wassenaar, Dillon, and Manz, 2015, p. 132). However, when we add cultural dimensions to what is authentic and what is responsible, we realize the core values and cultural differences add complexity and confusion. Unless the organization expands into a global perspective, responsible for knowing and understanding the cultures of all the countries in which it operates, misunderstanding and distrust tend to evolve.

For example, while working with a Japanese-owned American corporation, I was brought in to coach a recently promoted executive. When I asked about the purpose of the coaching, I was told that it was to prepare him for his next position. My American bias had made me assume that I was supporting the client to become competent in his new, current position, but it was clearly indicated to me that the individual was assumed to be competent already for the new position, and his immediate supervisor would support him in understanding any nuances. My assignment was to focus on his next position, scheduled five to ten years from now.

Had I not inquired deeper into the purpose, I could have made all sorts of mistakes, including applying American cultural assumptions to the situation and thereby setting the client and myself up for likely failure. Hence, what is authentic and what is responsible is culturally defined.

Identity and Role Identity

Our identity, or who we believe we are or should be, is a strong indicator of our predisposition for certain types of action. Identity has many different aspects that are influenced by our social roles. These role identities are shaped by our experiences, by our cultural knowledge of the role, as well as by our interactions with others while in the role. Hence, the value of organizations at all levels is that they can support new awareness while reinforcing existing perceptions of "what is the role." Unfortunately, many of these reinforcing perceptions are based on outdated values and unconscious perceptions about the organization and its operations in multiple countries.

For example, if a person is promoted from within the organization and has remained over an extended period of time within the same organization, the eventual role identity taken on by the individual will match the current characteristics of the organizational environment and its cultural norms, including the unwritten rules of how one succeeds. The role identities that leaders incorporate into their social identities reflect the expectations, norms, and values associated with the agreed-upon-over-time organizational identity that has evolved. However, as in the example above, where the Malaysian executive's company was purchased by the Dutch organization, the organizational environment and cultural norms can become blurred. Role clarity diminishes, self-identity becomes blurred, and self-efficacy becomes eroded.

I saw recent examples of this when I worked with a large city's metro-park rangers. Complaints and problems with park participants were becoming a noticeable problem. As the situation was explained to me by the client, I was aware that the park was enjoyed by many immigrant populations. Families and friends from the homeland would meet for picnics. The American cultural identity toward rules of authority and control of emotions was clashing with these other cultures, where relationships and emotional expressiveness were the norm. While having loud and raucous conversations, they did not meet the rangers with subordination and compliance. Often, loud arguments ensued when the rangers approached the families and requested more subdued behaviors. Using Mitchell Hammer's Intercultural Conflict Instrument (2005), which applied Trompenaars's and Hofstede's cross-cultural polarities to conflict, we recognized the cultural differences and reframed them into respectful understanding that could be reconciled to realize more satisfactory park experiences. Upon a return to the park and beaches, the rangers took more time to ask about the immigrants' homelands and if they were having a celebration or a joyful time with friends. Taking the time to personalize the conversations enabled the rangers to identify the countries and cultural conflict styles. This led to better relations and reconciling of the situations. The differences were neutralized through humanizing each other.

Cross-Cultural Authentic Irresponsibility

As indicated in prior paragraphs, irresponsibility occurs when people are not true to the embedded values that are part of their larger societal contracts. Their behavior is not consistent with the expectations that are part of this implicit agreement, either at their work or with their own moral code. Confusing this issue are the multiple levels that societal contracts imply (Wassenaar, Dillon, and Manz, 2015, p. 133). For example, societal contracts may involve (a) the role of being a citizen from the country of origin in a global organization, (b) the self-perceived role of being an officer or employee of the corporation, and (c) the core beliefs of what it means to be a local citizen in a foreign national organization. When these self-perceptions are muddled and confused, such as happens when organizations are imbued with people from many nationalities, misunderstanding occurs and leads to stereotypes and false assumptions. The act of irresponsibility is the unintended consequence of applying cultural assumptions and values onto other nationalities within an organization.

For example, when I worked with an Irish organization, it was global in reach, multinational (multicultural) in employment, and messy in relational dynamics. When confronted with several communications difficulties, it became apparent that the problem was as much how the Irish culture unconsciously permeated the organization as it was how the organization related to the cultural differences of the local employees at each national site. Using the above cited cultural dimensions, we began to create insights into unconscious behaviors that led to learning how to communicate better.

Complexity

The complexity of embedded cultural values, role clarification (within the organization and the larger societal system), and the behavioral contradictions resulting from the gap between one's intention and one's impact is difficult at best to discern let alone manage, and yet it is imperative that some semblance of understanding be developed if diversity is to transcend into greater inclusion and organizational effectiveness. Without an in-depth awareness of personal, professional, familial, organizational, and positional roles and how they interact congruently or create unconscious and unintended contradictions and consequences, an organization and all its leaders and associates may well be authentic and irresponsible when held to the higher standards of meeting the social contracts of all roles.

Common Symptom

A common example that cultural differences are impacting performance is when a change involves installing a foreign national leader or the organization is bought by a foreign national company. Without adequate cultural orientation between the different cultural perspectives, a negative turn in performance will likely occur. For example, when I was working with a U.S.-based global client, the executive team assumed that all employees understood the American way of doing business. However, due to the breadth of the company's business in multiple continents, rumblings surfaced about biases against non-U.S. (interpreted as non-Caucasian) employees. It was noted that all managers and leaders were from the U.S. even though there were extremely competent Latino, Indian, and Asian employees with equal or better education and years of experience. The employees felt they were doing the work and not reaping the benefits of their efforts. Unfortunately, in this situation, the executive team was not interested in the finding and simply ignored it.

The Behavioral Elements of Trust and Distrust

Global diversity increases the complexity of trust across cultures because our cultural differences are rarely factored into our awareness. I find that when engaged with clients and colleagues about diversity and inclusion, there is a tendency for trust and authenticity to become part of the conversation. Though I agree that the goal is for people to be authentic, I've found that most people in cross-cultural organizations truly believe they are authentic and struggle to grasp that trust and authenticity are embedded within cross-cultural values. In basic terms, until organizations and their leaders have a breakthrough in their conscious awareness, they will be blind to the cross-cultural perceptions surrounding them. Moreover, regardless of difference, culturally based behavior is tested against the local culture to determine if the person can be trusted to behave in ways that are generally beneficial to the individual. D. Harrison McKnight and Norman L. Chervany, in *Trust and Distrust Definitions: One Bite at a Time* (2001), reinforce this concept by indicating that trust is not situational so much as it is person-specific. A relational trust belief is established if the individual believes that another person has created a sense of psychological safety. When we bring the conversation back to authenticity, we begin to see why trust is directly related to transcultural competency. If, in my competency, I am culturally illiterate, I may be authentic in my national-centric beliefs but will not likely be trusted by other cultures.

In the following paragraphs we will focus on trust, organizational and individual, how it is developed and how we can support our clients to truly understand that people are constantly cross-culturally scrutinizing all behavior while formulating their trust beliefs about others.

Propensity: Internal Consistency of Trust

The propensity to trust surrounds being willing and able to cooperate, to share information, to make and honor informal agreements, to provide freedom to act (without burdensome controls or rules or micromanagement), to be influenced, and to grant decision-making authority (true power to decide without anyone looking over one's shoulder).

When we add the cultural dimension to the trust equation, we begin to understand why so many global acquisitions and expatriate assignments become a train wreck. Each of the cultural dimensions discussed earlier reveals that the reference point for making meaning prevents trust from developing between cross-cultural individuals. In short, the lack of understanding cultural differences leads to misunderstanding and therefore the lack of full inclusion. Instead of discerning cultural differences and applying them to the benefit of the organization, cultural biases often lead to moral judgments against those of different cultural processes.

TRUST = OBSERVED BEHAVIORS (OF INCLUSION)

Regardless of culture, people develop their trust beliefs from direct observation of those surrounding them. Generally, behaviors can be placed into four general categories for deciding whether to trust:

- Benevolence: caring and being motivated to act in another's interest rather than acting opportunistically for him or herself.
- Integrity: making good-faith agreements, telling the truth, and fulfilling promises.
- Competence: the ability or power to do for the employee what he or she needs done.
- Predictability: actions (good or bad) are consistent enough to be forecasted in each situation.

Case Study

A client was promoted to a senior leadership position in another country. He had successfully developed the necessary technical expertise and mastery of management systems in prior positions, and now he was given his first expatriate position. However, the new position entailed more organizational and strategic decisions involving multiple countries. Slowly and progressively his behavior became erratic as he became confused about why some directives worked in one country and not another. Subsequently, his instructions became inconsistent, and his capacity to influence the system became ineffective. At the end of his first six months, the executive team realized he was struggling. To support his development, a confidential 360-degree feedback process involving the employee's manager, peers, and direct reports was performed. The results indicated the following:

- He lacked cultural competency, having neither the organizational influence to get the needed resources, the expertise to guide the unit to success, nor the support to get the job done through the people surrounding him. He simply did not understand cultural differences or how to reconcile them into working solutions.
- He was perceived as unable to make good on his commitments, as he often returned without needed resources or with something, like more work, without including his staff when representing his organization.
- He was perceived to act in his own best interest when he encountered resistance from other areas of the organization by caving in or blaming others, especially his direct reports from the local country, for not being able to get the job done.

- He was perceived as inconsistent, as he floated back and forth among coercing, pleading, and demanding better performance, often loudly.
- He showed favoritism in performance reviews by rating males that shared his work experiences, nationality, and culture higher than local males, regardless of actual performance; moreover, he rated women even lower regardless of actual performance.

As we reviewed the results, it was clear that the client was overwhelmed both with the 360 results and the new position in a foreign country. Besides feeling pummeled from the feedback, he realized that he was in over his head. He was struggling with the fact that what had worked in the past no longer worked, especially with the locals. Most of all he was clearly upset that he was behaviorally perceived with distrust. To fully understand what we were looking at, we used a diagram of behaviors that create distrust and correlated it with his feedback. Though disheartening at first glance, it was clear to the client that many of the behaviors on the diagram were being cited in the 360 report. The important paradigm shift for him occurred when I reminded him that the feedback reflected perceptions based on prior and existing behaviors. Perceptions could be changed with concerted efforts to own up to what had led to the feedback and then to begin to change his behavior. His initial reaction was not pleasant; however, he realized he had no choice but to try to rectify the situation.

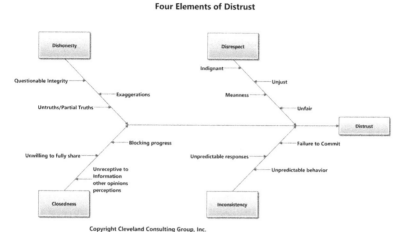

Four Elements of Distrust

Copyright Cleveland Consulting Group, Inc.

We reviewed the diagram in detail, searching for examples that could deepen his understanding of how these behaviors, which might not have seemed dysfunctional individually, had collectively created a perception of distrust among the employees. Even though he partially accepted the feedback, he had a massive reaction to being accused of favoritism. As we unraveled how this might be an accurate perception by reviewing how he had come to the assessments, it became clear that he had been internally weighting individual performance differently based on race, gender, and nationality. He recovered and moved to further assess his values and inbred beliefs that had blinded him to his process.

I introduced the four trust behaviors described above to show how perceptions of trust and distrust are developed by employees. As we explored the perceptions (benevolence, integrity, competence, and predictability), he began to realize that the new position had completely ungrounded him, causing panicked responses and a feeling of being out of control. He was surprised at how different the new job was compared to all his prior experiences. Moreover, he began to see from the table that he used a similar internal process to determine whether to trust everyone he was exposed to—direct reports, peers, bosses. He recognized that he had not been aware of how he had internally processed people different from himself and therefore had carried an implicit bias against them, and so these employees, judging him by his actions and behaviors, had perceived with some degree of confidence that:

- he did not hold all employees in positive regard based on performance and appeared to be motivated to act in his own interest or within his biases, even if it was unconscious;
- he did not make good-faith agreements, did not tell the truth, and did not fulfill promises with all employees;
- he did not have the desire, ability, or power to do for all employees what each one needed to be done to be successful; and
- his actions (good or bad) were consistent enough that one could forecast them in each context to be unfair.

To say the least, this was a turning point for the executive. After a slow start, he began to understand that his actions and behaviors had led to authentic irresponsibility for employees different from himself. He focused on learning about his own biases and incongruences that were leading to the unintended consequences of authentic irresponsibility. He initiated fact-based performance measures that were shared publicly. He committed to understanding the cultural differences of each of the nationalities within his team. He committed to being more open about getting work done in ways unnatural to himself yet effective. His team slowly learned to trust him, and as result the performance metric and climate surveys steadily progressed into outstanding results.

Global Diversity Requires Transcultural Competence

Glover and Friedman indicate that transcultural competence is imperative to success in a globally diverse organization. In their view, "transcultural competence involves being able to adapt to various sociocultural settings anywhere in the world, with or without prior knowledge of the cultural orientations of those people and societies they are encountering" (Glover and Friedman, 2015, p. 8). To attain such competence, there are four major aspects of transcultural competence that are critical to global diversity (Trompenaars and Woolliams, 2006, p. 6):

- **RECOGNITION:** What is the dilemma or point of friction preventing effective execution across cultures? Leaders need to ask, How competent am I to recognize the cultural differences around me? How do I define myself, culturally speaking, to understand, articulate, and negotiate my cultural identities?

- **RESPECT:** Acknowledging the cultural dilemma requires knowing that both sides have legitimate opinions. Leaders must ask, How respectful am I about those differences? Respect for those differences is crucial for one's competence to deal with cultural differences. (Glover and Friedman, 2015, p. xii).

- **RECONCILIATION:** Coming to some sort of cross-cultural agreement is reconciliation in global diversity. Leaders need to ask, How competent am I to reconcile cultural differences? Holding onto one's own cultural biases will lead to subpar performance and failure. A true opening into understanding the other's culture and finding bridges toward solutions is imperative for successful global diversity.

- **REALIZATION:** Translating the reconciled differences into inclusive behaviors that meet the needs of the organization and the multiple cultures within it leads to the recognition of a new culture. Leaders need to ask, How competent am I to realize the actions necessary to bring the reconciliation and implementation of cultural differences into greater acceptance and application?

Closing Thoughts

We are in an ever-growing world facing technological explosions that are rattling our various national and cultural predispositions to the core. Brexit was a cultural revolt from the fear of cultural dilution. National identities were threatened, as well as people's sense of safety and job security, by the inflow of immigrants. Similarly, it could be argued that the election of Donald Trump was a cultural reaction to immigration, an expression of a general sense that "I struggle so much, and I am not my brother's keeper, if he is different." Highlighting religious differences triggered a reaction from the embedded national belief, though constitutionally false, that Christianity is the only sanctioned U.S. religion. Highlighting health care as too costly triggered a reaction from many voters who, due to their own financial plights, had no interest in supporting fellow Americans' access to health care. A simplistic conclusion: the world is a mess. A more realistic conclusion: the world is a massively diverse, highly interdependent social system that struggles with how to create a sense of belonging and financial and personal safety. Differences can divide or enrich. We need to find a way to engage, embrace, and emulate these differences into a new definition of who we are as a people of this planet.

The hope for our future is to become culturally competent so that we can drive global diversity within each nationality as well as within each organization. We need a deep awareness that we are all human. We need to understand that inclusion is the full and complete acceptance of other people and cultures combined with the courage to build bridges for a better world, together. A complex conclusion: global development is a challenge that needs courage, commitment, and compassion to make the global community safe for all people. "Might take some time," as a wise friend once said, "so let's get to it."

REFERENCES

Bloom, H. (2002, March/April). Can the United States export diversity? *Across the Board*, 39(2), 47–49.

Burrell, L. (2016, July/August). We just can't handle diversity. *Harvard Business Review*, reprint R1607E.

Castilla, E. J., & Benard, S. (2010). The paradox of meritocracy in organizations. *Administrative Science Quarterly*, 55, 543–576.

Covey, S. M. R. (2006). *The speed of trust*. New York, NY: Free Press.

Dover, T. L., Kaiser, C. R., & Major, B. (2016, January 4). Diversity policies don't help women or minorities, and they make white men feel threatened. *Harvard Business Review*. Retrieved from https://hbr.org/2016/01/diversity-policies-dont-help-women-or-minorities-and-they-make-white-men-feel-threatened

English, P. Four stages of trust. Retrieved from http://paulenglish.com/trust.html

George, B. (2003). *Authentic leadership*. San Francisco, CA: Jossey Bass.

Glover, W. G., & Friedman, H. L. (2015). *Transcultural competence: Navigating cultural differences in the global community*. (Fundamentals of Consulting Psychology series). [Kindle version, 120–134]. American Psychological Association.

Goffee, R., & Jones, G. (2005, December). Managing authenticity: The paradox of great leadership. *Harvard Business Review*.

Hunt, V., Layton, D., & Prince, S. (2015, February 2). *Diversity Matters*. Report from McKinsey & Company. Retrieved from https://assets.mckinsey.com/~/media/857F440109AA4D13A54D9C496D86ED58.ashx

Ibarra, H. (2015, January/February). The authenticity paradox. *Harvard Business Review*, reprint R1501C.

Kramer, R., & Cook, K. (2007). *Trust and distrust in organizations: Dilemmas & approaches*. New York, NY: Russell Sage Foundation.

Kellerman, B. (2004). *Bad leadership: What it is, how it happens, why it matters*. Boston, MA: Harvard Business School Press.

Luthans, F., & Doh, J. P. (2012). *International management: Culture, strategy & behavior* (8th ed.). New York, NY: McGraw-Hill.

McKnight, D. H., & Chervany, N. L. (2001). *Trust and distrust definitions: One bite at a time*. In R. Falcone, M. Singh, & Y. H. Tan (Eds.), *Trust in cyber-societies*, pp. 27–54. Retrieved from https://www.msu.edu/~mcknig26/Trust%20and%20Distrust%20Definitions.pdf

Trompenaars, F., & Hampden-Turner, C. (2013). *Riding the waves of culture: Understanding diversity in global business*. New York, NY: McGraw-Hill.

Trompenaars, F., & Woolliams, P. (2006). Cross-cultural competence: Assessment & diagnosis. Adaptive Options, Spring, *The Newsletter of the Hawai'iPacific University Organizational Change Program*, Volume 2, Issue 1.

Waldman, D. A., & Galvin, B. (2008). Alternative perspectives of responsible leadership. *Organizational Dynamics, 37*(4), 327–341.

Wassenaar, C. L., Dillon, P. J., & Manz, C. C. (2015, April–June). Authentic (ir)responsibility: Quo vadis? *Organizational Dynamics, 44*(2), 130–137.

CHAPTER FIVE

Diagnosing Diversity in Organizations

Deborah L. Plummer

INTRODUCTION

IN THE EARLY 1980S PICTIONARY, the popular board game, was introduced to America. The object of the game is for participants to identify through sketched clues difficult words, persons, places, animals, or objects. The "picturist" is further challenged by having to depict the word in just sixty seconds. The game begins with the picturist having five seconds to examine the word before he or she begins to sketch. In those five seconds the audience can see the picturist struggling to take apart the word and break it down into recognizable clues. The picturist may not use physical or verbal communication to teammates and must rely solely on the sketch for the players to guess the word. Teammates strive to identify what the picturist so clearly visualizes in his or her mind. Often, after the sixty seconds has elapsed, teammates scream at the picturist for his or her poor representation of the word ("How did you get that from that word?" "What was that supposed to be?"), or they congratulate and high-five the picturist for his or her achievement. Many times teammates are amazed that they were able to identify a word from a poor or limited sketch. The interplay of picturist and teammates in this game is what has made Pictionary a best-selling game and provided a great deal of fun for many families and friends.

All aspects of the process we will be examining in this chapter are contained in the game of Pictionary. The game employs *methods* of sketched clues for participants to *identify*. The picturist continues the *process* of sketching and the players keep guessing until the sketch has been correctly *interpreted*.

Like the game of Pictionary, approaching the process of diagnosing diversity in organizations is a challenge. Unlike some other diagnostic procedures, diversity diagnosis requires a great deal of emotional preparedness on the part of the organization and the practitioner to begin the assessment. You probably can recall what it is like being a student on the day that test results are given. I can certainly remember the butterflies in my stomach and feeling the anxiety in my body listening to the instructor make general remarks about how the class did as a whole on a test. The anxiety was heightened even more if the professor chose to categorize the grading: "Only two people received A's, three B's, twenty-five C's, five D's, and two F's." Suddenly, whatever confidence you had about how well you might have done on the test disappears. In just a few minutes you have taken a roller coaster ride with your emotions.

Similarly, approaching diversity diagnosis creates an emotional roller coaster ride for organizations and for practitioners. Often considered to be an ancillary function for many organizations, diversity is only dealt with if there is a "problem." The "problem" may mean poor morale, team conflict, a threat of a lawsuit, or a filed grievance. The diagnosis appears to be simple—diversity or managing human differences in the workplace creates problems that need to be solved, typically by personnel in human resources. It can be easy to understand why approaching diversity diagnosis is not at the top of desirable interventions to undertake in an organization. Yet without an accurate diagnosis, any diversity intervention initiated will be like a shot in the dark. Smart companies know that managing diversity well is one of a company's greatest assets, so it is necessary to assess and measure diversity in the organization's current state if the desired state is to be achieved. Managing diversity well leads to enhanced performance and greater productivity. Managing diversity well means beginning with an accurate diagnosis of exactly where the organization stands in regard to managing human differences and leveraging those differences for organizational effectiveness.

The aim of this chapter is to help you understand the process of diagnosing diversity in organizations. It focuses on the process of identifying the current state of an organization and the methods for analysis. Topics to be explored include:

- the process of organizational diagnosis through the lens of diversity
- diagnostic tools that support inclusion
- application of the process of data-gathering and analysis to diversity
- feeding back diagnostic diversity information
- challenges in diagnosing diversity

Arguably not as fun as playing Pictionary, diagnosing diversity in an organization can be exciting for diversity practitioners. It requires using a number of skills and competencies to achieve the goal, which many professionals find intellectually stimulating. The process can be quite rewarding, especially when the diagnosis is identified and it guides the organization to organizational change and significant improvement.

Preparing to Undertake the Diagnostic Process

Because the diagnostic step is a critical one in the journey toward a diversity-proficient organization, it is important for diversity professionals to pay particular attention to the following conditions before starting the diagnostic process:

- **TIMING.** Diversity initiatives require a great deal of valuable time and resources (financial as well as emotional) from an organization. Is this the right time to examine how differences are managed in the organization?

- **READINESS.** How mature is this organization? Is the organization in a position to look internally at its operations, procedures, and policies? Will the present culture support this process?

- **INTENTION.** Is the organization clear about its intention for beginning a diversity initiative or examining its diversity efforts? This does not mean that there are right or wrong reasons for doing it. Whatever the motivation (business imperative, threat of lawsuit, moral integrity), the organization needs to be clear about its intention.

- **CANDIDNESS.** How willing is the organization to hear the many voices of its employee base? What has been the organization's history when it comes to implementing suggestions and managing feedback on company policies and practices?

Similarly, as a diversity professional, one must carefully consider the following aspects when beginning this kind of work in organizations:

- **CONFIDENTIALITY.** To increase the effectiveness of the process, confidentiality must be managed in a professional manner. All data must be held confidential and revealed only to appropriate parties.

- **OBJECTIVITY.** Although we know it is a myth for any practitioner to be truly objective, the diversity diagnostic process particularly requires a balance of objectivity and sensitivity. The practitioner must conduct an impartial representation of the data yet be insightful enough to give meaning to the interplay of hard and soft data. Hard data are facts that are measurable and observable, such as workforce profile data, engagement survey results, and work-life balance indicators such as absenteeism, early leaves, and tardiness. Soft data are personal anecdotes and experiences about how employees are treated, perceptions of feeling valued, and the emotional connection that employees have with the organization.

- **CREATIVITY.** The diversity diagnostic process requires managing the creative tension that exists in diversity. Diversity, or divergence from the prototype, introduces tensions that can be conceptualized as good and that produce new ideas, new products, and new processes. For the organizational system, this means deconstructing the perception of *us versus them* to create *we* in order to achieve the mission and drive the business objectives of the organization. For the individual organizational member, it means deconstructing the concept of *I get it* or *I am not [racist, sexist, homophobic, classist, ageist, etc.]* or that valuing diversity means one always engages in inclusive practices. Managing the creative tension of diversity requires remaining in a state of responsiveness and acting with cultural humility.

The practitioner needs to rely on experience, intuition, and hunches as well as diversity theory, research, and scholarship when gathering and analyzing data and formulating conclusions and recommendations.

Diversity Management Approaches

It is critical to understand the organization's approach or understanding of diversity as well as to know the approach of the diversity practitioner or consultant who will be guiding the diversity effort. The term "diversity" holds perhaps as many meanings as there are organizations, communities, and educational institutions that practice it. For a comprehensive understanding of the many dimensions of diversity and the frameworks that support them, refer to the chapters in the first section of this book—but one or more of the following four frameworks seem to operate in most businesses, communities, or educational settings:

Diversity as social justice. This approach grows out of the history of diversity management's roots in the civil rights movement. Eliminating oppression or the ways in which inequitable practices of power are used is the focus of this approach. Eradicating the "isms" or destructive beliefs and attitudes that individuals may have about race, gender, sexual orientation, or other human differences is also a goal. Community-based and faith-based organizations often approach diversity from this perspective. Corporate organizations that concentrate on affirmative action and equal employment opportunity also share this perspective, since these initiatives are designed to account for the wrongs of discriminatory employment practices in the past. "Leveling the playing field" is a phrase often used in organizations, reflecting the notion of equitable use of power and equitable distribution of resources and opportunities. Group-membership identities according to race, ethnicity, gender, class, sexual orientation, age, disability, and religion become critical components for measuring diversity success.

Diversity as equity. Similar to the social justice approach, this framework focuses on ensuring fair opportunity for everyone. Equal treatment does not mean the same treatment.

Diversity as economic empowerment. This approach does not hold central the issues of oppression and "isms" but holds as its focus increasing the bottom line. Diversity from this perspective translates into practices that make good business sense—and cents! If a byproduct of increasing the bottom line is better race and gender relations, then it is a bonus. If establishing better race and gender relations will increase the bottom line, then we need to have it as a critical part of the strategic plan. Diversity research helps to inform target markets and strategy. For example, if the multicultural buying power is over $3.4 trillion, then we need to know what to do to tap into this market. If recruiting information and technology talent is the goal and the pool of talent includes younger people and people of color, then we need to go after them. If stakeholders require that the company is socially responsive, then community partners in diverse neighborhoods will support our goal. Measurement of diversity is critical. Employment practices such as recruitment, retention, and promotion are analyzed from a dollar amount. Similarly, effective employee relations are measured by reduced employee complaints or grievances and avoidance of lawsuits. Most for-profit organizations recently have widened how they measure economic power by including a quadruple bottom line: profit, people, planet, and performance.

Diversity as inclusion. This approach is born out of the human-resource framework that capitalizes on the interdependence of people and organizations. People are not only seen as the greatest asset of an organization but key to its effectiveness. Thus diversity means establishing an organizational culture that promotes inclusion of differences. This approach perceives diversity as a tool for growth and a means for assuring the organization's future. Diversity is an organizational asset because differences enhance work practices by redefining markets, products, and strategies. From this perspective, organizations manage diversity to enable all employees to bring their full selves to the table in order to enhance creativity, morale, and productivity. Diversity success is measured by employee satisfaction, lower turnover rates, ability to recruit and retain the best talent, productivity, and an increased bottom line. Many organizations—profit and nonprofit, community, and faith-based organizations—operate from this approach.

In reading about these four approaches, you may already have positioned your organization in one of the four slots or in a combination. Or as a diversity practitioner, you may already have identified the approach that you most lean into. Perhaps you may be thinking that parts of your organization fit one approach and others operate out of another framework. Likewise, you may work as a practitioner from one frame with certain organizations and from another frame with other organizations.

No one approach in and of itself holds precedent over another approach. Each approach is neutral. You may have had to read those two sentences again. Before you prepare for a debate on the topic, understand that it is not the approach but the organizational fit (approach with organizational culture and mission) that is the primary intent of the process of diagnosis. The meaning of diversity must work for the organization—if not, little will be achieved. Thus it is important for the organization and the diversity practitioner to be clear on the meaning of diversity for an accurate diagnosis to take place.

What Is Diversity Diagnosis?

Consider the following case study:

Company Bigbucks, a moderate-sized insurance company, has been in existence for close to seventy-five years. Originally a family-owned business, it prides itself on treating its eight thousand employees as its greatest asset. Demographics in each of its three sites have changed over the years, resulting in a considerably more diverse workforce. Because its reputation is good, the company continues to make a profit; however, profits have been slower as domestic competition and global markets have increased. The company is interested in being the premier insurance company while maintaining the values that have been part of its tradition.

In the tradition of Company Bigbucks, the organization holds to openly expressed values of hard work and excellence for all of its employees, but particularly for managers and top leadership, these values are a requirement. Hard work translates into long work days that extend into the evenings and Saturday mornings spent in the office with coffee and doughnuts and a less formal atmosphere. Managers and top-level leaders know each other and their families well. Most socialize together and even take vacations together. They often discuss and evaluate work projects at social gatherings, and vacations may incorporate "working lunches." Performance excellence means that one follows the prescribed methods and procedures for proven successful outcomes. Evaluations are based on how the work is done as well as the outcome.

After a mailing of the company newsletter to its stakeholders, a consumer calls one of the men pictured in the brochure and asks for information about the company's diversity commitment. The picture of the company leaders paraded on the cover of the brochure shows a group of all white males, and the consumer wonders whether the company reflects the client base it serves. The consumer is told that the company does indeed employ some women and a few people of color, although their upper management (pictured in the newsletter) is all white males. When the consumer expresses dissatisfaction with the response and notes that the director only considers diversity in relationship to group-membership identity, the director offers to send a representative to meet with the consumer and address any further questions.

At the next leadership meeting, the director who received the call relates the incident to his peers. After a brief discussion, they congratulate their colleague for dealing with the issue in a direct and courteous manner, especially because the consumer is perceived to be a complainer. The leadership team believes the incident is just representative of the political correctness sweeping the country. The leadership team further assesses that no other action is necessary.

This is not an unusual case for contemporary organizations. As a business, Company Bigbucks is holding its own when it comes to reviewing the bottom line. The company also considers itself to be performing competitively and that its organizational culture is healthy. Company norms are considered open and the culture believes itself to be clear in its requirements for employment and promotion opportunities. Employees are valued and treated well from a compensation standpoint. But would you vote this company one of the top companies to work for based on the information provided? How would you evaluate their relationship to diversity? What do you believe to be the working definition of diversity for Company Bigbucks?

While reading this case study, you may already have started the process of diversity diagnosis. Diversity diagnosis is the process that guides the development of diversity proficiency in an organization. It is an assessment of how well the organization is doing with managing a diverse workforce and utilizing its benefits to increase organizational effectiveness and achieve business objectives. The process of diversity diagnosis is the initial step in developing interventions that will be linked to a strategic plan to support organizational change and improvement.

What is diagnosed?

- Organizational culture (values, traditions, norms, artifacts)
- Business rationale (organizational history and its mission)
- Employee morale (work identity and spirit)
- Physical space (décor, design)
- Employee demographics (group-membership identity of employees)
- Turnover patterns (reviewed according to group-membership identity)
- Promotion patterns (reviewed according to group-membership identity)
- Brochures (any written descriptions of company)
- Websites (internet presence)
- Social media (participation in social networking)
- Organization's working definition of diversity
- Board membership (reviewed according to group-membership identity and leadership roles)
- Mentoring practices (formal and informal)
- Reward systems (reviewed for cultural flexibility)
- Strategic plans (for inclusion issues)

Redirect your thinking to the case study of Company Bigbucks. Considering the list of what aspects of the organization are part of the diagnostic process, you may be acutely aware of the lack of information you possess to support your initial assessment. You may have considered Company Bigbucks to *not* be diversity affirming but were unaware of a benchmark to support your claim. You may consider Company Bigbucks to be diversity affirming but lacked a framework to defend your position. As a CEO, manager, supervisor, member of a diversity council, consultant, or diversity practitioner, this chapter will help you assess how well your organization is doing with managing a diverse workforce and the related diversity issues.

Diversity Diagnosis Skills

Practitioners of diversity diagnosis are a special kind of change agent. Unlike diversity innovators or diversity champions, professionals who engage in diagnosing diversity in organizations possess a distinctive set of skills and competencies:

- Clarity on the meaning of diversity for a company and how diversity differs from the practice of affirmative action, equal opportunity employment, or social justice
- Ability to engage in dialogue as a communication structure that supports inclusion and objective research
- Mastery of systems thinking—understanding the interrelationships that shape the dynamics of differences
- Ability to hold multiple realities and perspectives while still appreciating individual identities
- Competent utilization of mixed methodology—both qualitative, a type of research that produces findings not arrived at by statistical procedures or other means of

quantification, and quantitative, a type of research that
produces findings based on statistical procedures

- Utilization of the art of giving and receiving feedback—
understanding the process of giving, getting, and
analyzing advice

Diversity Diagnostic Process

These are the steps of the diagnostic process:

1. Understanding the working definition of diversity for the
   organization
2. Choosing the right method(s) for diagnosis
3. Determining the level of analysis
4. Applying frameworks for interpretation
5. Developing appropriate reporting procedures

Although it would appear to be most logical to proceed in a step-
by-step manner for diagnosing diversity, there are occasions when the
level of analysis may precede the choice of method. For example, the
results from a prior questionnaire or focus group study may be available for reinterpretation from a diversity lens, allowing you to begin
determining the level of analysis before you have a working definition of diversity. In the best conditions, however, gathering fresh data
with this particular diagnostic process in mind is recommended to
allow you to choose the appropriate method aligned with the desired
end results.

Understanding the Working Definition of Diversity

The process of diagnosing diversity in any organization begins with
understanding the organization's approach to leveraging people's
differences in the organization. If an organization does not have a

working definition and is a novice in the area of diversity management, it may mean developing a process that unveils their approach. An organization may be a novice in its formal management, but that does not mean it does not have a working definition of diversity informally operating within the system. Because we are assessing what diversity means in an organization, it is important to ensure that the definition is representative of the collective voices of the organization and is not derived from an assumed understanding of the term. If diversity means respecting one another in the workplace, the approach for managing it will be very different from an organization in which diversity means enhancing the bottom line by effective performance from all employees.

Start where the organization is. If the organization does not have a working definition, begin the process of defining what is already in existence. This is different from a visioning process where the work is to determine the preferred future or desired state. You are simply labeling the "what is" of your organization in order to accurately diagnose how well it is doing at achieving what it believes to be diversity. The process of identifying an organization's working definition of diversity uses a similar methodology to the process of diagnosis— review of hard and soft data, interviews, questionnaires, and focus groups are appropriate choices. These methods will be fully discussed later. As the working definition is a dynamic entity and not a fixed state, the process of discovering the organization's working definition will not be a completed task. Thus you merely want to ascertain what is already present rather than stir up the need for evaluating whether or not the present definition is a good fit. That information will clearly come out in the diagnostic process. The important aspect is to make sure the working definition represents the collective voice and is not simply lifted from a book or video on diversity management. It needs to really work for the organization.

Once the definition is clearly in place, it is easy to understand that definition from the framework that it represents. Table 1 provides some examples.

Table 1. Definitions and Frameworks They Represent

Definition of Diversity	Diversity Management Approach
Organizational effectiveness	Inclusion
Dignity and respect	Social justice
Competitive advantage	Economic empowerment
Organizing business processes and establishing policies to ensure success, particularly for women and underrepresented groups	Equity
Creating policies, practices, and procedures that leverage differences	Inclusion
Creating an anti-racist, gender-fair, multicultural organization, community, or educational institution	Social justice
Full compliance with all regulatory aspects of labor laws	Equity
A business imperative for the twenty-first century	Economic empowerment
Innovation: new ways of knowing, thinking, and behaving	Inclusion

Think for a moment about your own organization. What words or phrases characterize the meaning of diversity for your organization? Skim through your organization's promotional material, examine your mission statement, visually assess your company's décor, think about your organization's values and its senior leadership. What does this information tell you about the meaning of diversity in your organization? Jot down some of these phrases in Table 2. Next to each phrase put the basic approach the concept is born out of.

Table 2. The Meaning of Diversity for Your Organization

Diversity Phrases	Diversity Approaches
1.	
2.	
3.	
4.	

What does this information tell you about your organization's basic approach to diversity?

The aim of diagnosis is not to change or influence an organization's approach or where an organization should or could be, but simply to lay out the data in a meaningful way for the organization's development of diversity competencies. Building a credible database including quantitative and qualitative data, hard data (historical and present-day facts) and soft data (psychological facts), is the ground from which accurate diagnosis takes place.

Choosing the Right Methodology

How the data is collected will determine the kind of data that is available for interpretation. Thus asking the right question and choosing the right method to support getting the appropriate framework is critical to obtaining the diagnosis that will lead to a measurable outcome. Get the sequence?

> **Right Question → Right Method → Appropriate Framework → Accurate Diagnosis → Measurable Outcome**

Like a set of dominoes displayed to stand up one against the other, good positioning will allow the structure to stand erect. Poor positioning on the part of any one of the dominoes will collapse the entire setup!

Asking the Right Question

Asking the right question begins with being clear about what the intended outcome is. What do you want to see change in the organization? How will you know when you have the answer? What is the desired goal? How will you know that you are successful after this intervention? These questions will lead to responses that will set the direction for the inquiry process. For example, if your desired outcome is to build an inclusive learning community for your educational institution, then start with examining what inclusive means and explore what inclusive behaviors look like. With this data, you can then reach consensus on what is meant by a learning community and how those inclusive behaviors might be practiced in that community.

With the specific understanding of what an inclusive learning community is, you are now armed with how to diagnose whether the culture is aligned with those behaviors. You can now choose the appropriate method for getting the answer to your question.

Choosing the Right Method

The methods for gathering data to support an accurate diagnosis are the practitioner's tools for success. Choosing the right tools will not only get the job done correctly but get it done in an efficient manner. If you have ever watched a professional worker repair something in your home, you know the difference a correct tool can make in getting the job done efficiently and effectively. Similarly, in diagnosing diversity, the appropriate choice of methodology will assure the desired outcome. The data gathering tools most often used in diversity diagnosis are the following:

- Questionnaires and surveys
- Individual interviews
- Environmental/cultural scans
- Observation/sponging/scouting
- Focus groups
- Historical timeline analysis
- Benchmarking
- Best practices/current-struggles profiles
- Career path process mapping
- Diversity dialogue sessions
- Critical incident interviewing
- Large group interventions

Table 3 depicts the advantages and disadvantages of each method when conducting diversity work.

Table 3. Advantages and Disadvantages of Data-
Gathering Methods from a Diversity Perspective

METHOD	ADVANTAGES	DISADVANTAGES
Questionnaires/ surveys/rating scales: Paper and pen measures with questions focused on general diversity issues and topics.	Gathers information effectively and efficiently. Can be used with a very large to a very small employee base. Gives the opportunity for everyone to have a voice in the process.	Not always sensitive to the affective realm or subtle complexities of diversity management. Often data is reduced to numbers, which in turn do not influence organizational change.
Individual interview: One-to-one responses to open-ended questions or structured questions on diversity issues.	Can be sensitive to the complexities and affective realm of diversity. Interpretations can be checked.	Time-consuming and costly, and interactive bias can occur. Yields data that often gets lost by either having it interpreted only on the individual level or because of the data's expansiveness, and so does not influence organizational change.
Environmental/cultural scans: A process of exploring the physical and social context within which the organization functions. Its purpose is to discover the relationship of the organization to the external world.	Contextualizes diversity; yields information that provides direction for the organization's diversity mission and vision.	Big-picture emphasis does not attend to details. Presents only a theoretical framework. Data requires being translated into action plans.

METHOD	ADVANTAGES	DISADVANTAGES
Best practices/current-struggles profile: An inventory process of cataloguing the organization's best diversity practices and its current struggles in diversity management.	Can involve the entire organization in the identification of the profile. Simple, inexpensive process that can yield rich data.	Only provides information on the current state of the organization, and without careful analysis does not support creating a meaningful organizational diagnosis or provide direction for future desired state.
Career path process mapping: Visual representation of the process for promotion and retention in an organization. Data is gathered from career path interviews with leadership teams and key individuals.	Reveals the subtle and complex systems interactions of an organization. Identifies the soft data (psychological facts) that often lie behind the "glass ceiling, race ceiling, or pink ceiling" in organizations.	Requires senior-level diversity-consulting skills and deep understanding of organizational culture and how institutional "isms" work.
Diversity dialogue sessions: An open but guided conversation on diversity issues in an organization	A communication structure that supports the exploration of complex issues such as diversity. With the right groundwork and guidelines, can create a climate where rich data can surface.	Requires skillful facilitation. Not always a good method to use in early stages of an organization's diversity effort. Better for mid-stage diagnosis.
Critical incident interviewing: Reports from employees of behavioral descriptions observed in the organization that support or detract from inclusion efforts.	Reconstructs specific events or certain processes that create organizational culture. Can identify specific behaviors that support inclusive environments.	Requires good interviewing skills and careful analysis. Unless training is created that is directed toward development of identified behaviors, the data remains dormant.

METHOD	ADVANTAGES	DISADVANTAGES
Large group interventions: Planned meetings or conferences for organization members and stakeholders to address problems and opportunities. Example approaches include Appreciative Inquiry, Future Search Conference, Whole Scale Change, Open Space Technology, and World Café, to name a few.	Inclusive, engaging, and energizing interventions. Inherently diversity-affirming.	Requires long-term planning and skillful facilitation. Deceivingly simple processes can be a disaster if not well planned or executed by experienced facilitation.

Determining the Level of Analysis

You may have heard the phrase, "If you only have a hammer, every-thing looks like a nail." For many organizations, the diversity toolbox has only a hammer in it. Thus, when diversity issues surface, the "fix" becomes training for the entire employee base. This often happens with minimal or no preparation for employees and there is often a mandatory requirement for attendance. The workforce easily peers through this thin veil and wonders why the initiative is starting at this time. They quickly determine that the diversity effort is just the "flavor of the month" or a way to manage potential legal risks.

However, with good facilitation and a stimulating training agenda, the sessions are not always a complete loss for the company. Often, training roll-outs serve to get everyone on the same page when it comes to a baseline knowledge of diversity. It also sends a strong institutional message on the importance of diversity. Yet this one-size-fits-all approach is not the ideal recommendation for creating condi-tions that will leverage differences for the benefit of the organization as a whole. Attention needs to be given to the organization's definition of diversity and its readiness for implementing change. With these factors, the level at which to intervene in the system can be determined. Table 4 outlines the best diversity change effort in relationship to levels within the organization.

Table 4. Diversity Change and Levels of System for Intervention

Level of System	Source or Catalyst for Change	Recommended Intervention
INDIVIDUAL	Individual diversity dimension that affects the quality of an individual's work life that may or may not reflect an organizational pattern. The impact prevents the individual from fully tapping into his or her potential for the organization's benefit— e.g., religious affiliation, gender identity, nationality differences, childcare.	Coaching Personality inventories Workshop, classes Track data to determine if there is a larger organizational pattern
INTERPERSONAL	Dyad has problems in teams or work groups—e.g., race or gender-based conflict.	Mediation Team-building sessions
GROUP	Individuals who share the same group identity experience the same phenomena. Data identified through surveys, ratings, or anecdotal information.	Network and affinity groups Employee and business resource groups Focus group evaluations Career path analysis Diversity dialogue sessions Policy review

Level of System	Source or Catalyst for Change	Recommended Intervention
ORGANIZATIONAL	Norms, policies, and procedures systematically work against or underutilize differences in the workplace—e.g., hiring and promotion practices.	Leadership briefings Diversity competency training Establishment of diversity councils Policy review

Applying Frameworks for Interpretation

A limited number of theoretically based diversity frameworks are available for defining and measuring organizational effectiveness in diversity management. These models delineate the broad arena for guiding choices for diversity progression and change. Most practitioners find that the data collection process generally yields a vast amount of data for interpretation—frequency charts, percentages, themes, anecdotes, case studies—all of which need to be deemed useful for supporting the organization in moving toward diversity proficiency. Using any of these frameworks to articulate your diagnosis is one way of interpreting data. Two of the most frequently cited frameworks—Continuum of Cultural Competence (NIMH, 1989) and Diversity Paradigms (Thomas & Ely, 1996)—are summarized in Tables 5 and 6. Frameworks such as the Continuum of Cultural Competence and Diversity Paradigms can be used by organizations as external markers for charting diversity progression. Encouraging an organization to design its own continuum to chart its progression is perhaps the most meaningful way to support an organization in achieving diversity success. After a feedback session presenting the data, the leadership team or diversity council creates labels that mark the current status of the organization and labels for its future state.

Descriptors of each marker can be gleaned from the data. An example of an internal marker for a fictitious company is outlined in Table 7.

Another internal marker for measuring organizational effectiveness in managing its diversity is a simple report-card process modeled after an educator's assessment of a student's progress. Table 8 provides an example of an organizational diversity report card that can be easily customized to include agreed-upon conditions for achieving diversity proficiency. As an exercise during workshops, training, or meetings, evaluating the conditions as a group yields robust data with a minimum response burden for participants.

CONTINUUM OF CULTURAL COMPETENCE

Table 5. Frameworks for Interpreting Diversity
Diagnostic Data—External Markers

CULTURAL DESTRUCTIVENESS	CULTURAL INCAPACITY	CULTURAL BLINDNESS	CULTURAL PRE-COMPETENCE	BASIC COMPETENCE	CULTURAL PROFICIENCY
Attitudes, policies, and practices destructive to cultures and individuals.	System is biased. Supports segregation. Ignorance and unrealistic fear of people of color.	Philosophy of being unbiased and well intentioned, but ethnocentric. Ignores cultural strengths, encourages assimilation.	System realizes weakness and attempts to improve. Experiments. False sense of accomplishment.	Acceptance and respect for differences. Continual self-assessment. Committed to practices that flow from philosophy.	Holds culture in high esteem. Seeks to add to knowledge base of cultural competence. Advocates for cultural competence.

Source: National Institute of Mental Health (1989). *Towards a culturally competent system of care.* (CASSP Report.) Washington, D.C.: CASSP Technical Assistance Center.

Paradigms for Managing Diversity

Table 6. Paradigms for Managing Diversity:
A Framework for Interpreting Diversity Diagnostic
Data Using External Markers of Progress

The Discrimination-and-Fairness Paradigm
Focus on equal opportunity, fair treatment, recruitment, and compliance with federal Equal Employment Opportunity requirements.

KEY = ASSIMILATION

The Access-and-Legitimacy Paradigm
Focus on a more diverse clientele by matching the demographics of the organization to those of critical consumer or constituent groups.

KEY = DIFFERENTIATION

The Learning-and-Organizational Effectiveness Paradigm
Focus on incorporating employees' perspectives into the main work of the organization. Enhance work by rethinking primary tasks and redefining markets, products, strategies, missions, business practices, and even cultures.

KEY = INTEGRATION

Source: "Making Differences Matter: A New Paradigm for Managing Diversity," by David A. Thomas and Robin J. Ely. *Harvard Business Review*, September 1, 1996.

Table 7. An Example of a Customized Diversity Continuum
with Internal or Customized Markers of Progress

Exclusive/Perpetuating Organization	→	Engaging/Forming Organization	→	Inclusive/Transforming Organization
• Decisions made by dominant group membership without input from diverse membership and those whose lives will be most affected by those decisions		• Analysis and implementation of diversity is superficial		• Policies and procedures are reviewed systematically for inclusion
• Ownership of property, fiscal decisions made by dominant group		• Token recognition of people of color and women given for image or political reasons		• Individual identity is appreciated as an organizational strength
• Financial gain dictates behaviors rather than organization's vision		• People of color hired but relegated to lower positions or culturally specific positions		• People of color and women included outside of culture/ gender-specific roles
• Public political affiliations are not representative of the whole or decided on		• Consensus is used for decision-making		• Organizational effectiveness is the driving force for any business decision
• Unwritten rules and practices go unquestioned		• Organization experiments with new initiatives and evaluates results in a positive manner		• Collaboration and dialogue used for decision-making
• Community contacts limited to select few		• Community contacts are made for convenience and expediency		• Practices, procedures are clearly written and public
• Mentoring practices limited to dominant group		• Conflict related to diversity is managed		• Organization is continually in a learning mode
• Conflict related to diversity is suppressed		• Board membership includes demographic diversity but not diversity of thought or expression		• Diversity-related conflict viewed as opportunity to enhance appreciation, support empowerment, and develop creative outcomes
• Board membership and governance exist to serve and support leadership				• Board membership exists to hold moral ownership on behalf of the community

Table 8. Diversity Report Card with Sample Conditions
for Use in Workshops or Training Sessions

REPORT CARD

Conditions that will assist Company XYZ to become diversity-proficient	GRADE (circle one for each item)				
1. Succeed in recruiting and retaining diverse individuals	A	B	C	D	F
2. Provide equal opportunity for advancement to all	A	B	C	D	F
3. Hold high standards of performance for all	A	B	C	D	F
4. Treat all individuals fairly	A	B	C	D	F
5. Value variety of opinion and insight	A	B	C	D	F
6. Make workers feel respected	A	B	C	D	F
7. State policies and rules clearly	A	B	C	D	F
8. Make the organization's mission clearly understood	A	B	C	D	F

Developing Appropriate Reporting Procedures

Most seasoned practitioners find that creating a picture—through words, symbols, charts, etc.—that is customized for the organization is the best way to capture the diagnosis for an organization. The following "Benchmark Box" is an example of how a great deal of data could be synthesized for an organization. It includes data from the external and internal markers described in the previous section.

DIVERSITY BENCHMARK BOX	
Name	Company XYZ
Location	123 Diversity Highway
Type of Corporation	Service/Small Business
Services	Communications Delivery Systems
Number of Sites	3
Number of Employees	1,100
External Paradigm	Between "Discrimination & Fairness" and "Access & Legitimacy"
External Continuum	Between "Culturally Blind" & "Culturally Pre-competent" Organization
Diversity Report Card Rating	B-/C
Internal Benchmark	Between "Exclusive/Perpetrating" and "Engaging/Forming" Organization
Strengths	Long history of successful process and procedures for direct service delivery. Integrated service delivery system. Dedicated leadership and staff.
Improvement Agenda	Engaging the whole system. Inclusion. Communications and measurement accountability for diversity. Enhancing the principle of full participation.

When providing diversity diagnostic feedback to an organization, it is important to ensure that the feedback is given in a collaborative manner with ample time for organizational members to make meaning of the data and to even challenge the findings if warranted. Presenting the data or findings as themes, or as growth opportunities, sets the stage for a cultural change process to occur. Remember, unlike sales figures or stock market results, diversity data is dynamic and can position the organization for positive movement to leverage all of the human talent available.

Factors to Include in Reporting a Diversity Diagnosis

1. Identify the sources (hopefully multiple) that have contributed to the diagnosis.
2. Assess the organization's ability and readiness for change.
3. Describe snapshots of diversity competence already existing in the organization. Most organizations are doing something right, even if it is just by initiating the diversity diagnostic process.
4. Define where the organization is positioned in relation to being fully functioning in regard to diversity. Frameworks help to clarify the progression.
5. Present a menu of interventions, identifying those that are "quick fixes" or easily attainable interventions that do not rely on a great deal of human or financial capital. (E.g., removing the picture of the leadership team in the Company Bigbucks brochure and replacing it with pictures of the diverse workforce would get a lot of diversity mileage with a diverse client base.)

Challenges in Diversity Diagnosis

At the beginning of this chapter, we stated that readiness on the part of the organization and drivers for cultural change are important success ingredients. In other chapters of this handbook, we will emphasize use-of-self as a tool in diversity management. Use-of-self as a tool for behavioral change is particularly important in the diagnostic process. It is critical for the diversity practitioner to be aware of his or her own personal interests, beliefs, and attitudes in forming the lens through which the data is interpreted.

Many diversity practitioners who engage in this work are driven by personal convictions and experiences that have led them to a strong commitment to valuing human differences. Most diversity practitioners are passionate change agents. Using the energy of this passion in a way that first and foremost serves the organization can prevent potential diversity dilemmas.

In doing diagnostic work it is helpful to keep in mind a basic systems principle derived from gestalt psychology—a system is always doing the best it can at any given moment. From this perspective, the diagnostic process is enriched and diversity practitioners have the ability to effect positive change.

REFERENCES

Bunker, B. B., and B. T. Alban. *Large Group Interventions: Engaging the Whole System of Rapid Change.* San Francisco: Jossey-Bass Publishers, 1997.

National Institute of Mental Health. *Towards a culturally competent system of care (CASSP Report).* Washington, D.C.: CASSP Technical Center, 1989.

Seashore, C. N., E. W. Seashore, and G.M. Weinberg. *What Did You Say? The Art of Giving and Receiving Feedback.* Columbia, Maryland: Bingham House Books, 1997.

Thomas, D., and R. J. Ely. "Making Differences Matter: A New Paradigm for Managing Diversity." *Harvard Business* Review. September-October 50-61, 1996. Reprint No. 96510.

"The Making of a Multicultural Super Consumer." Nielsen, March 18, 2015. http://www.nielsen.com/us/en/insights/news/2015/the-making-of-a-multicultural-super-consumer-.html

Weisbord, M., and S. Janoff. *Future Search: Getting the Whole System in the Room for Vision, Commitment, and Action.* 3rd ed. San Francisco: Berrett-Koehler, 2010.

Worley, C. G., S. A. Mohrman, and J. A. Nevitt. "Large Group Interventions: An Empirical Field Study of Their Composition, Process, and Outcomes." *Journal of Applied Behavioral Science,* 47(4), 404–431, 2011.

CHAPTER SIX

Assessing, Measuring, and Analyzing Diversity

Laura Castillo-Page, Jennifer Eliason, Norma Poll-Hunter

Introduction

WHEN IMPLEMENTED IN A comprehensive manner, diversity can challenge people to think in new and different ways, expand their understanding of the world and its cultures, and develop critical thinking skills that better prepare them for success. However, in order to reap these benefits, a focus on diversity must not only increase compositional or representational diversity but also infuse the institution's mission and vision, strategic plans, policies, programs, structures, systems, practices, and procedures (Chen, Liu, & Portnoy, 2012; Mor Barak, Cherin, & Berkman, 1998; Pugh, Dietz, Brief, & Wiley, 2008).

Embracing diversity, equity, and inclusion as core elements of the institution's mission is an important step toward creating an inclusive climate that ensures equity for all (Nivet, 2015). In order to support such inclusive environments, we must routinely monitor our performance and progress pertaining to our diversity, equity, and inclusion efforts. Thus, the purpose of this chapter is to discuss promising practices in developing, collecting, assessing, and evaluating diversity, equity, and inclusion metrics.

In recent years, there has been a wide range of factors that have caused businesses with wide-reaching impacts to rethink how diversity is valued within organizational priorities. Those factors include shifting demographics and their impact on the workforce and consumer base, as well as a widening global economy that affects businesses' bottom lines (Balter, Chow, & Jin, 2014; Levine, Stoudemire, & Polonskaia, 2014). For many organizations, business success and a competitive advantage are critically tied to leveraging diversity through a strong diversity and inclusion strategy (Balter et al., 2014; Vermeulen & Jenkins, 2016). However, creating a diversity and inclusion strategy can be challenging; by nature, diversity is broad, and determining what diversity metrics to track, how to track them, and how to remain accountable to stated diversity goals can be difficult (PeopleFluent, 2015; Vermeulen & Jenkins, 2016).

Measuring Diversity vs. Inclusion

Many organizations house diversity and inclusion strategy and efforts within human resources. Human resources functions include talent acquisition (employee recruitment and pipeline development), learning and development (professional improvement and leadership training), employee engagement (employee resource groups and recognition programs), compliance and regulatory aspects (labor relations, equal employment opportunity), total rewards (compensation and benefits), and people management (employee relations, diversity and inclusion, wellness, and work-life balance). Tethering diversity and inclusion to human resources has been experienced by seasoned diversity and inclusion practitioners and progressive organizations as a limitation of their roles and functions. Many argue that diversity and inclusion belong at the center of the organization and should not be considered as part of a cost center that has to compete for resources (Dobbin & Kalev, 2016; Plummer & Jordan, 2007).

Similarly, while most company strategies do not disentangle diversity from inclusion, diversity refers to "any dimension that can be used to differentiate groups and people within the organization," while inclusion "refers to the involvement and empowerment of people within those groups" (Vermeulen & Jenkins, 2016, p. 3). Gaining conceptual clarity on what diversity and inclusion mean for the organization is the first step in knowing what is being measured and assessed (Thomas, 1996).

Collecting, Analyzing, and Interpreting Diversity and Inclusion Metrics

While organizations may face similar challenges in collecting, analyzing, and interpreting diversity and inclusion metrics, diversity practitioners have employed several methodologies successfully in organizations. What follows is a description of these approaches.

Randstad Sourceright's Approach. This talent and management consulting firm describes a "Six-Pack Strategy" for workplace diversity and inclusion. The first of six components, "Acquiring Talent," asks institutions to assess the diverse talent groups they wish to attract to their organization (Vermeulen & Jenkins, 2016), and advocates setting priorities/goals in relation to diversity groups based on benchmarks established by looking at the industry, organizational role, and geographic location. The second component, "Developing and Advancing Talent," directs institutions on how to support the abilities and develop the skills of newly acquired diverse talent to advance their careers (Vermeulen & Jenkins, 2016), and examines the internal talent-development pipeline as well as how organizations track the progress of employee advancement within the organization in relation to diverse groups. For example, questions like, "Are women succeeding or failing at a higher rate than men?" or, "Are disabled workers, veterans, or ethnic groups succeeding or failing at disparate rates?" or, "Are comparable roles being paid at the same rate?" are helpful tracking measurements when considering how diverse talent is developed and advanced (Vermeulen & Jenkins, 2016). The third component, "Rethinking Talent," reviews how successful the organization is at retaining diverse talent (Vermeulen & Jenkins, 2016), and looks closely at retention metrics, which are measured against external industry averages as well as within internal categories (e.g., business manager, department, worker type). The fourth component, "Representation," compares the proportion of diverse talent at the organization to the diverse talent available in the field (Vermeulen & Jenkins, 2016), and measures proportional representation of diverse groups by simultaneously benchmarking employee diversity trends against average market availability and internal/organizational representation trends. The fifth component, "Success Planning Pipeline Strength," addresses future strategic planning for recruitment and succession of diverse talent (Vermeulen & Jenkins, 2016). This component recognizes succession planning as a "direct predictor of what talent diversity looks like in the future" (Vermeulen & Jenkins, 2016, p. 11), and supports the creation of a succession plan that includes objectively identified candidates for the talent pipeline and alignment with future business needs and goals. Randstad Sourceright's sixth and final component measures inclusion, which is different from the first five components that measure diversity. The component, "Engagement," strives to understand the organization's culture and climate for a diverse talent workforce (Vermeulen & Jenkins, 2016) and utilizes tools like regular employee satisfaction and/or climate surveys, exit interviews, and cultural competence assessments to measure how well diverse talent is able to work once inside the organization.

Cornell University ILR School's Approach. This particular approach argues that in order to be successful, diversity initiatives should be quantifiable and closely aligned with organizational goals (Balter, Chow, & Jin, 2014). In recognizing the value of quantified diversity initiatives that push beyond the boundaries of federal regulations (i.e., affirmation action), Cornell University's ILR School provided several examples of best practices for quantifying diversity initiatives from well-known global brands. Each company quantified their initiative to track their progress toward diversity goals as well as toward overall organizational goals. The first example is Aetna's successful implementation of a number of new diversity initiatives (including publishing a diversity page on the internal company website and starting a diversity speaker series). Aetna then used assessment metrics, measured against company business outcomes, to maintain the efficacy of their strategic diversity initiatives. The second example is Nextel's creation of quantitative measurements on the company's return on investment (ROI) from "higher employee retention rates as a result of diversity training" (Balter et al., 2014, p. 2). The third example is Sodexo's senior-level commitment to diversity. Sodexo's executive committee members and senior leaders all commit and carry out mentorship and sponsorship of employee resource groups.

The fourth example is Cummins's high number of resource groups and diversity-reflective performance reviews. Cummins has "more than 100 resource group chapters nationwide" (Balter et al., 2014, p. 2) and includes organizational diversity goals in performance reviews for company executives. The fifth and final example is Pfizer's implementation of talent-development initiatives focused on underrepresented groups. Pfizer has initiated formal mentoring programs for women and other underrepresented groups, and utilizes employee resource groups for "recruitment, on-boarding, mentoring and talent development" (Balter et al., 2014, p. 3) of new employees. In working toward achieving diversity goals, Cornell University's ILR School recommends conducting employee climate surveys and implementing diversity initiative plans on strategic and tactical levels.

Diversity Best Practices' Approach. In the past few years, predictive analytics has gained traction as an innovative tool that can be used to hone in on the areas in which companies will need new talent, assess the market for available candidates, and determine comparison points for compensation. Predictive analytics works by "applying formulas and equations to raw data to predict what may happen in the future" (Baker & Collins, 2013, p. 4). Organizations have used predictive analytics to a) predict which candidates will be most likely to succeed by challenging assumptions about where the most talented candidate come from, b) develop metrics to predict which types of managers are most successful at retaining talent and use those measures in staff training and development, c) develop predictive data sets to improve talent management by utilizing interview output data, and d) predict which employees are most likely to quit by utilizing data pools (e.g., salaries, raises, performance ratings). Using examples from well-known global brands, Diversity Best Practices demonstrated how companies utilize big data and/or internal company analytics to further diversity and inclusion goals. The first example, Google, uses a hiring algorithm to predict which candidates will have a high probability of success once on board, an evaluative/predictive algorithm to determine which employees are most likely to leave, and predictive modeling to anticipate upcoming people-management challenges and opportunities. The second example, Whirlpool, utilized historical data on hiring, promotions, attrition, employee engagement scores, performance ratings, retention risk, recognition, and learning and developing to create a diversity scorecard, which was in turn used to develop organizational action plans toward diversity and inclusion goals. The third example, Walmart, uses big data and predictive analytics to forecast customers' needs, enhance their experiences, and better serve them through multiple channels. And finally, International Paper used big data to develop a global workforce planning tool that helps calculate the retirement risk of the organization's employees.

Mercer's Approach. Mercer created an Internal Labor Market (ILM) map to illustrate lateral and vertical moves by workforce segment (e.g., gender). The map can be particularly useful in tracking where and when individuals leave the organization. Furthermore, the ILM map can be combined with a cultural dynamics assessment to "obtain a holistic understanding of what employees and managers say vs. what employees and managers do" (Levine et al., 2014, p. 16). Additionally, projection modeling can be used to determine the number of hires and retentions an organization needs to complete in order to meet an aggressive goal. Finally, Mercer advocates embedding diversity and inclusion strategy within "key business and HR processes and practices" (Levine et al., 2014, p. 25).

Hubbard Diversity Return on Investment (DROI) Analysis Model.
Calculating diversity's return on investment requires asking key
questions and performing key tasks along the way. To achieve a successful result, measuring diversity return on investment (DROI)
requires a systematic approach that takes into account both costs and
benefits. The Hubbard Diversity ROI Analysis Model, born out of a
need realized by Drs. Edward and Myrna Hubbard to demonstrate
and measure the value of utilizing diverse human and other resources
to drive measurable results to the financial bottom line, provides a
step-by-step approach that keeps the process manageable so users can
tackle one issue at a time. The model emphasizes that this is a logical, systematic process, and applying the model provides consistency
from one DROI calculation to another. In essence, it suggests that the
major aspects of diversity measurement you need to address include 1)
knowing what you want to know, 2) collecting data and analyzing it,
3) isolating diversity's contribution, 4) converting the contribution to
money, 4) calculating the costs and benefits, 5) reporting it to others,
and 6) tracking and assessing progress (Hubbard, 2003).

Benchmarking Diversity and Inclusion Metrics

Benchmarking on human capital and institutional diversity is anec-
dotally perceived to be widespread in many fields, yet academic scholarship on the topic is considerably less prevalent. A true challenge
of benchmarking for diversity and inclusion change is identifying
appropriate benchmarking partners. Organizations with dissimilar success equations and outcomes would not make strong benchmarking partners despite similar performance services and measures
(Saul, 2004, p. 54). Comparative benchmarking between peers and/
or competitors requires more than accumulating and comparing data

sets. Saul (2004) refers to this process of comparative benchmarking as "gap analysis." Exemplary performance outcomes that cannot be reproduced because of factors specific to the host institution—such as charismatic leadership, geographic factors, or self-selected, limited samples that exclude unsatisfactory performance—are not best practices (Saul, 2004). Essential in benchmarking is institutional support, not only from leadership but throughout the organization, for the implementation of new best practices identified as a result of the benchmarking practice.

A 2014 study completed by the Diversity Collegium "identified 280 possible diversity benchmarks across 13 different categories" (PeopleFluent, 2015, pp. 3–4). With a variety of definitions of what diversity is, organizations may have a hard time determining what to track and how to track it, and may find it easier to default to maintaining compliance with regulations. Vermeulen and Jenkins (2016) recognize three distinct levels on which organizations can enact diversity and inclusion strategic plans. Level one is compliance with diversity mandates, level two is an ideological/theoretical commitment to diversity through setting goals (but without action), and level three is a core value or belief in diversity that is integrated into the company's culture and operations. While some organizations utilize vendors (external consultants) to help develop diversity strategies, PeopleFluent (2015) notes that as companies develop the internal capacity to engage and manage diversity goals, they become less likely to depend on vendors to assist them in developing and enacting diversity strategies. While PeopleFluent also notes that the overwhelming majority of organizations face similar challenges in achieving diversity and inclusion goals, they argue that measurement is the key to implementing a successful diversity and inclusion strategy. The most effective organizations track more, measure more, and reward more (PeopleFluent, 2015, p. 10).

An example of a measurement tool designed to turn data into action is the Diversity Engagement Survey (DES). The DES is designed to identify the workplace conditions that support inclusion of all employees. The twenty-two items of the DES assess levels of employee engagement as a means to develop a meaningful inclusion scorecard that characterizes the institution's progress toward creating an inclusive work environment (Person et al., 2015). Developed by researchers at the University of Massachusetts Medical School (UMMS) and the Association of American Medical Colleges (AAMC), the DES functions in three ways:

1. Descriptive—describes the inclusiveness of the environment by determining its level of engagement by demographic categories
2. Diagnostic—defines areas of strengths and areas of improvement for diversity and inclusion efforts through benchmark comparative data
3. Prescriptive—points to the strategic direction for change by identifying which engagement domains and which inclusion factors to target for improvement

The DES Impact Planning Tool, a companion to the DES, is an easy-to-use charting system that provides action-planning steps and tracking interventions designed to improve DES scores.

Quantitative approaches are often framed as the "gold standard" of diversity and inclusion metrics data collection and data-driven strategic planning. This is often driven by the axiom that "what gets measured gets done" (Balter et al., 2014, p. 2). Establishing quantitative diversity and inclusion metrics is often the most accessible pathway to introduce employees to diversity and inclusion goals. Furthermore, institutions set quantitative targets and benchmarks for a range of organizational goals, from increasing their profit margin to expanding their customer base. However, quantitative metrics alone may not capture the full scope of the diversity and inclusion culture and climate. Tracking progress over time is key, in part because the strengths and weaknesses of diversity initiatives are at times subtle, and improvements often occur only incrementally (Vermeulen & Jenkins, 2016). A mixed-method approach to diversity and inclusion metrics data collection and assessment, one that employs quantitative and qualitative methodologies, can offer the most robust understanding of organizational culture and climate "as it can more reliably surface hidden impediments to progress and ensure that as many voices as possible are included" (AAMC, 2013, p. 1). Marrying quantitative and qualitative metrics also ensures data validity (AAMC, 2013). Qualitative data collection, such as focus groups and interviews, is often eschewed as costlier and more time-consuming than quantitative data collection, but qualitative findings can add much-needed institutional context to quantitative data collection. The deeper understanding of organizational culture and climate that a mixed-method approach can give will better position your strategic planning for success by aligning it with key organizational goals.

Launching Diversity and Inclusion Metrics Research

Embarking on any diversity and inclusion data-collection project will require leadership support and institutional buy-in for the trustworthiness of the process. Quantitative diversity and inclusion metrics data may bring less than desirable results and difficult conversations to the forefront. It is pivotal that organizational leadership is in full support of collecting and reporting diversity and inclusion metrics as part of a strategic goal of advancing institutional culture and climate. A diversity and inclusion data-collection initiative without leadership support for engaging in an honest fact-finding process can be stifled or even fail. A successful diversity and inclusion data-collection effort requires leadership support for the objectives and goals of the entire process, including a robust analysis of the findings to drive institutional improvement. Leadership commitment is demonstrated through public statements, open support, and full participation with the diversity and inclusion research effort. Further, leadership prioritization of diversity and inclusion is noted by designating appropriate resource and staff capacity to successfully complete the project.

Any diversity and inclusion metrics data collection should begin with the key institutional stakeholders convening. These initial meetings should narrow the inquiry to prioritize select diversity and inclusion areas and ensure the data collection and analysis process is an attainable goal. The area of diversity and inclusion inquiry selected by the stakeholders should then drive the project planning, including the type of data collection (quantitative, qualitative, or mixed-method). Stakeholders should also conduct a review of the resources and talent required for diversity and inclusion research projects against a needs assessment to execute the project. This process should result in the designation of stages of the project to individuals or teams, thus creating a chain of accountability for the project's success. Many institutions may not have the experienced internal talent or capacity to implement such a data-collection and analysis project, but they would benefit by using resources to hire consultants or contractors.

Quantitative and Qualitative Diversity and Inclusion Metrics

Quantitative Data Collection

Organizational-level diversity and inclusion quantitative data collection most often includes a two-pronged approach: collecting longitudinal institutional data and conducting a survey. There is no "correct" method to engage in quantitative diversity and inclusion data collection, and organizations must adapt data-collection strategies that work best for their institutional needs.

A longitudinal analysis of institutional data is often a starting point for a quantitative analysis of structural diversity metrics. This review should include collecting human-capital demographic data on applicants and current employees. Further, data should be collected on employee promotions to management and executive-level positions by demographic metrics. Most organizations' human resources, affirmative action, or equal opportunity staffs have already collected this data. The designated researchers should identify a set period for their analysis, such as over the last ten or twenty years, so progress on key metrics can be tracked over time. This human-capital data can then be disaggregated by the key diversity and inclusion metrics (e.g., race/ethnicity, gender) for further analysis. The organization may also wish to conduct a salary-equity assessment by key diversity metrics during this preliminary stage of data collection and review.

Surveys remain the most common tool for efficient data collection since the perceptions and experiences of many individuals can be gathered simultaneously. Diversity and inclusion surveys measure an individual's level of satisfaction and/or engagement with their institution's culture and climate. Organizational culture consists of the deeply instilled values and beliefs of an institution (AAMC, 2013, p. 2). If an organization were a plant, culture would be the roots, as culture is embedded within the fabric of a place but is often unseen and undefined. Organizational climate consists of the perceptions, attitudes, and behaviors reflecting the beliefs and values, the culture, of an institution (AAMC, 2013, p. 2). Climate represents the branches and leaves that individuals can see, interact with, and use to form their opinions about their experiences with the plant.

Organizations can develop their own climate and culture survey or contract with a vendor. An organization that develops its own climate survey may have the advantage of being able to uniquely tailor the survey item to its own context. However, many institutions do not have the time and expertise to conduct their own survey development, administration, and analysis. Vendors may be costly, but with an experienced survey vendor, it is likely their survey instrument has already been validated. Further, if the vendor offers survey analysis, you may have the option to incorporate comparative benchmarking into your analysis using data from the vendor's prior customers to compare your institution to peer institutions. A self-designed culture and climate survey is unlikely to include the option to benchmark against peers or competitors in your field.

Survey-response anonymity, a hallmark of ethical survey design, is essential in diversity culture and climate surveys. Collecting data in a manner that might allow a respondent's identity to be revealed in the analysis and reporting stage compromises the integrity of the results. If users believe their responses are not fully anonymous, the data may be corrupted by inaccurate responses. This is particularly true when responding to sensitive survey questions, inherent in diversity and inclusion surveys that explore the relationship between the employee and the work environment. These steps will encourage respondent confidence and validity in the process, which will ensure that the data collected will be more accurate.

Quantitative Data Analysis

Data collected from surveys can be easily quantifiable to develop future target metrics or benchmarking goals. The level of statistical analysis your organization chooses to deploy is best guided by the statistical and data sophistication of your audience, your own institutional stakeholders. At a minimum, descriptive statistics such as frequencies, means, and standard deviations will be useful in addressing the culture and climate survey items. The next step in your analysis of the survey data may include disaggregating the results by demographic groups. For example, you might want to know if employees feel a higher level of trust in the organization by race and ethnicity. This analysis will allow you to develop base-level metrics to compare your institutional results across select demographic groups. Ideally, an organization conducts a culture and climate survey in hopes of seeing parity across demographic groups when analyzing the results. However, this is rarely the case in most organizational settings; women, people of color, people with disabilities, and LGBT individuals often report lower levels of satisfaction and engagement with their institutions. If your organization undertakes a more sophisticated analysis that includes statistical correlation or regression analysis, it will allow for more in-depth meaning-making of the data. Those survey items that yield differential results for social identity groups can then be given further attention. Advanced statistical techniques will allow you to identify areas where true demographic differences exist, and to target future investment of resources and initiatives for those areas of key concern.

Benchmarking Survey Data

Benchmarking allows an organization to utilize the data previously collected and analyzed and harness it into a lever of institutional improvement. First, the longitudinal institutional demographic data gathered prior to implementing the culture and climate survey (e.g., employee demographics by gender) can also provide important baseline metrics for the organization. A systematic review of employment practices and trends at your organization and in the field at large over time will aid in setting realistic and attainable diversity recruitment, hiring, and promotion targets for the upcoming years. Second, the data collected from a climate survey analysis can serve as the baseline metric for the perceptions and attitudes staff hold about the organization. This baseline sets the level for the organization to build on as it moves forward with diversity and inclusion strategic planning. Climate and culture surveys are traditionally reengaged every three to five years. The baseline metrics identified in the survey analysis can be targeted for set areas of improvement, either across the entire institution or by select demographic groups for the next iteration of the survey.

Benchmarking internally over time has its limitations. External benchmarking promotes transparency, best-practice comparison, and shared knowledge, and it advances industry standards. Participating in external benchmarking also provides recognition for those organizations who rank in the top percentiles. However, a true challenge of external benchmarking for diversity and inclusion change is identifying appropriate benchmarking partners. As noted earlier, organizations with dissimilar purposes, resources, values, and goals would not make strong benchmarking partners. Working with external survey-management services to build the best possible comparative peer benchmarking group ensures the validity of the comparison data. Some organizations may seek out benchmarking peers at an aspirational level or lower-tier level for political or public relations reasons. They may find institutional value in listing themselves as a peer with more prestigious brands. Alternately, selecting a benchmarking group of lower-tier organizations may artificially inflate the organization's benchmark, making them appear better than in reality. Aspirational or unambitious benchmarking for assessing diversity and inclusion functions does not support improving the organizational culture and climate and is generally perceived as window dressing rather than a true metric for diversity success.

Benchmarking is not just a comparative data-analysis method. Successful benchmarking collects not only raw data but also context information about the policies and programs that allow a particular institution to perform at the highest level. A best-practices checklist serves to record initiatives and innovations from inside successful peer institutions. As a result of placing the data in context, benchmarking becomes a vital tool for determining approximations toward achieving diversity and inclusion goals. The ultimate goal of benchmarking is to discover and adapt best practices, policies, and programs to improve organizational culture and climate.

Qualitative Data Collection
Gathering qualitative indicators of diversity, equity, and inclusion in an institution is also extremely important. Qualitative data-collection

strategies allow for the collection of rich data that cannot easily be captured via quantitative approaches. Focus groups, interviews, and the collection of existing documents are a few popular methods.

Focus Groups. Focus groups can be an effective way to gather information about participants' experiences, memories, and ideas (Krueger & Casey, 2014). When conducting focus groups on diversity, equity, and inclusion-related topics, it is important to keep the following general guidelines in mind. For the most part, groups should range from about eight to ten participants, since fewer might reduce idea generation and more will limit individual participation. It might be beneficial to invite ten to twelve participants per group, since a few may not ultimately attend. Meetings should generally be scheduled for ninety minutes, depending on the number of questions included in the moderator's guide. Shorter meetings may not give sufficient time to explore issues that emerge, but attention and energy wanes over longer periods of time (Bystedt, Lynn, Potts, & Fraley, 2010). The groups should be varied in composition so that social identity groups have representative voices. Depending on the topic of focus, these groups might also be varied with regard to secondary dimensions of diversity (e.g., geographic region, professional identity, marital status, educational background, or personal habits). Developing good questions that form a substantive moderator's guide and skilled facilitation are keys to accurate and complete data collection (Krueger & Casey, 2014). These conditions become even more critical when using focus groups to assess progress toward diversity and inclusion goals. Developing questions that are not socially loaded to solicit culturally acceptable responses requires preparing drafts that are vetted and revised accordingly to capture the intent of the study. Successful facilitation requires moderators who are culturally competent and understand group dynamics and communicating across differences.

Interviews. One-on-one interviews are also an effective method to obtain specific information from highly knowledgeable sources. Interviews typically utilize open-ended questions and can range in formality and standardization depending on the type of information you hope to gain (Kvale, 1996; Seidman, 2011). To develop a complete understanding of the components of a culture of diversity and inclusion, for example, it will likely be useful to conduct guided (but not highly structured) interviews with key personnel. In particular, interviewing those in the organization with diversity and inclusion functions embedded in their roles and functions as well as those most affected by the named goals would be critical to the assessment process (Seidman, 2011).

Document Analysis. One additional useful strategy is to conduct a systematic content analysis of existing documents such as strategic plans, employee handbooks, and public relations materials. These documents provide an opportunity to understand symbolic language and items that represent the institution as a whole (Hsieh & Shannon, 2005). While the specific documents collected and reviewed will vary from organization to organization, organizations should create a directed approach to document analysis, one that guides the assessment process of these documents by establishing a template for a common strategy of keyword and content analysis across document types and a final analysis that seeks to understand the underlying context that identifies the core mission and values of the documents (Hsieh & Shannon, 2005). In diversity and inclusion data collection, this will help to determine the extent and range of inclusion dynamics such as identity integration and social power.

Qualitative Data Analysis: Interpreting Focus Group
and Interview Data and Existing Documents
An effective way to analyze and interpret focus group and interview data is through *thematic* coding (Bystedt et al., 2010; Krueger & Casey, 2014; Saldaña, 2012). This is a process that involves using notes and/ or transcripts to reflect on the major themes that have emerged in discussions (Bystedt et al., 2010; Krueger & Casey, 2014). Ideally, more than one person who does not have a vested interest in the outcome of the assessment would reflect on each focus group or interview independently and make note of the predominant topics that emerged, a method known as inter-rater reliability (Bystedt et al., 2010; Krueger & Casey, 2014). These coders would then compare their independent reflections and identify common, central dimensions or issues (Bystedt et al., 2010; Krueger & Casey, 2014). This process could occur after each focus group or set of interviews so that the initial findings can shape later discussions and coding processes (Bystedt et al., 2010; Krueger & Casey, 2014). The use of multiple independent coders to generate common themes is recognized as a good strategy to ensure more rigor in the generation of qualitative findings.

The final product of these analyses would be a list of major themes common across discussion groups or interviewees that identify challenges and opportunities related to diversity and inclusion (Bystedt et al., 2010; Krueger & Casey, 2014). It might also be helpful to record direct (anonymous) quotes that help make the themes more tangible. In sum, the themes that emerge from the analysis should point to areas of strength regarding diversity and inclusion as well as areas of opportunity for improvement.

Conducting an Evaluation

This section offers practical guidance on how to plan and implement an evaluation of diversity, equity, and inclusion initiatives.

There are two main types of program evaluation: process evaluation and outcome evaluation (Banta & Palomba, 2014; Centers for Disease Control and Prevention, 2011; United Way, 1996). Both can be conducted for any intervention, but each serves a different purpose and requires a different evaluation design.

The Process Evaluation. The process evaluation, also known as a summative evaluation or implementation study, examines to what extent an intervention is being implemented as intended. Process evaluations measure fidelity to a model and execution of an intervention according to requirements, design, expectations, and standards (Banta & Palomba, 2014; Centers for Disease Control and Prevention, 2011; United Way, 1996). This type of evaluation reveals information on the challenges and lessons learned in reaching full implementation of an intervention. It measures how closely practice matches what the model is intended to look like.

Process evaluations use a number of approaches to answer the question, "How well is this intervention being implemented?" (Banta & Palomba, 2014; Centers for Disease Control and Prevention, 2011; United Way, 1996). Typically, data are collected from questionnaires or focus groups, interviews with individuals who are part of the intervention, and review of written records, such as participant files, program files, plans, or policies. Process evaluations can be helpful in making early adjustments to program interventions to maximize the implementation of the model and to decrease the influence of implementation issues on the outcomes (Banta & Palomba, 2014; Centers for Disease Control and Prevention, 2011; United Way, 1996).

The Outcome Evaluation. Outcome evaluations measure the ability of an intervention to achieve its goals by assessing both its direct and indirect effects on the target population (Banta & Palomba, 2014; Centers for Disease Control and Prevention, 2011; Sandars, Brown, & Walsh, 2017; United Way, 1996). These evaluations use information about an intervention (purpose, objectives, or goals) to define expected program outcomes.

An outcome-evaluation design should include only measurements that relate to the stated goals of an intervention and no measurements that relate to effects beyond those stated goals (Banta & Palomba, 2014; Sandars et al., 2017; United Way, 1996). Toward this end, it is important for evaluators to meet with those who develop programs and interventions to ensure that success or failure is measured appropriately and according to the intervention's goals and objectives.

There is overlap in the use of outcome evaluations and process evaluations (Banta & Palomba, 2014; Centers for Disease Control and Prevention, 2011; United Way, 1996). Outcome evaluations depend on components of process evaluations (e.g., fidelity measurements) to support their design (Banta & Palomba, 2014; Centers for Disease Control and Prevention, 2011; Sandars et al., 2017; United Way, 1996). Process evaluations help determine when evaluators should begin collecting outcome data to measure an intervention's effectiveness (Banta & Palomba, 2014; Centers for Disease Control and Prevention, 2011; United Way, 1996). While outcome and process evaluations should be planned in conjunction with each other, researchers should use process outcomes to drive the schedule for collection of outcome data and presentation of findings.

One outcome that is commonly measured is the cost-effectiveness or savings achieved as a result of a program or intervention (Banta &

Palomba, 2014; Sandars et al., 2017; United Way, 1996). This is often referred to as cost-benefit analysis. For example, educational benefits or scholarships may be intended to support staff professional development to promote career growth and reduce staff turnover. Therefore, an evaluation of the scholarship program might compare the total investment in such a program—administrative costs, financial commitment, and marketing or public awareness campaigns to promote participation—to the costs associated with staff attrition and talent recruitment.

Case Study
A director of employee programs has received the results of an organizational survey indicating that there are differences in employee engagement by race and ethnicity in her organization, in particular among black, Latino, and American Indian male employees. The leadership is concerned that they may lose key talent if this is not addressed. After conducting organization-wide focus groups to better understand the key issues and potential solutions, the director works with her team to develop a program to enhance employee engagement. Pilot funding is awarded to test the program with one of the departments. The program includes interactive learning sessions for each of the key target audiences—employees and managers. The director needs to demonstrate the effectiveness of the program and its impact to expand it to other departments and make it sustainable. She works with the research and evaluation team to plan the evaluation before the program starts.

Process and outcome evaluations will both play a critical role in determining program effectiveness and impact. For the process evaluation, the focus will be on how well each of the program components have been implemented and on program quality. The process evaluation may explore the following:

- Did the program components align with intended program goals?
- Did the program meet the target audience's needs?
- Did the program effectively engage participants in the session?
- Were there program components that worked particularly well compared to others?
- How well did the facilitator or instructor deliver the key program components?
- Were there any unanticipated changes or issues that influenced the program implementation?

Methods to assess this can include surveys at the end of each session. The team may enlist an outside expert to observe the program and provide objective feedback. The administrators can also review all the documents and communications that may influence the program's implementation. This will provide insight into what will contribute to an effective program.

The outcome evaluation will inform the director about the impact of the program. The key is to assess if there has been an observable change that can be attributed to the program, and how this is aligned to the program's intentions. The outcome evaluation may explore the following:

- Is there a difference in employee engagement for the target groups after participation in the program?

- Did the program increase manager behaviors that foster engagement?
- Did the program help to improve employee retention among men of color?
- Did the program have any other unintended impact on perceptions of the workplace?

Similar methods may be used to assess the program outcomes. The director can survey the participants before and after the program on key engagement indicators to assess for any change. She and her team can use the initial set of employee data as a baseline, and when the survey is re-administered, review the data by race and ethnicity and gender. There may be individual interviews or focus groups to learn more about employees' experiences after participating in the program. The employees may be enlisted to rate their managers on specific behaviors. Over time, the director can work with HR to review employee records or data on retention.

Together, process and outcome evaluations provide a comprehensive understanding of the intervention—what needs to occur for an effective program that meets the desired outcomes.

Planning Evaluations

Planning the program evaluation is critical to a successful process. Planning allows evaluators to determine key questions, what resources are needed, as well as the strategy and feasibility of an evaluation study. Further, well-designed evaluation studies enable evaluators to have data that can be used to inform interventions (Centers for Disease Control and Prevention, 2011; United Way, 1996). For diversity efforts, it is critical to have data that show the effectiveness and impact of policies and programs.

Step 1: Define Program and Evaluation Goals

- Identify the reason for conducting the evaluation and the program goals and objectives. Tools like a theory of change will be helpful in this process.
- Convene key program representatives and stakeholders to understand the program and the context in which the program is being implemented.
- Explore available data, documents, or other informational resources, including any past evaluations, to learn what data or information may exist and inform the current evaluation.

Step 2: Develop Evaluation Budget and Timeline

- Determine funding sources and any budget constraints that will likely influence the scale and scope of the evaluation. The larger the sample size, the higher the cost of executing a study.
- Create a detailed timeline, including milestones and deliverables, that takes into account budgetary and programmatic constraints. Always build in a "cushion" of time for unexpected delays.

Step 3: Plan Advisory Committee and Process

- Gather a volunteer advisory committee representing diverse areas of expertise, which will allow the evaluation team to gather a range of perspectives at a low expense.

- Ensure that the advisory committee represents a broad range of expertise, so that objective feedback on the evaluation design and procedures can be incorporated into the evaluation plan.
- Outline the role of advisors, including the expectation that they will review interim and final reports and engage in data-interpretation discussions.

Step 4: Develop the Logic Model

- Create the logic model that serves as a roadmap for the evaluation (Centers for Disease Control and Prevention, 2011; United Way, 1996).
- Logic models include inputs, activities, outputs, and initial, intermediate, and longer-term outcomes, when appropriate. (For examples, see Centers for Disease Control and Prevention, 2011; United Way, 1996.)

Step 5: Design the Evaluation Plan

- Identify surveys, questionnaires, focus-group protocols, or other tools and instruments that will help answer each evaluation question.
- Explore any potential factors that may facilitate or hinder successful evaluation implementation.
- Decide on the data-collection methods and procedures, including informed consent and recruitment.
- Review policies on data collection and the possible need for institutional review-board approval to execute the evaluation. If you want to make the data available to the

general public, it will be important to seek institutional review-board approval.

- Determine strategies for data analysis, reporting, and dissemination of findings.

Step 6: Conducting the Evaluation

- Provide necessary resources to execute the evaluation.
- Engage organizational leadership in the process.
- Anticipate impacts of findings and how they will influence your program.

Step 7: Reporting and Dissemination

- Consider how to present the evaluation results and the format—e.g., formal report, presentation, infographics.
- Develop a communications strategy to inform key stakeholders.

Conclusion

Diversity, equity, and inclusion data collection and analysis are central drivers in institutional culture and climate change. This chapter has outlined promising practices in quantitative and qualitative data collection and analysis, as well as evaluation planning and data, for diversity, equity, and inclusion metrics. Institutions often focus their diversity, equity, and inclusion data collection and reporting on increasing compositional or representational diversity alone. A robust diversity, equity, and inclusion metrics analysis, however, must focus on a broader understanding of diversity to encompass the institutional policies, practices, plans, and structures that create the culture and the climate. Further, this chapter strives to emphasize the importance of diversifying data-collection methods and analysis to gather rich data that can provide a validated underpinning to drive institutional change. Focusing diversity, equity, and inclusion on only compositional or representational diversity metrics has prioritized quantitative data collection. A quantitative focus alone, one that prioritizes staffing metrics and perhaps climate or satisfaction survey data, misses key factors about institutional culture. Implementing a systematic, mixed-method diversity, equity, and inclusion metrics plan will yield the richest and most robust understanding of institutional climate and culture. Quantitative data can generate answers to the "what" questions, but qualitative metrics and evaluation metrics can provide answers to the "why" questions. Institutions that are implementing a diversity, equity, and inclusion metrics plan not just to take the measure of the current landscape but to strive for institutional change will need metrics that can answer the what and the why.

REFERENCES

Association of American Medical Colleges (AAMC). (2013). *Assessing institutional culture and climate: Webcast supplemental guide.* Washington, D.C.: Association of American Medical Colleges.

Antonio, A. L., Chang, M. J., Hakuta, J., Kenny, D. A., Levin, S., & Milem, J. F. (2004). Effects of racial diversity on complex thinking in college students. *Psychological Science, 15,* 507–510.

Baker, B., & Collins, M. (2013). *The next generation of diversity metrics: Predictive and game-changing analytics* [PDF on Diversity Best Practices website]. Retrieved from https://www.diversitybestpractices.com/publications/next-generation-diversity-metrics-predictive-and-game-changing-analytics

Balter, R., Chow, J., & Jin, Y. (2014). *What diversity metrics are best used to track and improve employee diversity?* Retrieved from Cornell University ILR School website: http://digitalcommons.ilr.cornell.edu/student/68

Banta, T. W., & Palomba, C. A. (2014). *Assessment essentials: Planning, implementing, and improving assessment in higher education.* Hoboken, NJ: Jossey-Bass.

Bystedt, J., Lynn, S., Potts, D., & Fraley, G. (2010). *Moderating to the max: A full-tilt guide to creative, insightful focus groups and depth interviews.* Ithaca, NY: Paramount.

Centers for Disease Control and Prevention. (2011). *Developing an effective evaluation plan* (Report). Retrieved from https://www.cdc.gov/obesity/downloads/cdc-evaluation-workbook-508.pdf

Chen, X., Liu, D., & Portnoy, R. (2012). A multilevel investigation of motivational cultural intelligence, organizational diversity climate, and cultural sales: Evidence from U.S. real estate firms. *Journal of Applied Psychology, 97,* 93–106.

Dobbin, F., & Kalev, A. (2016, July–August). Why diversity programs fail. *Harvard Business Review*, 52–60.

Fink, A. (2008). *How to conduct surveys: A step-by-step guide.* Thousand Oaks, CA: Sage Publications.

Hsieh, H., & Shannon, S.E. (2005). Three approaches to qualitative content analysis. *Qualitative Health Research, 15*(9), 1277–1288.

Hubbard, E. (2003). Assessing, measuring and analyzing the impact of diversity initiatives. In D. L. Plummer (Ed.), *Handbook of diversity management: Beyond awareness to competency based learning* (pp. 271–305). Lanham, MD: University Press of America.

Jongbloed, B., Enders, J., & Salerno, C. (2008). Higher education and its communities: Interconnections, interdependencies, and a research agenda. *Higher Education, 3*, 304–324.

Krueger, R. A., Casey, M. A. (2014). *Focus groups: A practical guide for applied research.* Thousand Oaks, CA: Sage.

Kvale, S. (1996). *InterViews: An introduction to qualitative research interviewing.* Thousand Oaks, CA: Sage.

Levine, B., Stoudemire, T., & Polonskaia, A. (2014). Diversity and analytics: How to build and leverage diversity to outperform the competition. Mercer. [Webcast PowerPoint Slides]. Retrieved from https://www.mercer.com/content/dam/mercer/attachments/global/webcasts/140604-mercer-how-to-build-and-leverage-diversity.pdf

McKay, P. F., Avery, D. A., Tonidandel, S., Morris, M. A., Hernandez, M., & Hebel, M. (2007). Racial differences in employee retention: Are diversity climate perceptions the key? *Personnel Psychology, 60*, 35–62.

McKay, P. F., Avery, D. A., & Morris, M. A. (2008). Racial-ethnic differences in employee sales performance? The role of diversity climate. *Personnel Psychology, 61*, 348–374.

Mor Barak, M. A., Cherin, D. A., & Berkman, S. (1998). Organizational and personal dimensions in diversity climate. *Journal of Applied Behavioral Science, 34*, 82–104.

Nardi, P. M. (2005). *Doing survey research* (2nd ed.). Boston, MA: Allyn & Bacon.

Nivet, M. A. (2011). Diversity 3.0: A necessary systems upgrade. *Academic Medicine, 86*, 1487–1489.

PeopleFluent. (2015). Measuring diversity for success. Retrieved from https://mktg.peoplefluent.com/WP-MeasuringDiversityforSuccess_Landing-Page.html

Person, S. D., Jordan, C. G., Allison, J. J., Fink Ogawa, L. M., Castillo-Page, L., Conrad, S., Nivet, M., & Plummer, D. L. (2015). Measuring diversity and inclusion in academic medicine: The diversity engagement survey. *Academic Medicine, 90*(12), 1675–1683.

Plummer, D. L., Jordan, C. G. (2007).Going plaid: Integrating diversity into business strategy, structure and systems. *OD Practitioner, 39*(2), 35–40.

Price, E. G., Gozu, A., Kern, D. E., Powe, N. R., Wand, G. S., Golden, S., & Cooper, L. A. (2005). The role of cultural diversity climate in recruitment, promotion, and retention of faculty in academic medicine. *Journal of General Internal Medicine, 20*, 565–571.

Pugh, S. D., Dietz, J., Brief, A. P., & Wiley, J. W. (2008). Looking inside and out: The impact of employee and community demographic composition on organizational diversity climate. *Journal of Applied Psychology, 93*, 1422–1428.

Saul, J. (2004). *Benchmarking for nonprofits: How to measure, manage, and improve performance.* Saint Paul, MN: Fieldstone Alliance.

Saldaña, J. (2012). *The coding manual for qualitative researchers.* Thousand Oaks, CA: Sage.

Sandars, J., Brown, J., & Walsh, K. (2017). Producing useful evaluations in medical education. *Education for Primary Care, 28*(3), 137–140.

Seidman, I. (2011). *Interviewing as qualitative research: A guide for researchers in education and the social sciences.* New York, NY: Teachers College Press.

Thomas, R.R. (1996). *Redefining diversity.* New York, NY: AMACOM.

United Way of America. (1996). *Measuring program outcomes: A practical approach.* [Manual.] Retrieved from University of Nebraska Omaha DigitalCommons@UNO website: http://digitalcommons.unomaha.edu/slceeval/47

Vermeulen, P., & Jenkins, A. (2016) Turn diversity and inclusion into a talent strength: A six-pack strategy for driving measurable improvements. Retrieved from https://insights.randstadsourceright.com/h/i/247635727-turn-diversity-and-inclusion-into-a-talent-strength

Whitla, D., Orfield, G., Silen, W., Teperow, C., Howard, C., & Reede, J. (2003). Educational benefits of diversity in medical school: A survey of medical students. *Academic Medicine, 78,* 460–466.

CHAPTER SEVEN

Transforming Organization Cultures: Notes from the Field

Marilyn Loden

INTRODUCTION

TODAY AMERICA'S DEMOGRAPHIC destiny as a multicultural society is driving institutional change and simultaneously encountering backlash. Rather than work against those who experience this change as a threat, diversity practitioners must find more effective ways to include and understand the divergent perspectives and worldviews that are inherent in a multicultural, multiracial society. While most diversity practitioners believe that a respectful, just, and inclusive society benefits everyone, reaching this goal poses many implementation challenges—challenges that require humility, compassion, and understanding to ensure success.

For over three decades, organizations in all employment sectors, including private, public, and nonprofit, as well as universities, professional firms, and the military, have been focusing on workforce diversity. Early on, most categorized diversity as affirmative action with a new label and committed few resources to support it. Those who believed it deserved more attention often chose awareness training as the blanket solution to address diversity challenges.

Evolution of Diversity Programs

After two decades of false starts and an overreliance on awareness training, many institutions began to recognize the need for a more comprehensive approach to managing this important change. Targeted recruitment became a major focus in many companies, as did participation in minority supplier programs. CEOs began giving speeches about the importance of diversity for business success, and formal mentoring programs became a best practice across industries. While these focused efforts helped attract and retain (to a degree) a more diverse workforce, there remained one subtle yet powerful barrier to sustainable success that few institutions were prepared to address: *organization culture.* An organization's culture consists of the shared beliefs and values established by its founders and leaders. These beliefs are conveyed and reinforced through various formal and informal institutional channels, ultimately shaping employee perceptions, behaviors, and beliefs. Recognizing the ways in which many organization cultures welcomed and nurtured some identity groups as they minimized the talents of others was a powerful insight for diversity practitioners. It was also a threatening observation to those who were comfortable with the status quo. Thus, this was the juncture where proactive measures to support diversity collided with institutional myopia and an abiding belief among some that there was nothing discriminatory about the values, norms, traditions, institutional practices, or expectations informing the organization's actions. Not surprisingly, this was also the point where efforts to leverage diversity often slowed or even collapsed.

Thus, in many institutions, there were continuing cycles of progress and regression—as efforts to attract, develop, and retain greater diversity were thwarted by cultures that unwittingly limited opportunities, marginalized some members, and drove others away. This cycle of progress and regression was referred to as "our rotating door strategy" by one frustrated HR leader at a large manufacturing company, where a comprehensive plan to hire more engineers of color could not correct the high turnover that followed due to isolation and the "sink or swim" environment at many company plants.

Throughout the 1990s, working in the field as a diversity practitioner often involved employing strategies for change that skirted around the edges of the sacrosanct. Even when cultural barriers were obvious, they were often thought to be insignificant by those who had withstood them and prospered despite them. But the cumulative damage done by toxic cultures was building throughout the U.S. workplace. As more discrimination lawsuits were filed and stories circulated about Texaco, Smith Barney, Denny's, Walmart, Hobby Lobby, and many other organizations, the impact of culture could no longer be ignored. Not surprisingly, in companies that recognized the need to embrace change, such as Ernst & Young, IBM, Procter & Gamble, Unilever, and Xerox, building more welcoming and inclusive corporate cultures was at the core of their diversity efforts.

Eventually more institutions began acknowledging the self-limiting aspects of cultures frozen in the past, and they committed to making changes that no longer skirted the edges. It was at this point in the evolution of diversity implementation that many practitioners started using change adoption principles (Rogers & Shoemaker, 1971) and change management tools to guide their work. The era of culture realignment and holistic support for diversity as a key competitive advantage had finally begun. Today, leading-edge organizations recognize that while changing institutional systems to support diversity is often more tedious and time-consuming than offering the quick fix of awareness training, the difference in impact and sustainability is palpable. Fix the system, and the problem diminishes and may even disappear; "fix" the person with awareness training, and the biases will return once the workshop's effect wears off.

Many more organizations are succeeding today with holistic efforts to attract, develop, retain, and leverage employee diversity. A look at the results from *DiversityInc*'s Top 50 Companies annual survey makes it clear that the number of organizations committed to building healthy and inclusive cultures now far exceeds the list of yearly winners (DiversityInc, 2017). Their willingness to challenge old assumptions and rewrite the rules is making the critical difference.

This rise in institutional success with diversity implementation is not the result of a lucky accident. Rather, it is the product of careful and comprehensive strategic planning. Starting with a broad and inclusive definition of diversity, effective strategies rely on change adoption principles and employ eight powerful institutional levers to help build a solid, sustainable organizational infrastructure for diversity and inclusion.

Beginning with a broad and inclusive definition of diversity, this chapter outlines four key elements of a robust diversity strategy in use in many leading-edge organizations. The goals of this strategy are to:

- integrate diversity into the fabric of the culture as a core value;
- increase common ground across differences;
- build institutional cultures where all members can thrive.

Each element is essential in ensuring that diversity is understood, supported, and fully leveraged. While effective implementation takes time, commitment, and continuous oversight, the long-term benefits that can result for employees, institutions, and society make the extra effort worthwhile.

ELEMENT I: Utilizing a Broad and Inclusive Definition of Diversity

While much has been written about the primary and secondary dimensions of diversity (Loden & Rosener, 1990) over the last two decades, the updated diversity wheel (fig. 1; see also Loden, 2010) continues to be a useful model for acknowledging the complexities of social identity and ensuring that all members of an organization see themselves and are acknowledged as part of the diversity mosaic.

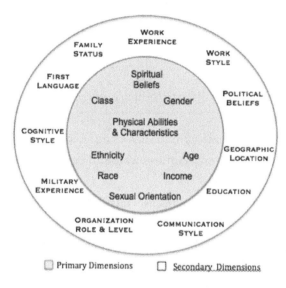

Figure 1

The diversity wheel is an inclusive framework and suggests every person has a distinct social identity that shapes attitudes, expectations, and behaviors. Within the wheel, we see many key dimensions of group identity—elements that influence who we are, our socialization, and how we relate to the world and those around us.

The wheel uses a wide lens to identify important differences, going beyond age, gender, and race to acknowledge the power that many other dimensions exert as well. By using this framework to define diversity, we set the stage for involvement by all members of the organization in efforts to build an inclusive and motivating culture. As individuals, we have more interest in the concept of diversity when we believe we are a legitimate part of the discussion. We are more likely to advocate for change when we see some personal benefit for ourselves.

This broad and inclusive definition allows every employee to consider the impact of diversity dimensions in her/his own life. As employees engage with others and explore their diversity profiles, each conversation has the potential to enrich understanding among all participants. Ultimately, this exploration allows participants to reveal more about many invisible dimensions of their social identities, building empathy, understanding, and support for others with whom they work while recognizing the many needs, aspirations, and goals they share.

In organizations that see diversity as descriptive only of underrepresented groups rather than everyone, resistance and opposition to culture change are often intense among those who believe they are being left out. The exclusion of mainstream members (such as straight white men) from the change process invariably leads to backlash and cynicism about institutional goals and the long-term career prospects for group members. Thus, at the start of any serious effort to transform the organization and leverage the skills of a diverse workforce, it is critical that diversity practitioners recognize and include all diverse groups. Leaving straight white men or any other identity group out of the process is a recipe for failure. The diversity wheel is a framework that can help dispel concerns about exclusion among employees as it reminds them that there is talent to be leveraged in every identity group.

ELEMENT II: Applying Change Management Principles to Guide Implementation

As with any change, perceptions of the risks and rewards associated with building a diversity-friendly culture vary within every organization. While some individuals eagerly welcome changes to increase access, flexibility, and inclusion, others persistently resist efforts to do this.

Based on extensive behavioral science research about predictable reactions to change (Rogers, 1995), the Diversity Adoption Curve (fig. 2) depicts the typical path that culture change in support of diversity takes (Loden, 1996) as it is introduced and adopted within an organization. All members of the organization fall into one of the five segments shown on this curve. Within each distinct segment, people share certain attitudes and assumptions about diversity.

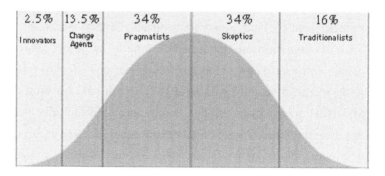

Figure 2.

Like a wave forming and rolling toward the shore, the benefits of diversity are initially recognized by a small, select group of innovators in an organization. As the concept of leveraging diversity gains momentum, change agents embrace it and speed up the wave, accelerating its acceptance. Slowly, after a period of successful testing and refinement, the wave gathers the strength required to become a change that pragmatists begin to accept. Ultimately, it will dash itself powerfully upon the rocks of the skeptics and traditionalists and begin wearing away their fear and resistance.

One's placement in a particular segment is based on the level of perceived opportunity and risk associated with leveraging diversity. For example, while innovators focus on the creative potential that diversity offers, pragmatists are motivated by bottom-line evidence of its benefits. In addition to wanting statistical "proof of concept," pragmatists often look to their more progressive peers for endorsement and are more inclined to support diversity once their change agent colleagues have tested and demonstrated its benefits.

Unlike innovators, the segment first to discover and quietly embrace diversity, change agents are opinion leaders, the people out front and visible in their support. Although extensive change management research (Rogers, 1995) tells us they represent just 13.5 percent of an organization, change agents are highly influential in promoting the merits of diversity and a culture of inclusion. As change leaders, they enjoy playing a proactive, visible role as "diversity champions." Successful diversity implementation and culture change hinge on the early and continuous involvement of change agents. This relatively small segment possesses the passion and commitment needed to build broad support for diversity across other segments and overcome resistance. However, while change agents can be highly influential with their pragmatist and skeptic peers, they can sometimes increase resistance within these groups through well-intentioned but inappropriate or ill-timed actions. In particular, communications that focus on "bias busting," "micro-inequities," and "isms" may backfire if they appear to target rather than inform more resistant segments. Similarly, some diversity training can lead to backlash and increase resistance among fearful employees when they perceive that their concerns are being dismissed or that they are being categorized as "part of the problem." To successfully promote diversity and inclusion, change agents must be able to recognize and defuse the concerns of their more resistant peers. For pragmatists, this involves providing a solid economic/business case for the benefits of diversity. With skeptics, it often means reaching out to understand and allay their fears—regardless of how distorted or exaggerated those concerns may appear to be.

To the extent that change agents are educated about change adoption and empowered to serve as change leaders, their impact as communicators, educators, and role models can accelerate culture change throughout an organization. Once they recognize the perspectives of pragmatists and some skeptics, they can customize their communications to emphasize the opportunities that diversity offers as they help increase understanding and openness in these groups.

Rather than assume everyone is ready to support and leverage diversity, today more organizations acknowledge the differences in openness and readiness that exist among change agents, pragmatists, skeptics, and traditionalists. To address their different perceptions, many organizations now employ a multi-pronged approach to communication, education, and systems alignment built on an inclusive vision of diversity. Rather than a one-size-fits-all approach, communications and education are tailored to the needs and readiness of each segment—while consistently emphasizing the organization's enduring commitment to building an inclusive culture where diversity is valued and leveraged. In some organizations, diversity council members are deployed to do peer outreach at their specific work sites and to provide basic employee education about diversity that defuses resistance and increases multicultural awareness and understanding. In these cases, it is largely the change agents who volunteer for this work—people excited by the prospect of delivering education and shaping peer opinions, particularly among pragmatists.

While change agents can be very effective at influencing the opinions of pragmatists, they are less able to reach past this segment to enlist support among many skeptics. Most skeptics are far more likely to be influenced by the evolving attitudes and beliefs of pragmatists, as well as by visible commitment from their organization leaders. Thus, the wave of adoption continues to spread from segment to segment with each group watching the group to its right for signs that diversity is becoming embedded in the organization's DNA. Once skeptics recognize that the integration of diversity and inclusion in the organization's core values is inevitable, they see that continued opposition to this change could have more negative consequences for them than embracing it. And when their "risk-reward proposition" shifts, most skeptics will slowly begin to comply.

Helping skeptics acquire the insights and behavioral skills needed for success in diverse teams and organizations is a key component of successful culture transformation, for it is the *severe lack of such skills* that is often the root cause of their embedded resistance to diversity and culture change. Until skeptics have the relationship skills, self-insight, and confidence required to step across cultural boundaries and interact effectively with others, most will remain guarded and fearful of change.

While segmented implementation occurs today in some organizations, it still happens more by accident than because of systematic and strategic planning. Unfortunately, advocates for diversity in many institutions remain convinced that attitudinal conversion of traditionalists is their primary goal. But direct attack, blame, and confrontation by advocates does not lead to acceptance and attitude change among members of this segment. Instead, it causes many to retreat further and engage in magical thinking about a "return to the good old days." Until organizations and diversity specialists commit to displacing the fears of resisters with knowledge and relationship skills to navigate effectively in a diverse world, neither skeptics nor traditionalists will be adequately equipped or motivated to embrace change. This is one of the principle tasks that now lie ahead. Until the growing community of diversity practitioners fully engages in this important work, organization and societal transformation will remain out of reach.

In the interest of accelerating adoption of diversity and minimizing backlash, utilizing the Diversity Adoption Curve to implement sustainable change is essential in organizations. By doing so, we will move toward the acceptance of diversity and inclusion, systematically and smoothly—with fewer obstacles to address on the journey. By ignoring the needs and concerns of any of the five segments, we increase the risk of having the wrong idea adopted—that diversity is destructive and must be curtailed.

ELEMENT III: Holistic Framework
to Strengthen, Modify, and Align
Institutional Systems and Practices

Thus far we have considered two important elements in comprehensive diversity implementation strategies:

- a broad and inclusive framework to define diversity
- change adoption principles to plan and guide the process

While these elements prepare people and organizations to adopt change, they cannot change institutional cultures on their own. Rather, they must be incorporated into a *holistic framework* designed to strengthen, modify, and align the organization's basic operating assumptions, practices, and systems with the goal of fully leveraging diversity.

This holistic framework relies on eight levers that organizations use to promote, support, and sustain desired change. These levers include:

- strategic planning and design
- ongoing communication
- senior leadership behaviors
- change management stewards

- aligned HR systems and practices
- performance standards and metrics
- recognition and rewards
- training and education

Whether we examine successful corporate efforts aimed at improving quality, safety, customer satisfaction, or any other important priority, we typically see all of these levers being utilized to build understanding and support for change. Successful organizational transformation requires every lever illustrated in the fishbone diagram in figure 3 be activated to guide the change process and embed diversity and inclusion in an institution's culture.

Levers for Organizational Transformation

Figure 3.

Borrowing from the work of Kaoru Ishikawa (1968), who developed the original fishbone model to illustrate cause-and-effect relationships in quality-improvement processes, this adapted model shows the levers that must be aligned and activated to produce a holistic and sustainable transformation in support of diversity and inclusion. When we evaluate the effectiveness of institutional diversity efforts using this model, it is easy to see why some succeed and many fall short. *Not a single box in the model can be overlooked or minimized* if the goal to transform the organization and build a welcoming, inclusive culture that leverages employee diversity is to be realized. What's more, the phased approach that the model illustrates is also critical for successful transformation. Rather than starting with training, successful and sustainable diversity change efforts begin with leader engagement, communications design and rollout, strategic planning, and process-infrastructure building. The last box in Phase I of the diagram, Change Management Stewards, refers to the leadership and local diversity council structures required to implement actions and monitor results at all organization levels. The following is a description of the important part each lever plays in facilitating comprehensive and sustainable change.

Figure 4 illustrates the strategic plan developed by a dynamic global corporation with a comprehensive diversity strategy in place. This is an actual, U.S.-headquartered business with operations and facilities on five continents. For over six years, the company has been working to transform its corporate culture and enhance efforts to attract, develop, promote, and retain a highly diverse workforce. For illustrative purposes only, the organization is referred to as "CHem Corp" in this chapter.

DIVERSITY & INCLUSION AT CHEM CORP

Strategy.
(*How CHem Corp will move from its current state toward the desire state*)

Employ a wide-lens definition of diversity, Change Adoption and D&I Guiding Principles (I CARE) to guide the company's efforts towards becoming a diversity-friendly employer of choice.

Tactics. (*The people and processes CHem Corp will leverage to achieve this strategy and sustain change*)

Align CHem Corp's organization culture through:

- Senior leadership involvement & behavior modeling
- Ongoing corporate-wide communications
- Identification of linkages between D&I and other strategic business goals
- Mobilization of D&I advocates across the company
- Implementation of aligned HR systems, policies & practices
- Development & deployment of relevant management metrics
- Identification of CHem Corp successes with Recognition/Rewards for proactive leadership, employee advocacy & role modeling
- Training & Education

    Initial Manager Education focused on:

        » Understanding mental models

        » Harassment prevention

        » Employee engagement

        » Diversity dimensions

        » I CARE Principles & behavioral expectations

        » Accelerating & managing inclusion in teams

        » Initial Employee Education focused on:

        » Understanding mental models

        » Harassment prevention

        » Diversity dimensions

        » I CARE Principles & behavioral expectations

        » Guidelines for giving & receiving feedback

Figure 4.

In reviewing the CHem Corp diversity strategy, we see how each lever on the fishbone has been incorporated into the tactics used to drive change. The company's intention is to exert pressure using these levers to build and maintain a welcoming, diversity-friendly business where the talents of its entire workforce are leveraged. As all eight levers are pressed and systems and practices evolve to better support diversity, new tactics are added to fine-tune and propel the process forward, while the original strategy continues to provide the basic foundation for sustainable transformation.

While the fishbone model lays out the tactical requirements for sustainable change, moving and aligning all eight levers with the goal of a culture of inclusion is a complex, labor-intensive undertaking. Consequently, many institutions and diversity practitioners opt to employ select levers from the model rather than commit to this holistic approach. Regardless of which levers are emphasized and which are ignored, these "cherry-picked" tactical plans will fail to deliver the desired result. Here's why:

- If **senior leaders** are not engaged, modeling appropriate behavior, and actively promoting change, many skeptics will perceive diversity and inclusion as a temporary fad.
- When **communication** about culture change and its importance to the enterprise is infrequent, incoherent, or fails to address the concerns of pragmatists and skeptics, disinformation about the benefits and intent of the change will begin to circulate, undermining the business case.
- Without a formalized infrastructure that enlists the ideas and enthusiasm of change agents as **change stewards**— through participation on local, regional, and executive

diversity councils—grassroots resistance and retreat from change are more likely to occur.

- When **HR systems and practices** do not align with diversity and inclusion, systemic problems like cronyism, discrimination, exclusion, and harassment will remain and, in some cases, increase. In addition, organizations with weak HR platforms are likely to be more vulnerable to legal actions due to employment discrimination and often experience higher turnover among "regretted loss" employees who believe they are being underutilized and systematically disenfranchised.

- When **metrics** for measuring progress toward the goal of building a welcoming, inclusive culture are not applied year to year, then both the champions of change and its detractors can point to subjective examples of its success or failure. And where there are no **performance standards** for manager and employee actions that enhance progress, there is limited motivation to behave differently.

- As with any change that has a significant value to an institution, **recognition and rewards** must be available to those leaders who stand out as superior role models as well as to employees who step up as change agent volunteers. Where recognition and rewards are not available, the lack of acknowledgment often leads to lowered engagement, apathy, and even burnout among these key thought leaders and advocates for change.

- Finally, no one can deny the important role that **training and education** play in building skills and increasing understanding and support for diversity and inclusion. If we begin with an inclusive definition of diversity and the assumption that all employees possess diverse identities, we open the door for broader volunteer participation in the educational process. When we offer education that exposes participants to greater cultural and experiential diversity as well as practical tools to improve interpersonal effectiveness, we make it easier for individuals to build both competence and the confidence required to step out of their comfort zones and effectively engage others from diverse identity groups. And when we avoid imposing the conscious and unconscious biases we may carry about the character and beliefs of skeptics and traditionalists, we increase the probability that deep and sustainable change will ultimately occur.

In organizations committed to building a welcoming and inclusive workplace, *there must also be recognition* that achieving this goal demands a rethinking and recalibration of the traditions, norms, systems, policies, and practices that inform the culture. By utilizing the three strategic elements already discussed in this chapter—

- a broad definition of diversity,
- an implementation process guided by change management principles,
- a holistic approach to strengthen, modify, and align systems, policies, and practices—diversity practitioners can maximize the impact of every action taken in building a vibrant, empowering, and inclusive culture—while minimizing the chance that this critical change will not be embraced across the organization. When every

important change lever—from senior leader behavior
through HR systems to training—is aligned to support
and leverage diversity, nothing can stand in the way of
sustainable success.

ELEMENT IV: Using I CARE to Set
Behavioral Expectations

While aligned institutional practices and systems are essential in
efforts to leverage diversity, it is the everyday interactions among
employees that often serve as a litmus test in gauging broad commitment, understanding, and support for change. Whether new employees are welcomed or isolated, the level of respect and cooperation
offered to coworkers of diverse social identities, the willingness of
more experienced team members to guide and assist new entrants,
and the collective monitoring of individual and team actions to ensure
that no behavior crosses the lines of civility and professionalism are
examples of the soft metrics that indicate buy-in and broad support
for change.

Building employee ownership for a healthy climate where diversity flourishes is the strategic change element most often overlooked
or taken for granted by diversity practitioners and organizations
alike. While much is made of the economic and demographic case
for diversity, these arguments do not translate into specific actions
that individuals can take in support of change. What's more, while the
business case for diversity is compelling for many pragmatists, it offers
less compelling evidence for endorsement within other segments.

Fortunately, a simple, elegant, and transformative solution
for building employee commitment can be found in four guiding

principles. When implemented effectively, these principles have the power to exponentially enhance the success of culture change. They are:

> → **Inclusion** → **Cooperation** → **Accountability** → **Respect**

Unlike elements previously discussed in this chapter, each of these concepts has been widely used in diversity work for many years. Yet, despite their popularity, they have rarely been treated as powerful catalysts in cultural transformation. All too often, they are reduced to tired clichés that are used in recruiting brochures or on company websites to signal commitment to diversity. Yet they have the potential to do much more to support change and build common ground in organizations.

In the CHem Corp strategy discussed earlier (fig. 4), several references were made to I CARE. The acronym stands for:

- INCLUSION
- COOPERATION
- ACCOUNTABILITY
- RESPECT
- EVERY DAY FOR EVERYONE

By embedding these behavioral guidelines in its diversity strategy, CHem Corp has greatly enhanced its success in building a welcoming and inclusive company culture.

By crafting ongoing communications, education, HR systems, metrics, and training to reflect and reinforce these guiding principles, CHem Corp has succeeded as few others have in preparing individuals to be effective actors in a diverse world. What's more, these guiding

principles serve as a soft metric in assessing how effectively CHem
Corp's HR systems and practices support employee diversity. While
it is certainly true that the words themselves are not new, it is the
way in which they have been defined and deployed by CHem Corp's
Executive Diversity Council (EDC) that has given them the power to
help transform the culture and build shared behavioral expectations
among employees.

The I CARE Story

Slogans and logos often have a short lifespan, but I CARE has been in
existence at CHem Corp for several years. As a global company with
business interests on several continents, CHem Corp has a mobile,
multinational workforce that continually crosses both national and
cultural boundaries to get work done. As an engineering-driven manufacturing business, the company understands from experience that it
is engaged in a fierce, ongoing competition for talent. Thus, the business case for building a diversity-friendly culture was quite apparent
from the start and relatively easy to articulate within CHem Corp.

Where the real challenge existed was in enlisting the support
of every employee to help create a welcoming environment for all.
Noting that many companies used diversity training to spotlight and
correct inappropriate behavior, CHem Corp's EDC was determined
from the start to provide more than a long list of "do nots" to build
understanding and employee support for change. They realized that
the bulk of cross-cultural challenges and conflicts occurred in day-
to-day interactions inside work teams and cross-functionally, so they
resolved to create a tool that would help employees choose appropriate behaviors in everyday interactions and, thereby, build rapport
while decreasing conflict and miscommunication.

Recognizing that CHem Corp contained the same distribution of skeptics and traditionalists as other organizations, the EDC set out to develop behavioral guidance for *all* employees that transcended identity politics. They used a global lens for their work, articulating a set of professional, success-oriented behaviors that, when used by employees in all job capacities, were more likely to enhance relationships and cross-cultural interactions, build trust, and improve business outcomes.

With additional input from the organization's diversity thought leaders, many of whom were members of local diversity councils throughout the company, each principle was then expanded to illustrate its importance in enhancing day-to-day team interactions. By linking I CARE to basic activities in which all employees participated, the principles became less abstract and more relevant and actionable.

To bind with the company culture across national and cultural boundaries, the principles also needed to be global in their reach. This meant the EDC had to consider how each principle would be interpreted and implemented in many diverse cultural settings. All of the decisions about purpose, positioning, language, use, and potential impact took the small committee several months and many lengthy meetings to resolve. But when the final document was published and the initial communication rollout plan was developed, every member of the team realized the importance of what had been created and the enormous potential I CARE offered in helping CHem Corp enhance its culture. Figure 5 contains the final version of the I CARE guiding principles developed at CHem Corp to support its diversity and inclusion change process.

In this document, each principle is defined and linked to the interactive process where its relevance and potential for positive impact are greatest. In addition, sample behaviors that support each principle are included to provide further guidance.

Today, there is no doubt that employees throughout the organization understand CHem Corp's commitment to I CARE. It remains a major focus in ongoing communication, education, and systems designed to attract, develop, reward, and retain a multicultural workforce. It is reinforced in "I CARE moments"—brief discussions of a principle in action that occur at the beginning of most team meetings. It is used by employees to challenge coworkers when their behavior crosses a line. It has been built into the company's annual employee satisfaction survey as a metric for gauging successful culture alignment and is also becoming an increasingly important component in assessing effective leader and manager performance. And because I CARE resonates with the desires of most employees to work in an inclusive environment where they are respected and their skills are well utilized, there has been little resistance to accepting this guidance as a positive step toward building a welcoming and inclusive culture for all. Thus, from the grass roots to the executive suite, employees are broadly supportive of the principles and are putting them into practice every day.

I CARE: Diversity & Inclusion Guiding Principles

1. **Inclusion** pertains to **How We Make Decisions.** We include *by ensuring everyone on the team is part of the team.*

   Examples of Inclusive Actions:

   - Soliciting others' ideas and listening to suggestions both within our teams and cross-functionally

   - Monitoring how the team works together to ensure that all relevant input is considered

I CARE: Diversity & Inclusion Guiding Principles

2. Cooperation pertains to **How We Work Together.** We cooperate **by** *helping each other succeed.*

Examples of Cooperative Actions:

- Sharing information and other resources to accomplish goals

- Building a collaborative climate where the level of trust is high by supporting others on the team

- Recognizing we are better off sharing what we know with others on the team and throughout the company so we can all succeed together

3. Accountability pertains to **How We Manage Our Work Environment.** We are accountable when we *ensure that our own and others' behaviors contribute to a welcoming, diversity-friendly workplace.*

Examples of Accountable Behavior:

- Ensuring that our personal actions align with the D&I guiding principles of inclusion, cooperation and respect

- Recognizing and reinforcing the actions of others that support the principles of I CARE

- Discouraging behaviors that may diminish or discriminate against any individual or group

4. Respect pertains to **How We Treat Each Other.** We show respect when we **treat others with dignity and consideration.**

Examples of Respectful Behavior:

- Often we will find that our coworkers want to be treated exactly as we do. For example, most employees like to be recognized and appreciated for their contributions. We all "expect respect" as CHem Corp colleagues.

- Sometimes, team members may have different expectations due to differences in values, priorities, family obligations, or culture. In such cases, we need to be mindful of these differences and make reasonable accommodations whenever possible.

I CARE: Diversity & Inclusion Guiding Principles

By applying these principles every day with everyone (including customers, colleagues, and community stakeholders), we will become a great company in which to work, with an organization culture that maximizes the contributions of its diverse workforce.

Figure 5.

Principles That Enable Behavior Change

The dissemination of I CARE began with a meeting of the top fifty leaders from CHem Corp, where the principles were positioned as a foundational element in the company's Diversity and Inclusion Strategy. Communication plans were developed to cascade the proactive message of I CARE throughout the organization, beginning with leader-led town hall meetings and cascading down in the organization with follow-on manager- and first-line-supervisor-led I CARE team discussions. Detailed discussion guides were distributed and reviewed with all managers and supervisors to ensure that consistency in messaging was achieved. As more diversity councils were formed at various plant locations, communication about the importance of I CARE became a major focus of their ongoing work. And to be certain the connection between I CARE and basic business priorities was clear to pragmatists and skeptics, a video was produced and shown throughout the organization in which each of CHem Corp's senior leaders discussed the importance of I CARE and diversity in the context of achieving key business priorities, including globalization, innovation, talent acquisition and retention, productivity, safety, and teamwork.

After the first "total immersion" communication cycle concluded, an ongoing communication plan was developed, focusing on examples of how I CARE could be used to build stronger, inclusive teams and cultural competence among employees. This follow-on communication plan continued to emphasize the benefits that I CARE offered to everyone and the importance of full employee participation in making the principles a part of the organization's DNA.

Over the past several years, CHem Corp has continued to relentlessly emphasize the importance of I CARE in building and maintaining a welcoming, engaging, and diversity-friendly culture. Because these principles apply to everyone, they offer the same advantages to members of all identity groups. No one loses in a culture that supports I CARE. The guidance also emphasizes that employees are not only accountable for their own actions, they are empowered to discourage inappropriate behavior if and when they see it. Thus, CHem Corp has taken the position that in matters of exclusion, disrespect, and discrimination, being a disengaged bystander is not an option.

Several years after I CARE was first introduced, it continues to be the glue that connects employees to organization transformation on a daily basis at CHem Corp. It has become a set of shared expectations that builds bridges across differences and increases support and a sense of common purpose among employees. At this point in the journey, the company has built I CARE into its hiring, training, performance management, and employee feedback processes. The EDC now uses a dashboard to measure progress toward recruiting, development, retention, and advancement goals and employs the I CARE lens when evaluating that progress and identifying opportunities for improvement in each area. Thus the magic of I CARE continues to work as employees from diverse backgrounds buy in and CHem Corp's culture continues to be transformed.

Looking Ahead

Today's rapid pace of change in the global economy and throughout U.S. society continues to pose new diversity challenges and opportunities for practitioners and the institutions and communities they support. Regardless of how far some have come in transforming their cultures, successful organizations will need to remain change hardy and poised for continuous adaptation to fully support and leverage diversity into the future. Together, the strategic elements outlined in this chapter form a solid platform on which to build more vibrant, engaging organization cultures where diversity is valued and leveraged. Because these elements transcend national boundaries, their applicability and appeal are almost universal. While the journey will differ in every society, it is one worth embarking on in all.

Although the term "global village" has been a part of the diversity lexicon for decades, that village has yet to reach consensus on the guiding principles it will embrace or the actions it will take collectively to increase cross-cultural understanding, trust, and cooperation while securing and maintaining the global commons for all. It is time for that important work to move forward. By leveraging the talent residing in the global workforce and using the principles of I CARE to define shared expectations, we can improve prospects for achieving breakthrough discoveries that enhance the quality of life and even address the planet's most critical challenges such as climate change, war, disease, hunger, and poverty. As citizens of the global village, we need only recognize the enormous resource at our disposal and then use it for the good of all.

REFERENCES

DiversityInc top 50 lists since 2001. (2017). Retrieved from http://
www.diversityinc.com/all-diversityinc-top-50-lists/

Ishikawa, K. (1968). Guide to quality control. Tokyo: JUSE Press.

Loden, M. (1996). *Implementing diversity* (p. 42). New York:
McGraw-Hill.

Loden, M. (2010). Diversity dimensions [Figure]. Retrieved from
http://loden.com.

Loden, M. & Rosener, J. (1990) *Workforce America! Managing Employee
Diversity as a Vital Resource.* Burr Ridge, IL: McGraw-Hill.

Rogers, E. M. (1995). *Diffusion of innovations* (4th ed., pp. 257-265).
New York: The Free Press.

Rogers, E. M., & Shoemaker, F. (1971). *Communication of innovations:
A cross-cultural approach* (pp. 183-185). New York: The Free Press.

CHAPTER EIGHT

Building Inclusion Through Conflict-Resolution Mechanisms

Patricia Bidol-Padva

A MAJOR OPPORTUNITY for the American workplace arises from the increased diversity present within the workforce and marketplace. Yet inherent in diversity are challenges that need to be addressed in order to create inclusive work environments. Persistent, systemic social inequality throughout organizations harms and decreases the capacity of organizations to be successful and sustainable. A sustainable organization is fiscally viable and agile and addresses the future impacts of current social, economic, and environmental factors (Lawler & Worley, 2006).

Individuals experience inclusion as a sense of belonging, respect, access to formal and informal communications and data, being appropriately rewarded fiscally, and feeling secure and able to exercise formal and informal power (Jordon, 2009). Inclusive systems, through a combination of individual behavior and attitudes, group norms, leadership approaches, and organizational policies, enable each person to flourish and develop in ways that are beneficial for both the individual and the collective system (Ferdman, 2014).

Inclusion reflects the interdependency between people and the organization. When individual employees perceive that they are appreciated, included, and have influence, they are likely to be more engaged and proactively do work that contributes to an organization's success. Their sense of being accepted by managers and coworkers is enhanced. Affirming diversity in its many dimensions serves as a catalyst for inclusion, allowing all employees to fully engage in the organization and resulting in bolstered creativity, morale, and productivity (Plummer, 2012).

For inclusion efforts to succeed, they must be integrated into a customized, system-wide diversity and inclusion initiative that supports the talents, engagement, and appreciation of all employees while enhancing the capacity of the organization to be successful and sustainable. The creation of a systemically inclusive organization emerges from successful transformative change. Transformative change occurs when there are fundamental changes in the organization's culture, mindset, values, and operations.

The transformation process emerges from system-wide visioning, trial-and-error discovery, and learnings. A critical mass of the organization must be engaged or positively impacted by the diversity and inclusion initiatives and operate from the new mindset and behaviors for the inclusive transformation to succeed and the new business model and direction to be sustained.

In order to create viable, systemic diversity and inclusion in an organization, a diversity and inclusion initiative must continuously address the creative and the dysfunctional conflicts that arise when inclusive changes are made. Conflicts regarding factors such as inclusion-exclusion, acceptance of social identities, and social power can emerge at all levels of the system (individual, social group, team, division, organization, and external environment) that are impacted by the changes. When transformative changes in the entity's culture, policies and practices, fiscal and other reward systems, and mission are being created and implemented, it is essential that creative and dysfunctional conflicts are identified and aptly addressed.

This chapter explores conflict-resolution mechanisms that support diversity and inclusion initiatives. Conflict is inherent in organizational life and within diverse work groups. When managed effectively, conflict is an essential and generative aspect of transformative organizational change and can be leveraged to improve all parts of the system.

The Nature of Conflict in the Diversity and Inclusion Process

Conflict is expressed in many forms ranging from discomfort to open disputes. Discomfort is a sign of a latent conflict, such as the perception that an individual's social group identities are not appreciated. Latent conflicts are often the source of continued feelings of tension, mistrust, and frustration. A latent conflict that is not expressed usually grows into either an open dispute or a covert withdrawal of an employee's energy and willingness to engage and share knowledge. This has an impact on employee engagement, performance, and organizational results.

A dispute is a specific and tangible expression of a conflict. Disputes may be functional or dysfunctional. High-performance groups need to disagree while exploring divergent options before they jointly decide on a solution. Spirited deliberations that produce quality decisions enhance relationships and improve productivity (Katzenbach & Smith, 1993).

Disputes can be expressed from lower to higher levels of discontent, such as mild complaints, angry exchanges, increased absenteeism, complaints, work slowdowns, grievances, and lawsuits. As the dispute escalates, the disputing parties and those impacted by the dispute usually change their perceptions of each other and of the issues. The phases of an escalating dispute are as follows:

- The dispute emerges, and a sense of crisis becomes manifest.
- Perceptions become distorted, and the parties begin to believe that the other person's conflict-related behavior is deliberate. Viewpoints become fixed positions, and the parties become defensive.
- The dispute moves beyond the original disputing parties when the disputants seek support from others.
- Direct communication stops, and messages become distorted. In response, the disputants and their supporters attribute negative assumptions and motives to the other party. They begin to seek evidence that their negative perceptions are correct, and they feel righteous and blame the other for the conflict.
- Positions harden, and the parties believe they cannot collaborate because the other party is unwilling to dialogue.
- The intense dispute fully emerges, and the organization's formal and informal systems are aware of it. External parties may know of the dispute and often enter into it.

- At this point, the dispute is now perceived to be a crisis (Carpenter & Kennedy, 2001).

Social Identity Disputes

Social-identity-driven disputes often arise because of lack of appreciation of an employee's social group identity and/or as a result of policies that result in the unfair treatment of members of a social identity group. Individuals often experience these conflicts in an ongoing manner, and the conflicts often arise from daily interactions between members of minority social groups and others.

Members of social identities that are underappreciated are often the recipients of ongoing social-identity-driven microaggressions. Microaggressions are verbal or behavioral indignities, whether intentional or unintentional, that communicate derogatory or negative slights and insults toward members of underappreciated social group identities. Perpetrators of microaggressions are often unaware that they engage in such communications when they interact with racial/ ethnic minorities (Sue, 2007, p. 271).

Managers often misdiagnose, ignore, or suppress the disputes arising from microaggressions, thereby creating larger challenges such as lack of retention of diverse employees or overt conflicts between employees from diverse social identity groups.

Diversity disputes are also often ignored because managers are not aware or choose not to be aware that their organization is implementing discriminatory policies (e.g., pay, promotion, or performance evaluations) that benefit members of the organization's dominant social identity group. When these discriminatory practices are not discussed and eliminated (if present), intense disputes often emerge.

Conversations about topics previously considered taboo in the workplace, such as race, religion, and politics, have invaded work life. These polarizing conversations happen daily in our work environments and, left unchecked, can impact productivity, engagement, retention, teamwork, and even employees' sense of safety (Winters, 2017). When managed appropriately, the initial complaints about discrimination or lack of appreciation for the tensions inherent in a diverse workforce can be "gifts" for the organization. They provide an opportunity for disputants to enter into dialogue about their needs and values. These dialogues are a key aspect of a diversity initiative's conflict-resolution process.

Creative and Dysfunctional Conflicts

Creative and dysfunctional conflicts arise when the leaders and the workforce respond to the opportunities and challenges that must be addressed when changes occur during the creation and implementation of a customized intervention. When an organization wisely leverages conflicts that emerge from an intervention at the individual, group, team, division, and system levels, it enhances its inclusion, growth, and sustainability.

Individuals can't change systems, but diversity and inclusion initiatives can create leverage points that support new systems, structures, and strategies.

Conflict-Escalation Cycle

In any system change, including a change of strategic direction, members of an organization have to deal with a loss of the status quo. Organizational conflict occurs at many levels of the system when one or more individuals, social identity groups, teams, divisions, senior executives, and/or outside stakeholders are dissatisfied. The sources of dissatisfaction in organizations with a diverse workforce often include factors such as unclear communications, the negative impacts of policies and procedures, incompatible interests, cultural differences, power discrepancies, and the perception that someone is not respected. Leaders need to be aware of the ways in which individuals and subsystems are dealing with any changes and be prepared to accept and respond to the tension in a manner that supports an appreciation of the entire workforce. Consensus-based conflict-resolution mechanisms can increase the appreciation and inclusion of diverse individuals and social identity groups and the elimination of discriminatory behaviors at all levels of the system.

Conflict-Resolution Mechanisms

Conflict-resolution mechanisms for diversity and inclusion initiatives usually include a variety of interventions or mechanisms such as prevention, collaboration, and an appeal to a higher authority to resolve conflict situations that range from latent conflicts to intense disputes.

Figure 1 illustrates a model of a conflict-resolution mechanism developed by the author. The model describes a conflict-resolution system that is flexible and enables decision-makers to refine their interventions as the conflict unfolds. The CRM has three components:

- assessment factors
- resolution interventions
- outcomes

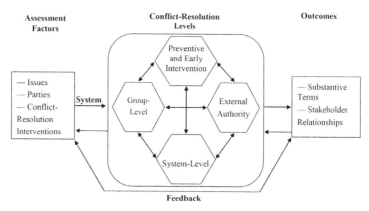

(*Bidol-Padva, 2000*)

ASSESSMENT FACTORS	INTERVENTIONS/MECHANISMS	OUTCOMES
Issues • Conflict characteristics • Central and secondary issues • Intensity level **Parties** • Main and secondary parties and their spokespersons • Impacted parties **Power and Influence Factors** **Relationships** **Feasibility** • Value-added options • Social justice	**Preventive and Early Mechanisms** • Diversity taskforce • Affinity groups • Training • Management practices • Interpersonal relationships **System-Level Mechanisms** • Leadership behavior • Intragroup behavior • Communication processes • Use of power and influence • Interface with external stakeholders **Group-Level Mechanisms** • Initiated by parties • Collaboration when appropriate • Use of internal and external facilitators **External Authority Mechanisms** • Litigation • Hearings	**Substantive Terms** • Appreciation of all social group identities • Elimination of discriminatory policies and practices • Support organization's success and sustainability **Stakeholder Relationships** • Positive feelings between involved parties at all levels of the system • Perception by all impacted parties that intervention was fair and inclusive

Assessment Factors

Assessment of a conflict situation enables the disputants or the conflict intervener (e.g., work-unit manager, ombudsperson, consultant,
or facilitator) to make informed decisions about conflict interventions. If an organization is conducting a systemic diversity and inclusion initiative, the chief diversity officer would have a tracking system
to know about organizational disputes in order to decide if they
need to be addressed through the CRM model. Equal Employment
Opportunity (EEO) complaints are required to be tracked for organizations that receive federal dollars.

The conflict-assessment process includes data-gathering and
analysis of the five dimensions present in every conflict situation:
the issues and interests, the parties, the power and influence factors,
the relationships, and the desirability of the proposed intervention
(see table 1).

Table 1: Conflict Situation Assessment Questions

DIMENSION	QUESTIONS
1. Issues (Substantive Terms)	• What are the issues for you and for the other parties? (Issues are behaviors or decisions that need to be addressed.) • What are the needs for you and for the other parties? (Needs are requirements that must be fulfilled.) • Is it possible that the solutions to the issues may cause negative or positive impacts on other factors (e.g., promotion opportunities, union contracts, personnel policies, and customer retention)? • What needs do you and the other parties have in common? • What is the major outcome you desire for each of the issues?

DIMENSION	QUESTIONS
2. Parties	• What parties are directly involved in the conflict? • What parties are indirectly impacted? • What parties can hinder or enhance the implementation of the project? • How do the social group identities of the parties influence the creation and the management of the dispute?
3. Power and Influence	• What types of power and influence have each of the parties used (or are likely to use) when they interact with the other parties? • To what degree is oppression (e.g., racism, sexism, heterosexism, anti-Semitism, ageism) present, and what is the impact of the overt or covert oppression? • Are multiple departments, divisions, and organizations with differing missions involved in the conflict?
4. Relationships (Social Contract)	• Do you and the other parties have to maintain an ongoing relationship? • What is the level of interdependency between each of the primary parties? • What is the level of interdependency between the other parties? • What is the past history of interactions between you and the other parties? Are there strong emotions or values at play? • Do you or any of the other parties belong to any groups that can consciously or unconsciously influence your management of the dispute?
5. Relevance of Collaboration (Value-Added)	• What incentives exist to motivate the parties to use a collaborative approach? • Will each of the parties obtain value-added benefits (substantive terms or social contract) if they participate in a collaborative approach? • Is there a desire to establish or maintain cooperative and mutually beneficial relationships between the parties? • What is the most collaborative way to resolve the problem? If collaborative negotiations are not feasible, what conflict-management mode should be used?

(Bidol-Padva, 1990; edited 2010)

Since all the actions taken during the conflict-resolution process are interrelated, the resolution mechanisms should not be selected until the assessment data have been analyzed. For example, the process of gathering data about an intense dispute could result in the disputants deciding to engage in collaborative decision-making rather than referring the matter to litigation. The assessment process is repeated during a lengthy resolution process to determine whether or not the resolution strategy needs to be refined.

In many cases, the disputing parties can also jointly assess the conflict situation. The conscious and routine use of conflict-assessment processes by parties who are involved in a dispute usually reduces the dysfunctional aspects of their communication patterns and increases the probability that their appreciation of other social group identities and their individual personalities will grow.

CRMs often include mechanisms to provide the skills individuals and team members need to dialogue with and actively listen to each other, engage in mutually beneficial decision-making, and make personal connections. Dialogue supports appreciation of the other because "ahas" arise from deep listening and self-disclosures. Dialogue is not just a means of communicating but enhances individual and collective learning. Apt dialogue and deliberations transform conflict and rejection into joint work and appreciation. Little healing of the emotional wound is likely to occur without an opening of the heart through genuine dialogue, empowerment through being heard, and a recognition of each other's humanity despite the conflict (Lewis & Umbreit, 2015). A systems-thinking approach enables the CRM change agents to appreciate the interconnectedness among and complex dynamics within humans and structures that make it possible for a change at any one level of the organization to set into motion ripple effects across the other levels—individual, group, organizational, and community (Bidol-Padva & Nukum, 2014).

The following are some other aspects of a system that describe how inclusion and resulting conflicts are managed during CRM creation and implementation:

- Constructive and dysfunctional disputes and changes in a system occur at system boundaries (e.g., interpersonal, within a team, between divisions).

- Factors present at a systems level include co-creation, resistance, rejection, conflict, power, social oppression or appreciation, trust, and collaboration.

- Boundaries need to be managed so that transactions across them enhance learning, support collective thinking and behaving, and support the achievement of the organization's desired outcomes. It is important to provide individuals, groups, and teams with the skills and mindsets to positively respond to conflicts.

- When there is a positive interaction between the parts of a system, there is a synergistic flow of energy between them. Synergy is the reality that the sum of the whole system is greater than its parts. A vibrant, inclusive culture is a synergistic culture that enhances all levels of the system.

Identification of Issues

The issues and interests of the conflict need to be well defined and understood. The parties in most conflicts have many issues and needs. For example, the issue could be that members of a group perceive that they are not given prime assignments and thus are not promoted.

Their interest (need) could be to immediately rectify the unfair policies and procedures. They could also want the organization to appreciate their social group identity.

In addition to identifying the current issues and interests of key parties, the assessment process needs to identify subsequent issues that could arise when an issue is resolved. For example, if unfair policies are changed, the parties that currently benefit from them may protest (i.e., charge reverse discrimination) if they perceive that their prime assignments would be reduced. On the other hand, the change in unfair policies could result in synergistic policies that create more opportunities for all involved parties. The new, mutually beneficial policies could then result in a positive substantive issue, such as how the new policies can be disseminated to other work units.

Parties, Relationships, and Power

The primary and secondary parties who might be affected by the resolution of the conflict, and their spokespersons, need to be identified. Most organizational disputes affect not only those who are directly involved but also other parties as well. For example, members of a group could assert their desire to have the performance-review process changed. If the review process is changed, it will affect all employees who use that process.

For example, involving representatives of all affected parties in a collaborative decision-making meeting might resolve the performance-review process. Or, instead of the collaborative meeting, the human resources staff could gather data about the process and design an inclusive review process. Or the matter, if needed, could be referred to litigation.

The assessment process also identifies how the parties currently relate to one another and the impact of these relationships on the resolution of the dispute. Relationships are complex and can be expressed in many ways, such as:

- *Blind inequity*: The dominant group, unaware of the lack of inclusion and equity, believes everyone is okay and happy.
- *Respectful divergence:* The parties respect each other but disagree about certain issues. They are willing to collaborate to resolve those issues.
- *Interactively suspicious:* The parties interact to do their work but are moderately distrustful of each other. Each party questions the motives and values of the other party.
- *Highly mistrustful:* The parties barely speak to each other, and each is sure that the other party cannot be trusted. Each is very suspicious of the motives, values, and statements of the other party.
- *Proactive hostility:* The parties are hostile and vengeful. Not only do they want to win the dispute, they want the other party to experience a humiliating defeat.

Data on the nature of the relationships are interrelated with the other assessment data. Even if the parties are hostile, they can engage in collaborative decision-making if they realize that this is the only way they can obtain the results they want.

The assessment process identifies the power and influence factors that each party may use when they interact with each other and the rest of the organization to obtain the results they want. The way that parties use their power is often determined by the approaches (e.g., assimilation, mutual adaptation, separation) they use to manage the interaction of their main social group identity with other members of the organization. Parties can use their power and influence by engaging in collaborative efforts, escalating the conflict, resorting to litigation, making administrative appeals, or staging community protests.

Feasibility Factors
During the feasibility phase of the assessment, the costs and value-added benefits of all the potential resolution interventions are assessed. Since collaborative interventions usually result in the resolution of the issues to the satisfaction of the parties and the enhancement of their relations, the underlying interests, needs, and values expressed by the parties are studied to determine whether or not a collaborative intervention can be used.

Many conflicts can only be resolved by the use of two or more interventions. Consensus-based approaches are usually the prime intervention, unless the situation needs to be resolved by litigation or administrative hearings. Even when litigation or hearings are used, collaborative processes are often used to design follow-through remedies (e.g., replacing unfair practices with inclusive options).

Types of Conflict-Resolution Mechanisms

CRMs that are embedded in the diversity and inclusion initiative are characterized by four types:

1. prevention and early mechanisms/interventions
2. system-level mechanisms/interventions
3. group-level mechanisms/interventions
4. external higher-authority mechanisms/interventions

Prevention and Early Mechanisms/Interventions

Preventive and early interventions include collaborative approaches that provide opportunities for dialogue and mutually acceptable decision-making on matters related to the diversity initiative. Some situations may require no action, but usually actions are required, and the following bullets are some proactive early interventions:

- Formation of CRM project teams responsible for a whole-system change or a change to a portion of the system. The project team could be an affinity group (e.g., African Americans, women, people with disabilities, veterans, interfaith).
- System-wide training in diversity management, consensus-based decision-making, and negotiating that enhances the appreciation of diversity, the mitigation of organizational inequities, and the capacity for collaboration by workers throughout the system.
- Consensus-based creation of diversity-desired outcomes and action steps by all sectors of the organization, such as individual work units, the diversity task force, identity-based affinity groups, or large-group sessions.
- Opportunities for individuals and teams to engage in dialogue and create mutually beneficial options to resolve their conflicts.

Large-group interventions for organizational change engage a significant representation of the organization in the development and implementation of diversity-desired outcomes and change plans. They use dialogue and consensus-based decision-making tools that enable participants to appreciate their differences, work through conflicts, and produce mutually acceptable plans that result in an inclusive and fair organization (Bidol-Padva & Greenwood, 2000). Several large-group approaches that effectively involve the total system have been developed, including Open Space Technology, Search Conferences, Whole-Scale Change, Preferred Futuring, Appreciative Inquiry, and SimuReal (Holman & Devine, 1999). Change leaders benefit from creating customized large-group interventions that are based on the current reality of the organization regarding inclusion and the desired outcomes.

Large-group interventions reinforce the concept of a learning organization that channels the energy, wisdom, and visions of its participants into a joint creation of options that allow the organization to grow. They provide opportunities for participants to explore assumptions and feelings and to develop goals that support the desired outcomes regarding inclusion as well as the functioning of the organization in the key areas of financial performance, customer outreach, and internal business processes.

System-Level Mechanisms/Interventions

Organizational leaders can mobilize the energy and power of the total system to increase support for diversity and inclusion initiatives and to aptly respond to any related conflict situations. The behavior of leaders influences the workforce at individual, interpersonal, and organizational levels. Employees constantly scan the words and actions of the leaders to determine whether they really support the diversity initiative. Leaders need to use system-level mechanisms to get CRM entrenched in the organizational policies and procedures at the level in which they work, and to support this occurring at all levels of the organization. They need to have CRM incorporated into the organization's code of ethics and/or the organization's espoused values.

Since diversity initiatives change the status quo, and the changes may be perceived as "reverse discrimination," leaders must proactively communicate that the diversity initiative is inclusive and will fairly benefit all employees, and provide learning and development for the participants of the CRM and the coworkers with whom they share their learning.

In order to increase the opportunities for diverse individuals and social identity groups to appreciate each other, they also need opportunities to participate in informal activities such as recreational events. The organization, through its formal and informal networks, can also communicate the positive impacts of diversity and inclusion initiatives with its key external stakeholders, such as customers, vendors, and the local community.

Group-Level Mechanisms/Interventions

Group-level interventions occur within a work unit. A work unit can be a team, a department, a division, or an ad hoc unit (e.g., a cross-departmental committee). Any impacted party can ask the unit manager to resolve the conflict. The impacted parties can include the individuals experiencing the discomfort, colleagues, the work-unit manager, and other organizational stakeholders. A group-level intervention can resolve many conflicts, such as a specific complaint, a perception that the team needs to improve its interpersonal relationships, or a need to develop protocols (e.g., team assignments and mentoring) that are inclusive and fair.

Consensus-based interventions are the primary conflict-resolution tools used to resolve group-level conflicts. In addition to being used for the prevention of conflicts and early intervention in an emerging dispute, they are used to resolve conflicts that have grown into an overt dispute. During the creation and implementation of a diversity and inclusion initiative, leaders and all participants in the change are trained in and proactively use consensus tools (e.g., brainstorming, active listening, and generative decision-making) to create mutually beneficial options for resolving the conflicts and implementing mutually acceptable changes. These tools can be used at interpersonal, team, group, or system-wide levels.

Consensus-based meetings, occurring at either the interpersonal, group, or system level, are designed to allow parties to share their needs, interests, and frustrations, so that they can jointly create options that meet their individual needs and those of the work unit. The following steps are usually followed during the collaborative meetings:

1. A climate is created in which the participants can safely share their stories about the issues, the impact of the dispute on their work, and their feeling of self-worth.
2. Parties share their desired outcomes and educate each other about their needs.
3. Parties actively listen to each other, in order to understand what the other parties are saying and to be able to explore the meaning of what they hear.
4. Parties engage in a collaborative decision-making process that enables the disputants to concentrate on the interests of all parties, explore possibilities, formulate mutually beneficial options, develop criteria to evaluate the mutually beneficial options, and select preferred solutions.

Consensus-based meetings usually increase opportunities for mutually beneficial outcomes such as:

- resolution of the disputes imbedded in the conflict situation;
- enhanced interpersonal communication;
- support for the relationships between the parties;
- support for the productivity of the impacted individuals, the work unit, and the total organization;
- increased appreciation of social identity groups and individual diversity;
- elimination of unfair practices and their replacement with inclusive practices;
- increased use by work units of collaborative decision-making tools that produce mutually acceptable options; and
- enhanced appreciation of diversity and inclusion and increased organizational success and sustainability.

External Higher-Authority Mechanisms/Interventions

External higher-authority interventions include such approaches as litigation, administrative hearings, arbitration, mini-trials, or fact-finding. They are used when the consensus-based interventions do not work or cannot be used. If the conflict situation is a case of actual harassment or discrimination, it is an illegal action, and a remedy such as litigation or administrative hearings must be used to resolve it.

Harassment and discrimination cases are governed by organizational personnel policies, union contracts, and federal, state, and local laws. In the United States, employees are protected by law from discrimination based on gender, race, religion, pregnancy, national origin, age, or physical ability. Harassment is a form of discrimination. Managers and leaders of diversity initiatives often do not understand harassment. They may mistakenly try to resolve a harassment case by the use of dialogue and coaching. During the conflict-assessment phase, the word "harassment" should not be used until an expert has determined that harassment has occurred. Until an expert has made that determination, the case can be defined as a conflict that has emerged due to inappropriate behavior.

In addition to litigation or administrative hearings, aggrieved parties may resort to community protests that represent the needs of their social identity groups, to ensure that the organization addresses their cause. Organizations can also belong to community partnerships, such as United Way, that create a network of inclusive and sustainable organizations and communities.

Conflict-Resolution Outcomes

Outcomes are the results of CRM interventions that have been used to resolve a conflict situation by preventing the emergence of a dispute, creating consensus options, communicating with formal and informal networks, or engaging in litigation. They are analyzed to determine whether or not the desired outcomes were achieved. The use of CRM in diversity initiatives produces two types of outcomes: substantive agreements and stakeholder relationships.

Substantive agreements are assessed to determine whether or not the intervention resulted in outcomes that resolved the issues of the dispute to the satisfaction of the impacted parties. In addition, the substantive agreements are analyzed to determine the degree to which they contributed to the appreciation of the workforce's diversity and the development of inclusive and fair policies and practices. Stakeholder relationships are assessed to determine whether or not the impacted parties' relationships are the same as or better than before the intervention. The outcomes are also carefully studied to determine whether or not the parties perceived that the resolution processes were done in a fair and inclusive manner.

It should be noted that it is difficult for external higher-authority interventions to make all the parties feel that the issues were resolved to their satisfaction. Litigation and administrative hearings produce outcomes that are based on objective criteria derived from laws, legislation, or regulations. These outcomes result in one side winning and the other side losing. The benefit from this type of intervention is that it contributes to the understanding of the impact of not being an inclusive organization.

Leading the Management of Conflict Resolution

A transformative diversity and inclusion initiative will impact the entire organization, making it critical to select leaders who are competent to guide diversity efforts and best positioned to lead change. The leaders who ensure that the diversity and inclusion change process will result in transformative culture change and who can demonstrate successive approximations to the goal are best positioned to manage the complexities of a diversity and inclusion initiative.

The leadership roles for any transformative change are important, and those asked to lead the change initiatives must have adjustments made in their current workload to able to do the change effort. In addition, all of those who serve in such roles are responsible for modeling the desired cultural mindset and behaviors that are required to achieve a high-performing, inclusive organization.

During systemic transformation change, the following leadership roles are normally included:

- *Sponsor.* The senior executive champion oversees what needs to be done to appropriately engage the workforce and ensure that the desired change outcomes are achieved. The organization's executive team also works with the sponsor to develop the desired outcomes of the diversity and inclusion initiative and CRM (these are developed based on the assessment data). The sponsor and the senior executive team support change mechanisms that enable the workforce to 1) create and act on a shared perspective on the meaning of inclusion for their organization, 2) increase their awareness and appreciation of diversity and enhance their capacity to be inclusive at all levels of the system, and 3) develop accountability measures for all levels of the system.

- *Diversity and inclusion initiative senior leader.* This leader reports directly to the sponsor, who has given her/him delegated authority to lead the initiative and ensure that the desired outcomes for all levels of the system are achieved. S/he is aware of and actively manages the entire CRM change work and any other organizational activities that may not be done by any of the change teams but that impact the organization's capacity to be inclusive.

- *Diversity and inclusion initiative leadership team.* The team is composed of stakeholders representative of the entire system. They report to and work with the diversity and inclusion senior leader or chief diversity officer. They are responsible for creating the initial change process and actions for the diversity and inclusion strategy and modifying it as the system reacts to the changes. They are also responsible for the ongoing assessment and for aligning all of the diversity and inclusion efforts and the embedded (CRM) actions. They ensure that the change initiative actions are provided with the needed fiscal and time resources.

- *Diversity and inclusion action teams.* These teams are composed of representatives of the entire system or of a portion of the system and are responsible for a particular CRM change effort. They often are accountable to the diversity and inclusion senior leader and her/his direct reports. These teams may be existing diversity councils or employee resource groups or business resource groups.

- *Diversity and inclusion change consultants*: A strategic diversity and inclusion change initiative may include a number of internal and external consultants engaged in the change work. They may consult at any level of the system, and include those who specialize in transformative organizational development and change, consensus-based systemic conflict management change, and diversity and inclusion assessment. Change consultants usually report to the chief diversity officer, who ensures that the diversity and inclusion initiative and CRM change work are aligned and support the desired change outcomes (Ackerman Anderson & Anderson, 2010).

Change Management Consulting Roles

Many organizational development consultants employing a CRM approach use applied behavioral science methods, research, and theory to enhance the health and effectiveness of organizations while affirming respect for human differences and racial and social justice. Both internal and external change agents can perform a variety of roles determined when contracting with the client. The three key consultant roles used for diversity and inclusion initiatives and CRM efforts are process consultants, collaborative consultants, and expert consultants. The table below describes the roles, when they are useful, and when they are not useful.

Table Two: Change-Consulting Roles

Role	Nature of Work	Most Useful When	Least Useful When
Process Consultant: Proactively focuses on ways client tackles interpersonal problems that directly impact interpersonal and group-level work and relationships	Helps client recognize and address the impact of their individual or social identities or group-level behavioral patterns on others and/or the organization	Client willing to take primary responsibility for experimenting with new behaviors Client asks for feedback When problems are interpersonal and/or group-level, there is interest in development	Client resists feedback and is not open to new learning Need for specialized expertise

Role	Nature of Work	Most Useful When	Least Useful When
Collaborative Consultant: Proactively focuses on ways to enhance client's capacity to respond to the challenge/ opportunity rather than on providing a solution	Helps system leaders recognize, define, diagnose, and solve challenges/ opportunities independently Work is collaborative effort	Client willing to take primary responsibility The current reality and desired outcomes are complex and not well defined Need for strong commitment to the creation and implementation of transformative changes	Client demands quick solution Need for specialized expertise Crisis needs to be resolved immediately
Expert Consultant: Doing something clients can't do for themselves, such as litigation.	Diagnose problems Generate solutions Predict consequences	Client has no expertise and doesn't need to develop it Crisis deadline where quick solution is best Client's buy-in to solution not crucial	Client system needs members to buy in to the changes to make it work No clear definition of the problem Early solution not practical or likely

(Adapted by NTL from Flawless Consulting: A Guide to Getting Your Expertise Used, by Peter Block. Learning Concepts, 1981.)

My work as an international organizational change consultant and facilitator/mediator of complex disputes has enhanced the capacity of organizations to create systemic diversity and inclusion initiatives that fully recognize all employees and enhance the organization's sustainability. From my work as a scholar, change practitioner, and senior executive leader, I have learned the following key factors for success in creating systemic diversity and inclusion change:

- Creation of a customized, system-wide diversity and inclusion initiative with an embedded CRM that addresses the current organizational needs and desired future outcomes by changing the system's culture, mindsets, and behaviors.
- Heightened awareness among all participants that change does not occur in a linear fashion. In spite of perceived setbacks, the desired change can occur. A systemic and ongoing assessment enables a diversity and inclusion initiative and CRM to be refined as the system reacts to the changes.
- Increased understanding that courageous shared leadership enables an organization's culture to positively change.

Case Study

One of the largest state education unions in the United States (130,000 members belonging to 750 local unions) faced a need for change after a bitter dispute between members and leadership. During a post-strike meeting of the executive team, the board, and the staff unions, they jointly decided that the major issues facing the organization were changing member demographics, lack of representation of the diverse social groups at all levels of the organization, political and economic challenges, and untapped technological opportunities. At this meeting they decided to engage in a system-wide, transformative change effort that would clarify and communicate a vison of what an inclusive state union can and should be, and identify and establish the culture, structures, and systems that would ensure mutual success.

They also recognized that the organization needed to engage in a "whole system transformative change model" that would engage the hearts, minds, and spirits of all their stakeholders. They thought that it would take about three years to achieve their desired change outcomes, and they wanted to have tangible results occur within the first year. During this meeting, the group formally became the Change Leadership Group (CLG) and decided to add representatives of local unions. They created a committee that selected organizational-change consultants, a communication consultant, and a technology consultant. The consultants reported regularly to the CLG. The communication and technology consultants worked with the CLG to create and implement a comprehensive outreach strategy.

Organization Development consultants began their work by conducting an organizational assessment that measured factors such as engagement, conflict management, joint decision-making, and productivity. The results of the assessment were used by the consultants and the CLG to create a transformative process that engaged stakeholders in a series of action-learning, small and whole-system meetings that addressed the substantive issues and enhanced the engagement, appreciation, and inclusion of all the stakeholders. The mega-goal was a paradigm shift. Here were some of the key transformative interventions:

- Fifteen interactive meetings held throughout the state to jointly think through, question, and create drafts of what might be done for the organization to be inclusive at all levels of the organization.
- A two-day Whole System Engagement (WSE) event in which the participants, who represented all stakeholders, used consensus-based tools to put the inclusive vison and values

into practice by identifying behaviors and relationships that would make the vision and values real.

- After the WSE, the leadership team reviewed the input from the event and created seven Implementation Oversight Teams (IOT). Each IOT was a cross-section of the union's stakeholders and addressed one of the key factors that needed changing.

  □ The IOTs were to review programs, structures, and systems; improve two-way communication; promote member engagement and inclusion; enhance organizational learning; and identify methodologies to measure success.

  □ The IOTs worked for several months, and their recommendations were submitted to the Representative Assembly (which represented the local unions and state board). The assembly met a year after the WSE.

- After the Representative Assembly, teams were created to implement the recommendations that the assembly wanted adopted. The teams' members represented the diversity of the organization's stakeholders, and all of them created action steps that were successfully implemented.

When most of the implementation actions were done, the organization evaluated the organizational transformation efforts. The assessment showed that the change work had empowered its members, leaders, and employees to express their dreams, create their desired future, and foster system-wide inclusion and engagement of other minds, hearts, and spirits in the business of the organization.

Conclusion: Moving Forward to Systemic Inclusion with Wisdom

CRM approaches can change an organization's culture, mindsets, and behaviors to make it an inclusive and sustainable entity that is fiscally viable and agile and addresses current social, economic, and environmental factors. Implementing CRM initiatives can create changes that are needed across the globe today. Inclusive organizations honor the minds, hearts, and spirits of themselves and those with whom they interact.

REFERENCES

Ackerman Anderson, L., & Anderson, D. (2010). *Beyond change management: Advanced strategies for today's transformational leader* (2nd edition). San Francisco, CA: Jossey-Bass/Pfeiffer.

Bidol-Padva, P., & Greenwood, B. (2000). *Collaborative environmental and land use conflict management.* Davis, CA: University of California, Davis.

Bidol-Padva, P., & Nukum, J. (2014). System perspectives and organization development. In B. B. Jones & M. Brazzel (Eds.), *The NTL handbook of organizational development and change* (2nd ed.). San Francisco, CA: Wiley.

Brown, L. D. (1983). *Managing conflict at organizational interfaces.* Reading, MA: Addison-Wesley.

Carpenter, S. L., & Kennedy, W. J. D. (2001). *Managing public disputes: A practical guide to handling conflict and reaching agreements.* San Francisco, CA: Jossey-Bass.

Catalyst. (2014). *Women CEOs of the Fortune 100 list.* Retrieved from http://www.catalyst.org/knowledge/women-ceos-forune-1000

Costantino, C. A., & Merchant, C. S. (1996) *Designing conflict management systems: A guide to creating productive and healthy organizations.* San Francisco, CA: Jossey-Bass.

Diversity Inc. (2014). *Where's the diversity in Fortune 500 CEOs?* Retrieved from http://www.diversityinc.com/diversity-facts/ wheres-the-diversity-in-fortune-500-ceos

Ferdman, B. M. (2014). The practice of inclusion in diverse organizations: Towards a systemic and inclusive framework. In B. M. Ferdman & B. R. Deane (Eds.), *Diversity at work: The practice of inclusion* (pp. 3–54). San Francisco, CA: Berrett-Koehler.

Holman, P., & Devine, T. (1999). *The change handbook: Group methods for shaping the future.* San Francisco, CA: Berrett-Koehler.

Jordan, C. G. (2009). *Rethinking Inclusion: Case studies of identity, integration and power in professional knowledge work organizations* (Dissertation). Case Western Reserve University, Cleveland, OH.

Katzenbach, J. R., & Smith, D. K. (1993). *The wisdom of teams*. New York, NY: Harper Collins.

Lawler, E., & Worley, C. (2006). *Built to change: How to achieve organization effectiveness*. San Francisco, CA: Jossey-Bass.

Lewis, T., & Umbreit, M. (2015). A humanistic approach to mediation and dialogue. *Conflict Resolution Quarterly, 33*(1), 3–17.

Miller, F. A., & Katz, J. H. (2002). *The inclusion breakthrough: Unleashing the real power of diversity*. San Francisco, CA: Jossey-Bass.

Plummer, D., et al. (2012). *Diversity engagement survey (DES): Building an engaged and inclusive work environment*. Amherst, MA: University of Massachusetts.

Sue, D. W., et al. (2007, May–June). Racial microaggressions in everyday life. *American Psychologist*, p. 271.

Winters, M. F. (2017). *We can't talk about that at work! How to talk about race, religion, politics, and other polarizing topics*. Oakland, CA: Berrett-Koehler.

Going Plaid: Integrating Diversity Into Business Strategy, Talent Management, and Work Design

Deborah L. Plummer and C. Greer Jordan

IN THE VERSE "The Blind Men and the Elephant," John Godfrey Saxe describes six men from Indostan who are eager to learn about the physical nature of an elephant but, because they are all blind, must rely on other powers of observation. They engage in a robust dialogue, yet because they lack collaborative problem-solving skills, they never achieve a useful analysis of the whole concept and leave the experience with only partial truth.

At this critical stage in the life cycle of the work of diversity in organizations, our approach to managing diversity resembles the blind men from Indostan. Static models and step-by-step approaches to diversity have provided organizations with descriptions of interventions and action items, but they have left organizations without a manual for how these interventions can be integrated to effect culture change and achieve business objectives. Thus, organizations are not able to realize the full potential of diversity beyond the value proposition of endorsing it as a worthwhile initiative (Kulik & Robertson, 2008).

Conceptually, the business rationale for embracing diversity and inclusion practices reflects the espoused belief of many organizations that human capital is the most important asset of an organization (Flumer & Ployhart, 2013). The business case for diversity and inclusion that is based on this premise ties directly to the mission of the organization and the clients and constituents who represent our increasingly multicultural, multiracial society. A further rationale is that managing diversity effectively and developing inclusive practices, policies, and procedures minimizes legal risks and protects the organization from legal action by its own employees, customers, or even the communities or countries in which it operates. Data comparing diversity practices and policies to legal costs associated with lawsuits demonstrate that this is true. Research has demonstrated the data-to-dollars conversion of effective diversity leadership to increased productivity and profits (Herring, 2009; Rosenbaum, 2014; Reagans & Zuckerman, 2001). Progressive organizations have taken heed that diversity needs to be woven into the overall business strategy and integrated into every aspect of the organization—very much like producing a vibrant plaid fabric. Yet challenges remain, as the diversity and inclusion initiatives of many organizations still focus on training as the primary intervention instead of integrating inclusion efforts into the culture and then leveraging the resulting performance and innovation to support the organization's overall strategic plan.

This chapter aims to offer some clues for how to integrate diversity into business strategies, systems, and structures. The authors propose that diversity is not a problem that must be managed, but rather a vital input into the dynamic process of inclusion by which the perspectives and worldviews of a diverse workforce are integrated into organizational systems and structures to compel the organization toward its business and mission objectives and to maintain a sustainable source of competitive advantage. In other words, we "go plaid" with diversity by integrating and creating organizational conditions that are sustainable beyond changes in senior leadership, downsizing, financial variability, or other organizational changes (Figure 1).

We have identified four strategic areas into which diversity must be integrated for sustainable competitive advantage: talent acquisition and talent management, contemporary work design, leadership performance, and globalization. It is our hope that this examination will strengthen the work of diversity practitioners and support the advancement of this field and the organizations in which diversity and inclusion are practiced.

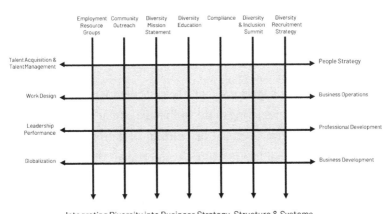

Integrating Diversity into Business Strategy, Structure & Systems

Figure 1: Going Plaid

Talent Acquisition and Talent Management

Finding, developing, and retaining people who will drive an organization's strategy is not a compartmentalized function of human resources, an office of equal opportunity, or an office of diversity. It is a core responsibility of contemporary leaders, even as short-term pressures vie for their attention and energy. Furthermore, people's daily experiences at work and whether they feel engaged or not are key factors in distinguishing great organizations from good organizations (Collins, 2001; Morgan, 2016). In short, creating an inclusive workplace must move from the HR section of the glossy recruiting brochure to functional and line leaders' strategies toward achieving the mission and business objectives for the organization.

To create sustainable success for the organization, senior leaders are charged with creating a work environment in which the values, goals, and objectives are shared, and people can see how their unique skills, perspectives, and experiences contribute to achieving the goals and related rewards. As a result, people find meaning in their work, feel a connection to the organization, and have a strong interest in the organization's success.

As leaders seek superior talent, the considerations can no longer be simply the ease of relating to the individual, attendance at the same schools, or similarity in social or cultural background—all factors that make a job candidate feel like a comfortable "fit" (Ibarra, Ely, & Kolb, 2013). Instead, superior talent or talent that will spur innovation and team performance will possess leadership competencies that enable them to build high-performing, diverse teams and/or work across human differences to achieve excellent outcomes. These leadership competencies include the ability to learn effectively in diverse teams, collaborative problem-solving skills, emotional intelligence competencies, collaborative conflict-management skills, change-management skills, systems thinking, group-dynamic skills, power and influencing skills, cross-culture adaptability skills, and assessing, measuring, and evaluating skills. These competencies are all necessary skills to work effectively in our increasingly diverse work environments. As the marketplace for talent is now global, we know that these skill sets are represented across a wide array of diverse people and are not the sole proprietorship of one cultural group.

Many organizations have made progress in changing policies and practices that were created for industrial-age, hierarchal workplaces operating in stable economic environments with little external competition. The ideal leader in such a context did not lead but managed the work of lower or no-status workers. The workplace mimicked the external social relationships and hierarchies between people.

While many of the outward signs of the industrial-age workplace have dissipated, remnants remain in protected geographic pockets of the world, and unconscious beliefs about people remain active influences on the selection, evaluation, and advancement of people who do not match the ideal type. These implicit biases have been repeatedly demonstrated to influence hiring decisions and employee evaluations (Goldin & Rouse, 2000). Furthermore, several larger sociopolitical factors have moved the rungs of the opportunity ladder out of reach for people around the globe. These factors include historical and de facto segregation, disenfranchisement of racial and ethnic identity groups from benefits afforded to dominant social groups, and—particularly in the U.S.—the loss of internships, apprentice programs, and employer-funded education that allowed people to build knowledge and skills through employment and move solidly into the middle class. Thus, talents of large swaths of the population are lost, or people find themselves unconnected and unqualified for jobs with success-ful firms in the growing knowledge economy. Regions of countries, industries, and communities are harmed, too, as the cost of finding talent increases, regions become less attractive to top talent, and the growth of local employers is stifled.

To respond to these concerns, institutional and organizational leaders must educate themselves as to the hidden costs of the status quo that are accumulating, to be paid in future competitiveness and growth. Automated human resources processes need particular scru-tiny as computer algorithms become increasingly prevalent, to avoid the appearance of objectivity when, in reality, biases and assump-tions have simply been built right into the processes. For example, minimum and preferred qualifications as well as evaluation criteria must be carefully unbundled for the social loadings that have led only certain groups and individuals to be considered "more qualified." At a recent diversity retreat for a civic leadership program of emerg-ing leaders in a metropolitan city, a robust dialogue ensued over the meaning of "more qualified." One of the participants reported that twice she had been denied a position and told that she was the "more qualified candidate" but the position had to go to a minority. She wanted to know what her African American counterparts thought about positions going to those who were less qualified and how they might feel if they were the recipient of such a position. Key ideas that surfaced during the dialogue focused on:

1. The meaning of "more qualified," which is often a code for "someone I am more comfortable with," or someone considered to possess the qualities of a potentially better team player because of perceived fit. It could also mean

someone who went to the same schools that are typically represented in the system, or someone with the same background—educational or otherwise.

2. The potential lack of candor of the hiring manager. Assuming the mandate for hiring more minorities is true, this phrase can be a cop-out for an inability to say, "We believe you could do a great job, but there are others we believe would be equally competent and would add value to our organization in other ways." Or it could possibly be that the hiring manager just does not know how to reject candidates without making up excuses that allow him and the candidate to feel good.

3. The examination of the assumption that minority candidates are not qualified or could not be comparatively equal or better qualified than majority candidates. Even the most liberal affirmative action policies do not support hiring minorities who are unqualified for a position. Qualified is qualified is qualified. It then begs the question: What is the true meaning of the term "more qualified"?

Although no quick resolution was made of this dilemma, another observation from this meeting revealed a key strategy in addressing accepted assumptions. There was clearly movement in attitudes and perspectives on both sides for these Generation X and millennial adults. As they listened for understanding, not rebuttal, and released the need to be right in the conversation, they were able to stay engaged and begin to explore and redefine the assessment processes for talent acquisition and management for a new generation of workers.

Without the diversity competency of being able to communicate across differences these insights would never have been realized. By one intense dialogue, carefully facilitated by a seasoned Organization Development (OD) practitioner, participants were moved to action around this hiring practice. White participants now pledged that if confronted with such feedback from a job interview, they would push back for more detailed information and applaud the value-added dimension of diversity as a component of "more qualified."

To address the drying talent pipeline, investment in programs that increase the pool of talented people that reflect the changing demographics of the communities and regions in which organizations are located is vital and good business. According to a 2016 Society for Human Resource Management (SHRM) study, the average cost per hire is $4,129. For an organization filling ten positions per year, that cost is $41,290, and for a hundred the estimate is $412,290. The reported average cost of a recruiter is $46,368 per year. Depending on local labor costs, a summer internship program for ten senior-level college students can be around the cost of a recruiter—to provide a pool of proven talent, create buzz that supports recruitment of their peers, and, with the addition of a mentoring program, engage the rich talents of current employees.

Contemporary Work Design: People-Centric, Performance-Focused

There are many factors that make contemporary work challenging. In a far cry from the utopian dream that technology would shorten the workweek, the workweek for workers around the world has increased.

For professionals in fields from medicine to business, the seventy-hour workweek of what Hewlett and Luce (2006) termed "extreme jobs" is dispelling notions of the forty-hour workweek as full-time. People working low-wage jobs are challenged to work multiple part-time jobs to attempt to make ends meet, even in large economies such as the U.S.

In the meantime, the composition of the global workforce is changing. These workforce shifts have been well documented and reported. This emerging workforce is more educated, more female, younger, and more racially, ethnically, and religiously diverse. It consists of more dual-career households, more single parents, more individuals whose cultural upbringing draws them to serve their communities, and more individuals who adhere to strict religious practices. The members of this new workforce are also likely to have lived at some point under the poverty line or come from lower-income families. The aging of the baby boomers will also place new demands on households in which two working adults are required to make ends meet. Furthermore, work, or a career, is not the only important pursuit and responsibility of people in this emerging workforce. They desire to have purposeful work, family and a good quality lifestyle. Thus, this emerging workforce does not fit cleanly into the profile of the "organizational man" whose ideal made the job or career the number-one priority of life at all times. Traditional notions of a career, and how and when work is done, will continue to be challenged by this emerging workforce.

Both employees and management are responsible for effective work outcomes through work design. However, in order to meet the needs of the emergent workforce and blend them into opportunities in the twenty-first century, approaches to work from the nineteenth and twentieth centuries must be redesigned for flexibility, effectiveness, and sustainability at all levels. By work design, we are referring specifically to work inputs, processes, practices, and outcomes that comprise any job. Work design, or tacit assumptions about it, have been found to play a key role in who has access to certain types of work and how they can be effective (Meyerson & Fletcher, 2002). Some of the more visible levers of work design are policies and benefits. Both progressive organizations and trend-followers have implemented various policies around telecommuting, flextime, parental leave, and nonstandard or flexible workdays, as a few examples. However, if the organizational culture about where and how work is to be done has not changed, people are not inclined to use these benefits or policies. Furthermore, as the gap between highly resourced companies such as Google or Apple and others increases, organizations are less inclined to offer flexibility or to empower employees with the tools they need to succeed at work and maintain a life outside of work.

The key to integrating and sustaining a diverse workforce is to strive for effectiveness, equity, and opportunity in work design for all employees. This is not a new goal, but a diverse workforce makes organizations already weak in effective work design more susceptible to workforce problems than in the days when workforce homogeneity, a norm of assimilation, and an emphasis on comfort level with others pushed ineffectiveness under the table or allowed it up the ladder. Organizations will need to continue to provide employees with both the tools and flexibility to create value for the organization internally, maintain healthy lives, and contribute to the larger community as parents, caregivers, and volunteers.

Contemporary work design focuses on flexibility such that the variability of individuals performing the work can be incorporated into the work in ways that create equity in opportunity and effectiveness in fully engaging talented individuals. Flexibility is usually associated with flextime or part-time work programs. However, flexibility also comes into play by development of diversity competencies that enable organizational members to identify and implement adaptive and/or innovative approaches to the work. In contemporary work design, standardization of work processes that serve only to increase managerial control is out. Standardization processes that reduce routine work and free people to use their talents in complex tasks, such as relationship management and problem-solving, are in. Lean and six sigma initiatives are more important tools than ever, as they offer ways for teams to design processes that are efficient and empower all involved in the work. At the same time, organizations must leverage diversity of thought, experience, and cultural background to identify opportunities to serve customers, patients, and clients better; for process and product innovations; and for nimble responses to changes in the environment (i.e., stakeholders, business models, or the natural or social environment).

The final element of work design for workforce effectiveness is sustainability. Already, highly skilled workers are taking extensive leave from high-demand jobs when they have family or elder-care responsibilities. Consistent with data from the smaller sample of emerging professionals we have coached, Hewlett and Luce (2006) report that young people, both male and female, acknowledge that they doubt they can maintain their work hours over the course of a career. Overlaying contemporary life and work demands on fifty- to one-hundred-year-old work designs is most likely unsustainable in the long run. Sustainable work environments are not only engaging to current occupants but attractive to new talent. Millennials are coming into the workplace with the expectation of using technology to reduce routine work. They are expecting development opportunities and opportunities to increase their skills. An organization's ability to replenish its workforce will rely on its leaders' ability to mesh technology with professional practices and workplace social norms, with worker expectations at least in the front seat of the people strategy of the organization.

Leadership Performance and Diversity

Leaders of contemporary organizations face flatter organizations due to restructuring, constant pressure for cost reductions, and the need for continuous value-added contributions from the workforce. They also face higher costs associated with health care, technology, and regulatory compliance. The old carrot-and-stick approaches to motivating and retaining an effective workforce will likely be less effective with Generation X and millennials than it was with baby boomers and veterans. Leaders have to communicate clear outcomes, provide tools and other supports needed to get work done, hold employees accountable for outcomes, and monitor how their own behavior supports or undermines work processes.

In contemporary life, for-profit and not-for-profit organizations have become such a prevalent influence on the lives of individuals that their contributions to the larger social fabric can no longer be ignored or considered simply a by-product—hopefully positive—of the initiatives the organization does for survival. The evaluation of the performance of organizations or their leaders can no longer be narrowly focused on improving shareholder value or soliciting large donations to a nonprofit. In an increasingly complex operational environment, performance must reflect progress across the quadruple bottom line—purpose, profit, people, and the planet. This assumes complete responsibility for economic performance and the impact of their organizations on the social and natural environment. To accomplish this, contemporary leaders will need the ability to understand the diversity dynamics of their environment and create intelligent responses both inside and outside of their organizations.

For example, while flattened structures were supposed to weaken traditional power structures that tended to exclude, research suggests that in practice they can have the opposite effect, as formal authority is replaced with informal relationships—typically between similar individuals who forge new, informal power substructures, which are even more difficult to recognize (Green, 2005). These informal relationships can involve the exchange of informational, material, and emotional resources that benefit those in the circle. Informal relationships can also create groupthink around what is acceptable appearance, behavior, and speech, which has a marginal impact on effective work processes and outcomes. It is a natural human tendency to believe that those who think and act like we do are wonderful human beings! Leaders must break free of their own unconscious biases to make quality decisions in the midst of the complexities of diversity (Thomas, 2006). If leaders believe that capabilities and performance should be the basis of status, rewards, and advancement within the organization, and that the capabilities and performance of the workforce are what drive organizational results, then allowing individuals to bring their whole self to work would maximize performance and thus outcomes for the organization.

Addressing these or any other type of workforce diversity dynamic begins with leaders who have confronted their bias toward considering those who appear to be most similar to them as the best qualified and the highest performing and individual performance. Diversity pioneer R. Roosevelt Thomas (2006) notes that this bias is one of the major obstacles to creating and leveraging a diverse workforce. To address such inequities, performance metrics in terms of a leader's success in developing and promoting capable, qualified diverse candidates may be established and tracked as part of a manager's overall leadership skills. Leaders can also create inclusive, effective work environments by creating open information networks, transparent decision-making processes, and both relational and task activities that cross diverse social or functional identities. Key to making any of these approaches work is the leader's self-awareness, diversity and leadership competencies, level of cultural competence, job analysis and design skills, and ability to engage employees and link performance to measurable outcomes.

Developing their own and others' diversity competencies is a challenge to all twenty-first century leaders of diverse workforces. Many leaders would credit themselves with having matured in their diversity competence such that they would not engage in openly derogatory remarks about women, racial or ethnic groups, or the LGBT community. However, while "political correctness," in the form of basic norms of civility and respect, provide the ground necessary to build relationships across differences, it is not by itself diversity competence. Diversity competence requires emotional intelligence, cultural competence, plus the ability to detect potential or occurring diversity fault lines, and the communication skills, commitment, and courage to address them. While for many this commitment may stem from a belief in "doing the right thing," we assert that diversity competence is as important to the strategy of achieving bottom-line results as other performance indicators.

Political correctness, in the form of stereotyping and fixed assumptions, can hamper communication around requirements to do the work effectively and prevent the building of trusting relationships required for teams to recognize, work through, and integrate differences that improve performance. Political correctness can also veil diversity conflicts and impede organizational members from engaging in constructive conflict. To move beyond suppressing biases and natural conflicts, organizations must first begin to incorporate diversity-competence training into leadership-development programs.

Keep in mind that training only introduces the concepts, and as with any learned behavior, leaders need others who support their learning and development. Leaders need to develop mentoring relationships and supportive relationships for the development of diversity competencies just as they do with networks for other aspects of their career development. This requires crafting and articulating clear performance standards and, many times, providing leaders with appropriate coaching or counseling to help them achieve those goals.

An example of this kind of leadership development initiative is the Diversity Learning Partners Luncheon, where senior leaders and employees are matched through a computer-based survey as learning partners. Together they attend a luncheon with a diversity speaker, and after the presentation they share their reactions and learn from each other. Partners hold each other accountable for the impact of their behavior on others and on the culture of the organization.

Globalization

The impact of globalization on how diversity is conceptualized and managed is now even more apparent. We navigate not only a multicultural but a flat, hot, crowded world in the age of acceleration, as Thomas Friedman (2005, 2008, 2016) describes in his best-selling books. The demographic change from monoracial and monolithic to multiracial and multicultural; the interdependence of the world's markets and businesses; technological advances; the growth of the internet; shifting employment practices; challenges to recruiting and retaining talented teachers in our educational system; the ability to purchase foods from around the world at Wal-Mart—all of these are evidence that "we are not in Kansas anymore." In this flat world, if we always do what we always did, we will no longer get what we always got. For individuals it demands cultural competence—gaining those skill sets that support us to successfully navigate this increasingly diverse world. For organizations it requires cultural competence too—creating conditions by which a diverse workforce can learn from differences and leverage these differences to achieve business outcomes.

Furthermore, as a result of globalization, diversity leadership has increased in complexity. The work of diversity in organizations is customized to fit the needs, mission, and values of each organization. Successful diversity and inclusion initiatives cannot be exported to other countries, nor do they necessarily meet the needs of a global workforce. Globalization intensifies the need for diversity to "go plaid" in organizations. Due to the hybrid nature of the field of organizational development, diversity practitioners are particularly suited to manage this process.

The Role of Diversity Practitioners

Practitioners doing the work of diversity in organizations recognize the broad and expansive nature of the required skill sets necessary to manage it—a reason why relatively few individuals are successful in this arena. From the early stages of diversity management, diversity practitioners grounded in organizational development theories realized that diversity and organizational change are interdependent. A changing market, changing workforce demographics, a shifting political landscape, and global imperatives have reinforced that diversity in organizations is the most complex human resource challenge of our time. Diversity, defined through its multiple lenses of representation, inclusion, equity, and economic empowerment, permeates every aspect of an organization's internal and external environment.

Process, systems, and structure are inherent core values of the field of organizational development. Doing diversity work requires process skills to discern the conditions for sustainable competitive advantage, the influencing skills necessary to educate senior leaders on these conditions, analytical skills to explore the assumptions underlying the current reality, and critical thinking to be able to determine the strategy for execution. Diversity practitioners with the requisite skill sets are uniquely positioned to drive this process.

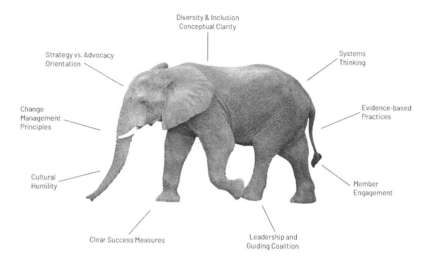

Figure 2: Diversity Elephant

What's Easy and What's Not

As an agent of change, the diversity practitioner must focus on system readiness, generating buy-in and identifying those sustainable conditions for the system rather than merely executing interventions and establishing programs unrelated to the mission and strategies of the organization. This approach can make it easier to get leadership to endorse the business case for diversity and sign on to honoring the values of diversity. A diversity champion or diversity advocate is not the same as a diversity practitioner. It is far harder to assess and hire for diversity competence than to hire an underrepresented individual under the assumption that a person of color or a woman or a LGBT individual or a person with a disability would espouse differing viewpoints, when contemporary theories on identity development suggest otherwise. It is far harder to change practices and create a mindset for supplier diversity than to simply mandate a percentage of spending for minority- and female-owned businesses. It is far harder to educate an employee base and create a learning organization characterized by cultural competence than it is to have a mandated, system-wide, one-day diversity training session, the results of which are never evaluated or integrated into the work-life experience. It is far harder to create an inclusive culture through transparent communication agendas, strategy-linked business objectives and rewards, and fair and unbiased performance appraisals than it is to set up affinity networks as employee resource groups that simply report out what the organization knows or wants to hear. It is far harder to restructure the design and assessment of how work gets done to create whole-person and friendly work environments than to simply grant women flextime. In other words, easy is characterized by compliance and simple adherence to best practices; hard is characterized by integration of differences into every aspect of organizational performance.

Going Plaid

The six men from Indostan, each being only partially right, needed the knowledge base of every individual to fully comprehend the nature of the elephant. Diversity has become the elephant of organizational development (Figure 2). Diversity practitioners are needed to advance diversity beyond awareness and competence training to integrating the different knowledge bases, experiences, perceptions, and ways of thinking about the world in new ways of fueling organizational performance.

REFERENCES

Collins, J. (2001). *Good to great: Why some companies make the leap and others don't*. New York, NY: Harper Collins.

Flumer, I. S., & Ployhart, R.E. (2013). Our most important asset: A multidisciplinary/multilevel review of human capital valuation for research and practice. *Journal of Management, 40*(1), 161–192.

Friedman, T. L. (2005). *The world is flat: A brief history of the twenty-first century*. New York, NY: Farrar, Straus and Giroux.

Friedman, T. L. (2008). *Hot, flat, and crowded: Why we need a green revolution—and how it can renew America*. New York, NY: Farrar, Straus and Giroux.

Friedman, T. L. (2016). *Thank you for being late: An optimist's guide to thriving in the age of accelerations* (First edition). New York, NY: Farrar, Straus and Giroux.

Goldin, C., & Rouse, C. (2000). Orchestrating impartiality: The impact of 'blind' auditions on female musicians. *American Economic Review, 90*(4), 715–741.

Green, T. K. (2005). Work culture and discrimination. *California Law Review, 93*(3), 623–684.

Herring, C. (2009). Does diversity pay? Race, gender, and the business case for diversity. *American Sociological Review,* *74*(2), 208–224.

Hewlett, S. A., & Luce, C. B. (2006). Extreme jobs: The dangerous allure of the 70-hour workweek. *Harvard Business Review,* *84*(12), 49–59.

Ibarra, H., Ely, R.J., & Kolb, D.M. (2013). Women rising: The unseen barriers. *Harvard Business Review* (September).

Kulik, C. T., & Roberson, L. (2008). 8 Diversity initiative effectiveness: What organizations can (and cannot) expect from diversity recruitment, diversity training, and formal mentoring programs. *Diversity at work,* 265.

Morgan, J. (2016). Five signs you are working for a truly great manager. *Forbes.com.* Retrieved from https://www.forbes.com/sites/jacobmorgan/2016/04/26/five-signs-youre-working-for-a-truly-great-manager/#63d6c6797e9b

Meyerson, D. E., & Fletcher, J. K. (2003). A modest manifesto for shattering the glass ceiling. In R. Ely, E. G. Foldy, & M. A. Scully (Eds.), *Reader in gender, work and organization* (pp.230-241). Malden, MA: Blackwell Publishing.

Reagans, R., & Zuckerman, E. (2001). Networks, diversity, and productivity: The social capital of corporate R&D teams. *Organization Science, 12*(4), 502–517. Retrieved from http://www.jstor.org/stable/3085985

Rosenbaum, E. (2014, April 23). The growing case for diversity as a profit source. *CNBC*. Retrieved from http://www.cnbc.com/2014/04/23/the-growing-case-for-diversity-as-a-profit-creator.html

Thomas, R. R. (2006). *Building on the promise of diversity: How we can move to the next level in our workplaces, communities, and our society.* New York, NY: AMACOM.

Consultation Skills: Creating an Inclusive Culture That Leverages Diversity for Higher Performance

Judith H. Katz and Frederick A. Miller

WE LIVE IN CHALLENGING TIMES, with organizations going through massive change and uncertainty. Organizations need people's problem-solving skills more than ever. Organizations need workforces that are talented, high-performing, diverse, and reliable—workforces that are willing and able to collaborate, contribute new thinking, and partner effectively among and across differences.

In this chapter, we outline the key approaches and skills that change agents need to create and implement strategies that ensure people feel included, differences are leveraged, and people are able to do their best work in order to achieve organizational goals and higher levels of performance. The labels "diversity consultant" or "inclusion consultant" lack the clarity necessary to adequately define the scope of work we do as change agents related to people, and they can inadvertently block effectiveness. We define the outcomes of our work in terms of a total systems change in *how* people interact and thrive in an organization, because it has implications for all aspects of an organization's work, culture, and performance. Consequently, we do not think of ourselves as "diversity" or "inclusion" in-a-small-box consultants, but rather strategic culture change consultants. The focus of this chapter, therefore, is on outlining the skills, competencies, and behaviors that are essential for individuals involved in strategic culture change. Throughout, we use the terms "consultant" and "change agent" interchangeably, and though we acknowledge that both terms can be applied to people internal to the system, much of this chapter reflects our experience as external consultants who partner extensively with internal resources for change.

There are several key assumptions we make with respect to the mindsets, behaviors, and skills a change agent needs related to people's interactions in organizations:

1. **YOU CAN'T DO THIS WORK ALONE** (Shephard, 1975). Working on strategic culture change—working to change the very fabric of an organization—is a major undertaking. No one individual has all the necessary skills and wisdom to transform an organization from a passive club to an inclusive organization (Jackson and Holvino, 1988; Katz and Miller, 1995). In fact, the very nature of culture change calls upon us to implement the factors of diversity in our approach. Namely, we must bring together a team representing human differences to accomplish the kind of change that makes building inclusion and leveraging diversity a way of life within an organization.

Members of change teams need to model not only the competencies related to organizational change, but also those related to diversity of identity, talent, focus, and expertise. Most importantly, the change team must be comprised of individuals external to the system and key partners within the system. The team must model facilitation, the behaviors of inclusion, the effectiveness of being diverse, and the high performance that is a possible result of these factors.

In many ways, the strongest message we send as consultants is the example of our own behavior—what we do, not what we say. How well we partner and leverage our own and others' diverse talents and how inclusive we are in our approach are informative to others. We must remember that people in the organization are watching our every move and learning from what we do.

2. **INDIVIDUALS CAN'T CHANGE A SYSTEM.** A system changes a system. All too often, practitioners believe that, with a good theoretical model, some great facilitation, a few tools, and the "right" client, they can change a system. As individuals, we can have some impact on other individuals, but the real goal is to create systemic change that impacts individual *and* organizational performance. Our challenge is to find leverage points within the organization to change the systems and processes while also changing individual and team interactions. We must, therefore, not only focus on educating people within organizations to increase their awareness and develop new competencies, but also concentrate on the systems and processes that will foster change. In essence we are working at multiple layers of the organization—identifying the levers that will move the system and be sustainable at the same time.

In working with individuals, we want to identify people who are leaning in and find areas that are ripe for change. We want to identify "pockets of readiness," leaders and teams who are ready to learn, model, and implement new mindsets and behaviors in order to demonstrate the business impacts that a more inclusive organization that leverages differences can make.

On the system level, if we are to create a high-performing, inclusive work environment, we need to focus on the people and management practices and behaviors that help shape the environment. How are people being hired? Developed? Promoted? Coached? Recognized? Rewarded? (Katz, 2006.) To what extent is the ability to leverage diverse talents and create a culture of inclusion seen as a vital and critical competency for being a manager and a leader? Are skills related to creating effective partnerships and collaboration within and across teams valued as much as or more than individual performance? Is the organization asking the right questions and getting the right people involved in making problems visible, solving complex problems, and enhancing results? How consciously does the organization link the success of its business strategy to leveraging differences and building inclusion? Are people within the organization being held accountable for delivering results in this arena, just as they are for other business objectives?

3. **CREATE ALTERNATIVE STRUCTURES THAT QUICKLY DEMONSTRATE IMPACT AND SUCCESS.** One way to jump-start or accelerate a change effort is to create alternative, temporary structures designed to enhance people's understanding of and fluency in the behaviors that will drive and sustain the change to the desired new culture.

Once you have leaders' buy-in and sponsorship and have clearly identified the organizational and business-strategy imperative, mechanisms to guide the effort and create momentum for change are necessary.

In addition to these new, temporary structures, networks, councils, action teams, policies, and other mechanisms may be needed to move the organization toward its goals in the area. Consultants need to be able to assemble the right people—those who can bring a coalition of individuals together with the requisite skill sets, experiences, backgrounds, and ability to influence others that will enable the creation of the structures needed to support strategic change.

For example, one of the most effective methods we have found for accelerating change is creating a peer-to-peer cohort of change agents who have experienced intense education and can model inclusive behaviors in their day-to-day work interactions. The power of this group lies in their ability to influence their colleagues to be different and create pull. People today can be more influenced by what their colleagues say and do than by what leadership and hierarchy proclaim (Baker, 2014; Davis-Howard, 2014; Guthridge, 2013). This cohort is able to get ahead of the change curve and demonstrate the positive impact that an inclusive environment can have on interactions, performance (individual, team, and organization), and results, creating greater momentum for change and a "proof of concept."

Skills for Change Agents

The skills a change agent needs are so interdependent and interwoven that dissecting them is not only difficult but potentially misleading. A strong vision is necessary early on, as well as the ability to connect new ways of interacting and operating to the organization's self-interest. Positioning and creating alignment are central to all phases of the intervention, especially getting leader buy-in.

Equally critical is the ability to partner with both clients and with other consultants and to connect and integrate the work of diversity and inclusion with other initiatives in place. Given the very nature of change, a change agent must not only be comfortable with addressing conflict—which goes beyond simply managing it—but be willing to raise issues related to differences and have the difficult and important conversations.

Measuring results along the way to include bottom-line impact and progress along the Commitment Curve (Conner and Patterson, 1982; Katz and Miller, 2017) is important for gauging and communicating the success of the change effort.

COMMITMENT CURVE to Mastery

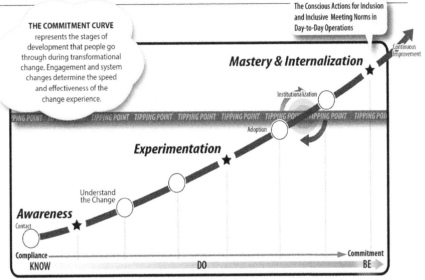

THE COMMITMENT CURVE represents the stages of development that people go through during transformational change. Engagement and system changes determine the speed and effectiveness of the change experience.

The Conscious Actions for Inclusion and Inclusive Meeting Norms in Day-to-Day Operations

Mastery & Internalization

Institutionalization

Continuous Improvement

Adoption

Experimentation

Understand the Change

Awareness

Contact

Compliance — KNOW   DO   Commitment BE

THE STAGES OF DEVELOPMENT describe the behaviors that an individual, team/group, organization, and sponsor are exhibiting and how interactions are changing. There is a risk of peole falling off the curve and losing commitment if engagement and systems are not sufficient.

It is also important to honor the strengths the current culture holds and to find ways to meet the leaders where they are and support them without justifying and colluding with elements of the culture that block progress and change.

Finally, there are a host of skills related to pacing. Practitioners must walk the line between acknowledging resistance and letting resistance stop the changes an organization needs. If the effort moves too quickly, it runs the risk of not being implemented deeply enough to truly take hold. If implementation is too slow, people may doubt the importance of the effort and its connection to organizational success. Figuring out the right level of pacing for true adoption of the effort, mastery of the new mindsets and behaviors, and institutionalization into systems and processes is critical for sustainability. And it is important to remind everyone involved that culture change is a continuous process that never reaches a final "we are there" state.

SKILL: Vision

Change agents need to have a clear understanding of what they are working toward. If you can't imagine an inclusive organization, you cannot create it. If you think all organizations are inherently "bad," you cannot create a good one. And if you don't have an idea of what success looks like, you will never know if you are moving closer to it. Consultants must question their assumptions and beliefs about organizations—their potential and their limitations.

However, a vision of success cannot be created solely by the change agent. Systems change requires that a team of people—internal change agents, leaders, stakeholders, and other members of the organization—be involved in setting the goals and working toward them. Consultants can assist in steering the process and share expertise and experiences about what kind of change is possible and how it may be achieved. But consultants also must reconcile their ideas with the organization's own vision for its future.

A key part of creating this vision is the ability to see the connection between creating a more inclusive organization that leverages differences and improving the organization's ability to achieve its objectives. The vision cannot be a standalone—i.e., inclusion for inclusion's sake. It must be connected to the strategy and performance of the organization (Katz and Miller, 2010).

In some ways, creating and collaborating on vision is a matter of positioning: the change agent needs to orient the organization to what inclusion will look and feel like and provide compelling reasons for adopting this vision. The proof-of-concept work through the peer-to-peer cohort has this impact. Aligning vision also requires the change agent to become familiar with the work and needs of the particular organization. The approach and even the goals of building inclusion and leveraging diversity are not one-size-fits-all. Change agents need to tailor initiatives to individual organizations so they can add value and respond to the market and contextual issues the organization is facing.

In some organizations—the ones most in need of diversity and inclusion efforts—envisioning success is not easy. The system may appear so broken or so steeped in privilege and oppression that the consultant despairs of ever making an impact. This, again, is why a strong sense of purpose and a clear picture of the ultimate goal are vitally important. Change agents and the effort itself need a focal point, a measurable goal—no matter how distant—to move toward, with measurable milestones along the way.

SKILL: Find The Self-Interest

Although many organizations talk about the need for greater diversity and a more inclusive workplace, many have fallen short of achieving that goal. They often talk about diversity and inclusion in the same breath, not recognizing that creating an inclusive environment and having and leveraging differences require very different strategies (Miller and Katz, 2008). In many organizations, diversity remains a human resources responsibility, unrelated to the organization's performance and frequently relegated to targets and goals and a focus on talent management: recruiting, development, and promotions. Making the connection to the system's self-interest (often the organization's bottom line) is one of the most important skills a consultant can have. It amounts to framing the issues in a way that motivates and compels the organization to create a comprehensive action plan that goes beyond training or recruiting and enables the organization's goals to be better achieved relative to its mission.

The connection is certainly there to be made. However, it is important that the organization truly tailor how a more inclusive workplace will impact their bottom-line results and individuals' ability to do their best work for the organization. It is clear that, to succeed, organizations need to have all people doing their best work, individually and collectively. Every organization can relate to the need for higher performance, attracting and retaining top talent, achieving a greater competitive edge, achieving the organization's vision and mission, and enhancing the bottom line (Katz and Miller, 2013a; 2017).

The failure of organizations to recognize the bottom-line advantage that leveraging diversity and inclusion can offer them is often a shortcoming of many change efforts. Many change agents base their approach on a social justice philosophy and bring with them an ingrained distrust of the profit motive (or fail to understand how to make the connection to profit and demonstrate results), creating a focus on diversity and inclusion efforts as the "right thing to do." The inability to connect such efforts to the bottom line—whether working in the profit or nonprofit sector—can be problematic. What good is a positive culture change if the organization goes out of business?

Only by connecting the change effort to the organization's ability to accomplish its strategies and mission can you address the sustainability of both the organization and the change.

SKILL: Positioning and Creating Alignment

To establish an atmosphere for a successful initiative, the consultant must do three things: position, position, position. We position the work itself as a valuable and attainable goal for the organization. We position the organization to accept and incorporate it. We position leaders to understand what inclusion is about and how to meaningfully enact it in their organizations and prepare them to be models and sponsors. Most, if not all, of the other skills discussed in this chapter require positioning and acceptance by the organization's leaders.

Positioning the effort for success requires not only a long-term strategy and an understanding of the internal politics of an organization but also patience on the part of consultants. Many people want to jump in and start making changes. They have clear ideas about what is wrong in the organization and are eager to roll up their sleeves and put it right. They don't see that the system has to change itself, that people in the organization need to take ownership of the change effort, and that there are developmental phases of the initiative that need to be properly paced.

We often only get one chance at doing this work, which makes positioning crucial. Whether we are external or internal consultants, we can't fail and then expect leaders to let us try a different approach. We can't ask for people's trust, fritter it away, and expect it to be given again. Just as important as gaining the support of hierarchical leaders is gaining the support of key thought leaders and influencers in the organization, some of whom may not believe the organization can change, or have been involved in previous change efforts that failed or fell short. Learning from those individuals about what went wrong and enlisting their involvement is a key to success. Learning about how the organization "shoots itself in the foot" is critical for avoiding pitfalls along the way.

To orient the organization and create alignment within it requires learning about the system, meeting with key stakeholders, enrolling people in the effort, and getting support from leaders. Many consultants dislike managing the political aspects of change efforts, but we cannot be successful without doing so. For us, positioning often takes months and involves multiple behind-the-scenes meetings. It is work that pays off when the initiative really starts to move. A change effort is like a rocket ship: when it first takes off, it may look like it's barely moving, but if the right combinations of chemicals are reacting in the ways they need to, the propulsion will ultimately carry you faster and faster to the stars.

Positioning is also a means for creating alignment. In the early stages of an intervention, it is crucial that everyone in the organization be aligned on several key factors:

- *Goals.* What exactly does the initiative aim to do? How is the organization defining and thinking about diversity? What is their understanding of inclusion? What do inclusion and diversity mean to the organization? And—an often overlooked question—how are diversity and inclusion positioned relative to each other? In our work, we lead with inclusion and, more and more, our clients treat the work as inclusion and diversity *in that order*, or even just inclusion. If the work is positioned right, and the goal is to have the right people doing the right work and to be able to tap their different views to see as much of the whole picture as possible, then diversity becomes a necessary and critical component of inclusion.

Without clear definitions of each of these terms and the initiatives needed to realize each element, it is hard to establish clear goals with clear outcomes and measures of progress. As practitioners, we must understand the difference between diversity and inclusion and the strategies to impact both. There must be clear goals at the outset so that people know what they are moving toward and can check progress along the way. Many people have misconceptions about diversity—they think it's about meeting targets and focusing on talent development rather than on individual, team, and organization performance. Only by articulating a vision of what the initiative intends to accomplish can the organization be clear and focused on why it is undergoing the changes and what each person's role in it must be.

- *Expectations.* What is required of a leader in the new organizational culture? What is required of all team members? What is required in all interactions? How long will the process take? What can you do—and not do—as a consultant to affect this process? Many well-intended initiatives have been abandoned or labeled a failure because people were not aligned on what they could expect from the change effort, leading to a lack of sustainability or a tendency to declare victory too soon. They thought they could achieve increased diversity by conducting senior staff education events or by having everyone attend a few hours of training on unconscious bias. These can be great foundational actions and have a place within the scope of an overall effort, but they alone cannot be expected to move an entire system toward sustainable inclusion, and without a clear end goal and comprehensive change strategy, they fall into a vacuum. The challenge is how to demonstrate the immediate results that today's environment seems to crave while also ensuring that the systems, processes, and structures also change in sustainable ways. Many organizations would rather focus on a three-month strategy than a long-term change effort. The change agent, then, has to demonstrate movement and results in the short term and also set and achieve medium and longer-term goals. The consultant has to educate people up front about what they can reasonably expect the effort to yield immediately versus what gains will take sustained time and effort, what kind of resistance they are likely to see along the way, and what it will take to overcome that resistance.

- *Process.* As Kaleel Jamison once said, "Change in the middle looks like failure," and leaders do not like the appearance of failure. The consultant must prepare everyone in the organization for the pockets of resistance, episodes of backlash, and the "two steps forward, one step back" nature of any change process. The goal is for the organization to get better and stronger in ways that are sustainable, not superficial. Everyone in the organization, and especially the leaders, must be clear from the start that success does not mean that every day sees incremental progress toward the goal. You can't start putting something entirely new in place and expect it to work not only perfectly but immediately. If people approach change with this expectation, they will be tempted to abandon the effort when the problems and challenges begin to arise.

- *Roles.* Alignment around who does what—and who can't do what—is critical. Some leaders feel their work is done when they hire a consultant. The consultant's job is to come in, wave a magic wand, and make everything better. Other organizations hire consultants for their expertise but then demand that they adhere to the internal systems and processes they were hired to change. Some team members believe that responsibility for an inclusion and diversity change lies with upper management and requires little or nothing from them. The consultant must align all people with what is expected of them and what they should and should not expect from the consultant. Failing to do this often leads to failed efforts. Consultants alone cannot carry an effort. For systems to change, the people within the system must also change and feel accountable for moving to new interactions and a new culture. They must understand that a culture that is inclusive and leverages differences will require a new set of competencies and a new way of engaging others. Everyone needs to "get different" in a process of culture change. This is an important component of educating them about the effort in general and what it means for an organization to be inclusive. It is also the benefit of starting with a peer-to-peer approach, so that there are examples to point to that begin to give people a better understanding of what the future state could actually look like, feel like, and accomplish (Kotter, 1995; Kronley, Steffan, and Katzenbach, 2012).

SKILL: Getting Leader Buy-In

Enrolling leaders at the start and keeping them on board is crucial. You cannot assume that by bringing you in as a consultant leaders have tacitly understood and acknowledged what creating a more inclusive organization is about and what the change effort will require of them. Most leaders start the process knowing only that change is needed and having some vague concept of what a consultant does. In a lot of organizations, the decision to start the process comes from a smaller subset of the leadership group, which means there may be some powerful people in the upper echelons who don't even have a vague understanding of why you were brought in or—worse yet—they oppose the idea. Your early work with leaders sets the tone and establishes what the partnership will be like. Your ability to be effective is a direct result of the partnership you build with senior leaders. Most importantly, leaders must feel that, by having a more inclusive organization that leverages differences, the effort will solve problems they see as important and that hold the organization back from greater success (Miller and Katz, 2002; Schein, 2013; Weisbord, 2012).

Getting leaders to buy into the process means getting them to buy into several main concepts:

- Leaders need to accept that the organization must improve. In theory, this should be easy. No one thinks their organization is perfect. However, when the exact nature and extent of the imperfections begin to surface, leaders' acceptance of this tenet sometimes wavers. They must be willing to hear how deep the issues are. Given that leaders are often insulated from the "true" voices of the organization by gatekeepers who ensure that bad news doesn't travel up, it may take some effort to open channels of communication. It is often shocking for leaders to see what is really going on.

- A powerful way to gain buy-in is to undertake a discovery process to understand the current state of the organization. This in itself is a major intervention, when people's voices begin to surface regarding what is working well, what they value about the organization, the barriers they experience, and the opportunities for change. By bringing those voices to the leaders, consultants help them understand the need for change and see the missed opportunities and waste that impede individual and overall organization performance.

- Sharing the data from the discovery process, so that leaders and all people have a common understanding of the current reality and a line of sight to the future reality, enables everyone to join the change effort. It is important to frame the work as a continuous improvement rather than a blame or judgment of the current state.

- Most leaders are people of action who like to immediately tackle problems. If Person A is not feeling included, it must be Person B's or Manager C's fault. Leaders may feel compelled to seek individuals to blame or "fix" rather than address the systemic nature of the problem. In these instances, how the work has been framed, and the larger organizational benefits that have been identified, can provide momentum for change.

- Understanding that the change isn't going to be easy or quick is critical. As much as people agree to this in theory, they usually still want a switch—one magic button that will make the organization inclusive and diverse. Leaders and consultants have to realize how unrealistic this expectation is.

- A shared understanding of the role of the change agent, the importance of the leader partnership, and the access the change agent needs is critical. Establish expectations and limitations up front so you don't set yourself up for failure or set the leaders up for disappointment. Of course, the relationship must be defined as you go. But this very fact should be clear to everyone from the start: change agents and leaders are in a partnership that requires support, trust, and clarity of roles. Leaders must be willing to learn, be reflective about their own behavior, and be willing to change, and they must enable the change agent to be their coach and their guide. There are times when leaders need to lead and times when they need to be led.

- Encourage leaders to be open to where the process will lead. Leaders are much more accustomed to contained projects with discrete beginnings and endings than they are to dynamic and organic processes. They need to understand that the change you are talking about goes to the very heart and identity of the organization and all the interactions the organization contains. They need to accept the uncertainty caused by the fact that all the changes will not be immediately apparent. You can only see so far down the road at any one time: you take a few steps, which lets you see the next few steps, and so on.

SKILL: Partnering

At its heart, creating a culture of inclusion is about people working together across the differences they have as humans. If consultants truly want to model the behavior they are endorsing, they need to work with partners and exhibit the collaborative and partnering behaviors that the organization needs for higher performance and is striving toward. You can't do this while working independently. What could be less diverse than a group of one? Working with partners also helps hone other critical skills: managing conflict, maximizing differences, taking advantage of your talents, and giving and receiving honest feedback.

Partners give you:

- more wisdom to make better plans;
- someone to bounce ideas off of and to brainstorm with;
- someone to watch your back;
- someone to lean on when you get tired;
- another set of eyes and ears;
- someone to celebrate successes;
- someone to confide in;
- someone to help you demonstrate new ways of interacting;
- confidence;
- a different perspective;
- the beginnings of a group that can grow toward critical mass;
- someone to challenge you;
- someone to support you;
- someone who can be honest with you.

Partnering with other consultants. Working with colleagues offers a great opportunity to model the partnership skills the organization needs to adopt. It provides many benefits and opportunities that are essential for culture change work.

We have been business partners for over thirty years: an African American man and a Jewish woman. We have worked hard together, built a business together, played together, enjoyed our families together, fought over and celebrated our differences. Critical to our success has been building a strong safety net—knowing what we could and could not count on receiving from each other. We have learned to be clear about our needs and willing to raise tough issues with each other. Clients see our partnership and learn from our example.

Partnering with allies in the system. In addition to other consultants, partnerships within the system are critical. No one can lead an organization through a culture change process without allies. Even a CEO needs partners, advocates, mentors, and a support system. If you are to be strategic about working for change, your first strategic action should be to forge key partnerships with leaders and other members of the organization. They can provide invaluable insight into the organization and how it works and also serve as a leverage point for enacting change. In working with them, you can teach, by example, the kind of partnership skills they need to develop. Also, look for thought leaders to partner with—people who are influential in the organization because of their experience, respect, or personality. They are not always the titled, formal "leaders."

Partnering with other initiatives. Part of a successful effort is to forge linkages to work that is foundational or ongoing in the organization. In many ways, these linkages strengthen the work on inclusion and embed it into other key aspects of the organization's work. In one organization, it may mean working with an initiative on process improvement or lean six sigma; in another organization, it might mean working with talent development as they create leadership attributes; in yet another, it might mean connecting with consultants involved in quality initiatives or safety. It is essential to see these not as competing efforts but as all working toward the same goal: the organization's ability to meet its objectives and create an environment in which all people can do their best work.

SKILL: Have a Joining Mindset

Underlying any effort or interaction is the mindset with which you approach others. Many of us have learned to judge others as our opening stance. Starting with a joining mindset is a conscious action that speeds up partnering and collaboration (Katz and Miller, 2012; 2013b). In joining mode, we approach each interaction with the assumption that we will partner and seek ways to build on others' ideas and thoughts. There is an assumption that the other person has something to offer us, something we can learn from, as we hear their perspective.

In joining mode, we enter with an assumption of trust.

Staying open and finding the point of connection and partnership, even with naysayers, is a critical skill for consultants. Even the most skeptical people can become allies when they feel heard, listened to, and partnered with—when they feel joined. The key requirement for the consultant is to truly understand others' points of view ("street corners") and to be curious about why they see and experience the organization the way they do. Only then can the consultant be most helpful to the organization. A key part of this is for the consultant to avoid judging others (such as, "He or she doesn't 'get it'"), since labels and judging continue to build resistance and defensiveness.

SKILL: Practice And Model Conscious Actions For Inclusion

The goal is to advocate and practice behaviors that:

- facilitate the creation of a workplace environment that allows every team member to do their best work;

- promote effective teamwork among all team members;
- create the opportunity for a joining mindset, connection, understanding, partnership, and safety.

Conscious Actions for Inclusion

4 Keys that Change *EVERYTHING*

1. **Lean into Discomfort**
   Be willing to challenge self and others. Speak up—bring your voice and street corner.

2. **Listen as an Ally**
   Listen, listen, listen and engage. Be a partner. Challenge as an Ally.

3. **State Your Intent and Intensity**
   Clarify intent: State Notions, Stakes, Boulders, and Tombstones. Say what you mean and how much you mean it.

4. **Share Street Corners**
   Accept others' thoughts and experiences as true for them. Hear others' differences as additive.

Practiced together, these 12 Conscious Actions create a Joining Mindset, which builds partnership, collaboration, and teamwork.

Inclusion Is...

A sense of belonging;

Feeling respected, valued, and seen for who we are as individuals;

There is a level of supportive energy and commitment from leaders, colleagues, and others so that we—individually and collectively—can do our best work.

Sustaining Behaviors

5. Greet people authentically—say "hello."
6. Create a sense of safety for yourself and your team members.
7. Work for the common good and shared success.
8. Ensure right people, right work, right time: Ask who else needs to be involved to understand the whole situation.
9. Link to others' ideas, thoughts, and feelings—give energy back.
10. Speak up when people are being made "small" or excluded.
11. Address misunderstandings and resolve disagreements—work "pinches."
12. Build *TRUST*: Do what you say you will do and honor confidentiality.

CHANGE THE INTERACTION · CHANGE THE EXPERIENCE · CHANGE THE RESULT

Demonstrating a joining mindset and the Conscious Actions for Inclusion detailed in the illustration will assist people in joining the effort and joining each other. These are the same ground rules that underlie inclusion itself—*creating an environment in which all people can feel valued, respected, seen for who they are, and able to contribute as partners.* They are behaviors the consultant needs to come in with and live and behaviors others in the organization need to learn and actively live as well.

SKILL: Managing and Valuing Conflict

More participants, more diversity, and more inclusion will result in more conflict. It is important to realize that conflict in itself is not negative; it can be positive propulsion for the organization if handled properly. A chorus of voices can be harmonious or chaotic, depending on how they are blended.

The consultant needs to model the kind of conflict management that the organization needs to practice. Consultants usually get plenty of opportunities to model it, since our work invariably creates conflict. For some the work may be moving too fast; for others the work is moving too slow. In other situations, we may witness disagreements between members of the organization and be in a position to mediate. If we can show through our actions that conflict is normative and additive, that availing oneself of a multitude of perspectives and ideas creates greater vision, and that disagreements don't have to be destructive, we will have gone a long way toward laying the groundwork for a culture of inclusion that leverages diversity. Framing conflict management as normative and valuable becomes an essential skill that the organization must lean into and learn if it truly wants a culture that values and leverages differences.

SKILL: Communication

Honesty is essential for change agents. If we don't speak the truth in an organization—especially the truths those in the system can't speak—who will?

At the same time, how and when we choose to speak those truths can make a big difference in how the message is received. Again, this is a matter of positioning. It is also a matter of modeling the kind of communication behaviors the organization itself needs to be moving toward.

Communicating clearly and directly WITH "Straight Talk": A Norm-Changing Intervention

One of the most helpful interventions that can be made in a group or an organization is to change its norms of interactions to enable people to communicate clearly and directly. In 1985 Kaleel Jamison framed this as "Straight Talk" (Covey, 1989, 2004; Jamison, 1985; Patterson, Grenny, McMillan, and Switzler, 2012). "Straight Talk" is the practice of speaking clearly, directly, and honestly. The foundations include:

- interactions of respect in which people are invested in engaging with other people in ways that address disagreements and misunderstandings;
- respecting others enough to be honest with them;
- sharing information in a way that produces an efficient, effective environment for communication;
- developing individuals by creating an environment in which it is okay to make mistakes, learn, and grow;
- utilizing differences to enable diversity of thought and experiences to be leveraged.

"Straight Talk" presumes that conflicting views, values, cultures, and styles are best addressed openly and that those differences—properly acknowledged—will enhance rather than detract from the human interactions and work of the group or organization. Communicating clearly and directly is not a byproduct of a strong and inclusive organization; it's a prerequisite.

Few people, groups, or organizations practice clean, clear, honest communications. We often value politeness (no matter how thin or destructive) over conflict (no matter how necessary and additive) and our interactions reflect this. We tend to use qualifying language, peppering sentences with "sometimes," "perhaps," "maybe," and other words that undercut the passion, authority, and precision of what we say. We use diminishing language that subtly undercuts our own voice ("I could be wrong, but ..." "You may not agree with this, but ...").

Such linguistic habits detract from effective communication and undermine the essence of what we need to say. "Straight Talk" eliminates these barriers and has the added advantage of enabling individuals in a group or organization to grow as individuals and as teams.

"Straight Talk" is not a license for rudeness, brutality, or disparagement. It should not be used to embarrass or humiliate, for public rebuke, or for a verbal "assassination." It is not a "hit and run" process and should always be conducted with respect for the listener. It is intended to enable honest, meaningful interactions—to enable people to lean into discomfort, to truly listen as allies to one another, to understand each other's perspectives and accept their frames of reference as true for them, and through those interactions to develop greater trust and understanding and, ultimately, to create breakthroughs together (Katz and Miller, 2012).

When people learn to use "Straight Talk"—in all their communications and interactions, both verbal and written, including email, texting, and social networking—they enhance their collective efficiency and information is communicated clearly, without second-guessing and without hidden agendas. Thanks to an uncluttered information flow, work is accomplished in a more timely and efficient fashion.

SKILL: Measurements that Matter

In most organizations, if you can't measure it, it isn't real. Yet some consultants are very reluctant to use metrics in their work on inclusion. This is probably the result of several factors: the misconception that culture change initiatives like building inclusion and leveraging diversity are resistant to measurement; the belief that it is too hard to attach numbers to initiatives like this (how can one quantify the degree to which people are accepted and allowed to bring themselves fully to their work?); and, the legitimate concern that treating people as "numbers" is part of what the initiative is trying to discourage. The metrics most often applied are associated with diversity targets for specific groups rather than connected to bottom-line results. This has backfired in many ways, as organizations talk about diversity in the broadest sense yet continue to measure only certain populations (Balter, Chow, and Yin, 2014; Brenman, 2013).

But if the impetus for doing this work is a bottom-line advantage, there ought to be some ways of demonstrating that advantage. If people are to be held accountable for moving the organization forward, there should be some way of marking that progress. It is important to have some concepts of what success looks like. If no attempt is made to track certain aspects of the culture change effort, it will be difficult to gauge its impact—or even to be sure it is having one.

Many organizations already track statistics that can be of use here, such as information on hiring, retention, promotions, and attrition. These metrics have obvious connections to the impact of efforts to build inclusion and leverage diversity (Hubbard, 2004).

There are many other opportunities for quantifying the effectiveness of a culture change initiative, though. Often they require being conscientious about what the goals of the initiative are and then checking to see if those goals are being met. Tools such as the Commitment Curve (Conner and Patterson, 1982; Katz and Miller, 2017) have been effective in measuring the progress of a change initiative to make inclusion a way of life. The Commitment Curve graphically represents the stages of development from contact to experimentation to institutionalization of a transformational change effort. It provides a simple framework for identifying the current state, setting goals for the future, and monitoring progress along the way.

Conducting measurements at the start of an initiative is crucial. They will provide the basis for a clear diagnosis of the system as well as a benchmark against which future measurements may be compared to mark the progress of the organization. Effort should be made to measure all aspects of the initiative across the organization: the degree to which the culture change is being communicated to everyone, the commitment of leaders, the extent to which people are responding to the call for change in their own behaviors, the effect the effort is having on key partnerships, the impact on competitive edge and financial success, etc. Survey instruments and performance evaluations (and the ability to meet specific goals) are some effective methods for assessment.

Considering all these elements is crucial for understanding what is key for the organization and then finding the strategic levers required to achieve change. Many consultants fail by merely going down the best-practices track. They often use boilerplate, activity-based approaches (e.g., mentoring, networks, training sessions), with the hope that something will resonate within the organization. The real skill here is to discern the relevant, core issues for each organization and then find the best approaches and strategies for affecting them and moving the organization to higher operating performance.

Most important is to understand what metrics matter to the organization. For example, if one of the key indicators for organizational success is customer service, then tracking how the inclusion change effort is impacting customer service should be a major component of the strategy. In other organizations it might be sales, or quality, or time to market, or output, or innovation. Having specific measureable outputs strengthens the sustainability of the effort. Also important is sharing the "success stories" along the way. For example, one client reported saving $50 million on a building capitalization project because inclusion efforts resulted in people feeling able to speak up and discuss innovative ways to do the building remodel. In another organization, people reported effective negotiation of difficult contracts based on using inclusive behaviors. Another client, struggling with rising quality defects caused by human error, began a multi-phase inclusion effort that included foundational education for people leaders, upskilling a change cohort, just-in-time coaching regarding inclusive mindsets and behaviors for teams, and the formation of compliance teams. Almost immediately, the rise in errors was halted, and over the next six months, errors decreased dramatically, from a high of 160 per month in June to 29 per month by December of the same year (Katz and Miller, 2017).

Talking about how inclusion and leveraging differences are making a difference in day-to-day interactions, teamwork, collaboration, making problems visible, problem solving, and decision making goes a long way toward demonstrating success and impact.

The limits of measurement. As mentioned earlier, change in the middle looks like failure. It is important to remember this when looking at metrics that, on the surface, may seem discouraging. For instance, it is not uncommon for the early stages of a culture change effort to result in some discomfort for people in the organization who don't fully understand the nature of the change effort or the need for it. This discomfort may be reflected in employee surveys and create the mistaken impression that the effort is failing. Engagement numbers actually might decrease the year following such an effort as people's expectations of the culture and organization are raised. Keep this in mind when establishing accountability. Leaders and others can be held responsible for the results that fall under their purview. It is important, however, not to hold people accountable for behaviors they have not yet learned or for pockets of resistance that may lie beyond their influence. This is particularly true at the early stages of the process.

In general, it is critical that consultants measure the organization's success, and equally critical that they recognize the challenges of such measurement.

SKILL: Honor The System

As consultants become familiar with an organization and its culture, it is often easy to see what is broken and what is wrong. The more we meet people, hear their stories, and directly observe the issues, challenges, and opportunities that are alive in the organization, the more dispirited we may become about the system itself.

A clear view of what is wrong with the system is, of course, essential for creating change. But a few other points are worth remembering, too:

- It is a privilege to be invited to work with an organization. The client organization existed before our involvement and has probably had a good deal of success. It is composed of people, not merely policies and practices. And it has reached out to us for guidance and help. No matter how discouraged we may become by the current state of the culture or its resistance to change, we must remember that it is an honor to be in a position to learn about, observe, and ultimately affect the systems in which we work. It is always important to build on what is working and to see the work as a continuous improvement journey.

- If the system knew better, it would do better. Malice, dysfunction, and/or low performance are not consciously embedded into the organizational cultures we are asked to assist; they come to accrue there. Most often organizations are passive clubs trying to do the best they know how. We are there to educate and share our knowledge so the organization can do better.

- The answers are already inside the system. The essentials for a successful change initiative reside within the organization—in its people, its ideas, its opportunities, its business strategy. Consultants augment the system with external aids, such as benchmarking, models, and experience in other organizations, but we must remember that the solutions for each system lie within it.

SKILL: Support Leaders Without Colluding

The relationship between a consultant and an organization's leadership is a delicate one. Consultants—especially in their early work with a client—are sometimes the bearers of bad news, and how that news is delivered can have a big impact on one's effectiveness. Obviously there is a constructive component to even the most discouraging of data gatherings, and the long-term goal of improving the system has to be kept foremost in people's minds.

Consultants can't let fear of a "kill the messenger" response from top leaders keep them from speaking the truths—no matter how ugly—that they discover about the organization. It is impossible to be an effective consultant while also shielding leaders or, by extension, the organization itself from what is going on in the organizational culture and what must be done about it.

At the same time, it is not wise to use such information in a way that harms or circumvents leaders. Remember, we are there to assist the leaders. That means, among other things, letting them lead. If we blindside them in meetings or fail to work with them in a way that allows them to do their jobs effectively, we are not helping anyone. Our job is to help them be as competent as they can be, as prepared as possible. It is not a test to see if they are committed to change. Our role is to assist them in being models of the new culture and give leadership to it.

When it is time to report our findings to leaders, we try to be careful: we don't want to give them all the information before we walk into that meeting, nor do we want them to be so surprised by the data that they end up looking out of touch or lost. We will talk to the most senior leader ahead of time, not to give them the full scoop before everybody else attending the meeting, but to give them the general direction and tone of what they can expect and need to be prepared to hear and respond to. They cannot lead their team and the organization and also deal with the material if they are sitting there stunned.

Again, this is not done to "stack the deck" in favor of the organization's leadership, but rather to enable them to do their jobs. Remember that you as the consultant will eventually leave and the leaders will stay. The success of the enterprise can't be predicated on your being there to do it all.

Another advantage to preparing leaders is that it enlists them as allies and advocates. The leader who stands before her or his staff ready for what they are hearing is able to function as a partner with the change agent. He or she is not distracted by their own reactions to what may be bad news, but is already on board with the process. The staff sees this immediately.

SKILL: Pacing

There is an initial start-up time when you need to build support and momentum for the change, and then a period toward the end when sustainability and long-term maintenance are the main thrusts. The middle period, however, is in some ways the trickiest. Consultants often find themselves caught between resisters, for whom the change is moving too fast, and champions, for whom it is moving too slow.

Each group needs special attention. Resisters have a lot of fear about the new culture and what it will mean for them. They have either not heard the message communicated clearly enough or their own insecurities and apprehensions about what change will really mean have not been overcome. Although a few resisters may never be willing to align themselves with the new culture and may need to leave, the majority simply need more time, attention, and information (Loden, 1996).

However, patience with skeptics is sometimes perceived as a mixed message by those who have been enthusiastically supporting the effort and are eager to enact the new culture as soon as possible. These champions get impatient with a slow pace; they sometimes feel the brunt of the backlash that comes from resisters and may resent the way in which such resisters are seemingly indulged by the organization. They may even accuse the organization and the change agent of not walking the talk.

This period of discomfort for both groups can be difficult to manage. One key to navigating this period successfully is to prepare people for it ahead of time. All parts of the change effort should be communicated early on. Once people recognize that what they are experiencing is a natural part of the process—that it actually indicates progress along some established continuum—they can see the larger picture and recognize that what may appear to be failure is actually part of the journey to success.

Managers need to be supported throughout this stage as well. They will feel forces pulling them in opposing directions. They need to remain resolute about sticking with the change process as it has been established. Their actions and words must consistently say that the organization is moving forward and that everyone needs to get on board with the new culture. The discontent that accompanies change in the middle must be taken as a specific leadership challenge and not as a failure of the initiative.

SKILL: Accept a Continuous Process

There will always be new challenges, new issues, and new opportunities. This is why long-term, permanent processes need to be in place, such as accountability procedures and strategic planning for building inclusion and leveraging diversity.

The consultant's goal, therefore, is not to completely eradicate all the problems in the organization; no consultant could do that. You cannot eliminate conflict, but you can establish a process for conflict resolution that maximizes people's contributions and finds additive value in multiple points of view. The organization, too, needs to understand that the work of building inclusion and leveraging diversity is not an isolated program or a discrete, finite effort with a clear endpoint. Ask them, When does an organization "stop" trying to be profitable or declare its drive for competitive edge "complete"? When does an organization determine that it has gotten sufficiently "smart" and doesn't need to learn anymore?

Culture change work is no different. Once the culture is aligned around the new goals, behaviors, and competencies, the emphasis moves from achieving the new environment to sustaining it and then creating what is needed next.

At the same time, it is important to celebrate milestones along the way and recognize the initiative's successes. This is another reason for setting specific goals: once they are reached, they provide snapshots of success. The successes create momentum for the rest of the initiative, help propel other areas of the culture change effort, and let people see that the organization is achieving something concrete as it goes through the change process.

Conclusion

It is impossible to catalogue every skill that consultants need—each client, person, encounter, and system is different from all others—and the finesse required is resistant to easy formulas and broad generalizations. Nevertheless, the skills we have outlined are called upon frequently and support some of the hundreds of finer points associated with consulting work.

More than anything, we as consultants need to remain open to our own continuous learning and honing of skills. We need to be conscientious about what we do and the effect it has on organizations. We need to make sure that the values we prize and espouse are the ones we are living and modeling in all our interactions with the organizations we aim to assist. Most of all, we need to remember that the biggest skill of all is Self as Instrument—we are the instruments of change—and how we show up and what we do (more than what we say) has a major impact on our success. At the same time, we cannot make change without a lot of joining and partnership from a lot of people who share the vision, see the self-interest, and are willing to do the hard work of change.

REFERENCES

Baker, M.N. (2014). Peer-to-peer leadership: Why the network is the leader. San Francisco: Berrett-Koehler.

Balter, R., Chow, J. & Jin, Y. (2014). What diversity metrics are best used to track and improve employee diversity? Cornell University, ILR School site: http://digitalcommons.ilr.cornell. edu/student/68.

Brenman, M. (2013). Diversity metrics, measurement and evaluation. Workforce diversity network. www. workforcediversitynetwork.com.

Conner, D.R., & Patterson, R.W. (1982). Building commitment to organizational change. *Training and Development*, 36 *(4)*, 18-30.

Covey, S.R. (1989, 2004) *7 habits of highly effective people: Powerful lessons in personal change*. New York, NY: Free Press.

Davis-Howard, V. (2014, July). Unleash change through a peer-to-peer approach. *T&D: Training and Development*, 76-77.

Guthridge, L. (2013). Change through smart-mob organizing: Using peer-by-peer practices to transform organizations. In Carter, L., Sullivan, R.L., Goldsmith, M., Ulrich, D., & Smallwood, N. (Eds.) *The change champion's field guide: Strategies and tools for leading change in your organization*. 2nd edition. San Francisco, CA: Wiley, 246-266.

Jackson, B.W. & Holvino, E. (1988, Fall). Developing multicultural organizations. *Journal of Religion and Applied Behavioral Science. (Association for Creative Change), 4-19.*

Jamison, K. (1985, June). Straight talk: A norm-changing intervention. *OD Practitioner, 17* (2).

Katz, J.H. (2006, October). Developing a comprehensive pipeline strategy: More than recruiting and retention. *ASTD Links* (atd.org.).

Katz, J.H. & Miller, F.A. (1995). Cultural diversity as a developmental process: The path from a monocultural club to inclusive organization. In Pfeiffer (Ed), *1995 Annual: Volume 2 Consulting* (pp.267-281). San Diego, CA: Pfeiffer.

Katz, J.H. & Miller, F.A. (2010). Inclusion: The *HOW* for the next organizational breakthrough. In Rothwell, W.J. Stavros, J.M. Sullivan, R. L & Sullivan, A. (Eds.), *Practicing organization development: A guide for leading change (3rd edition)* (pp.434-443). San Francisco, CA: Jossey-Bass/Pfeiffer.

Katz, J.H. & Miller, F.A. (2012). *Opening doors to teamwork and collaboration: 4 keys that change everything.* San Francisco, CA: Berrett-Koehler.

Katz, J.H. & Miller, F.A. (2013a, July). The hidden waste in manufacturing-and how to address it. *Manufacturing Net* (www. manufacturing.net).

Katz, J.H. & Miller, F.A. (2013b). Judging others has not worked…so let's join them. *Leader to Leader*. 51-57.

Katz, J.H. & Miller, F.A. (2017). Leveraging differences and inclusion pays off: Measuring the impact on profits and productivity. *OD Practitioner, 49 (1)* 56-61.

Kotter, J.P. (1995). Leading change: Why transformational efforts fail. *Harvard Business Review, 73*, 59-67.

Kronley, C., Steffan, I., & Katzenbach, J.R. (2012). Cultural change that sticks. *Harvard Business Review, 90 (7-8),* 110-117.

Loden, M. (1996). *Implementing diversity*. NY: McGraw-Hill Education.

Miller, F.A. & Katz, J.H. (2002). *The inclusion breakthough: Unleashing the real power of diversity*. San Francisco, CA: Berrett-Koehler.

Miller, F.A. & Katz, J.H. (2008). Compliance, leveraging differences and inclusion: They are not all the same. Unpublished manuscript. The Kaleel Jamison Consulting Group, Inc. (www.kjcg.com).

Patterson, K., Grenny, J. McMillan, R., & Switzler, A. (2012). *Crucial conversations: Tools for talking when stakes are high*. New York, NY: McGraw-Hill.

Schein, E.H. (2013). The role of leadership in the management of
    organizational transformation and learning. In Carter, L.,
    Sullivan, R.L., Goldsmith, M., Ulrich, D., & Smallwood, N. (Eds.)
    *The change champion's field guide: Strategies and tools for leading
    change in your organization.* 2nd edition. San Francisco, CA:
    Wiley, 595-602,

Shephard, H.A. (1975). Rules of thumb for change agents. *OD
    Practitioner.* 1-5.

Weisbord, M.R. (2012). Productive workplaces: Dignity, meaning and
    community in the 21st century. 3rd edition. San Francisco, CA:
    Jossey-Bass.

Diversity Management in Specialized Settings: Nonprofit and Faith-Based Organizations, Schools, Communities, and Government Agencies

Jim Henkelman-Bahn, Jacqueline Bahn-Henkelman

INTRODUCTION

Diversity Work Is Diversity Work

This chapter, concentrating on diversity work in nonprofit and faith-based organizations, schools, communities, and government agencies, will highlight the uniqueness of each of these kinds of organizations as it relates to leveraging differences and creating conditions that support them in achieving their mission. We begin with the acknowledgement that appreciating and managing diversity is essentially the same, whether the work is being done in a corporation, a nonprofit, a community organization, or a school setting. Diversity work is diversity work.

Individuals who make up organizations in specialized settings share the same multiple identities as other organizations, yet due to their social mission they may represent a broader range of human differences and social identities than for-profit organizations. It is precisely the richness of diversity within nonprofit settings that provides opportunities for driving organizational excellence. The traditional approach has treated differences as hierarchical, with some dimensions considered up or down, good or bad, or better than others. Embracing the simultaneity of race, gender, and class in organizations leads to identifying, untangling, and changing the differential impact of everyday practices in organizations. Whether the system is for-profit or nonprofit, it can and undoubtedly will experience challenges and tensions inherent in human diversity (Holvino, 2010).

Historically, there always has been and will continue to be misunderstandings, denial, and/or resistance in dealing with issues related to inequalities (or perceived inequalities) within our culture. When an individual or group within an organization believes that inequalities exist due to their unique difference, they often feel sub-optimized, and the organization needs to address the issue if it expects to maximize the input from all people and groups and optimize contributions for the betterment of the organization.

As we become a more multicultural society, the ethos of diversity and inclusion continues to be challenged at the individual, group, organizational, and national level. As a result, the role of diversity professionals to champion this effort becomes even more critical. We will draw on our experience as external consultants in framing this chapter, with the belief that all the skills and approaches discussed in other chapters of this book will be valuable and applicable to the work of diversity professionals dealing with nonprofit and faith-based organizations, schools, communities, and government agencies. We will seek to provide a heightened awareness of the uniqueness of these organizations and agencies, to enable diversity professionals who work in this arena to be more effective.

Since the examples in this chapter come from our professional experience as consultants, facilitators, or trainers working in these specialized settings, we acknowledge that our multiple and intersecting identities influence the framework presented, and we invite you to juxtapose them against your own experiences and perspectives.

The first section will set the stage for a discussion of nonprofit organizations and nongovernmental organizations (NGOs), then we will turn your attention to faith-based organizations. The next section examines the uniqueness of school organizations and will be followed by sections on community and government agencies. We end this chapter with some considerations for diversity professionals as they do their work.

Uniqueness of Nonprofit Organizations
The Bottom Line: A Mission to Achieve
By definition, nonprofit organizations are value-driven; they are motivated by a sense of mission and embrace a triple bottom line: people, planet, and profit (Elkington, 2004). From this holistic orientation, diversity can be a compelling force, and the complexity of human differences can just as easily create challenges that make it difficult for a nonprofit organization to become one truly committed to advancing the integration of diversity and inclusion goals into its mission.

Often, the mission of a nonprofit organization is aligned with the principles of social justice that work toward the elimination of oppression and other "isms" or destructive beliefs to create full and equal participation of all groups in society (Jagpal & Laskowski, 2016). As a result of this alignment, it is logical to assume that nonprofit organizations would be able to more effectively manage diversity and have inclusive practices. However, this is not always the case. The following example of a consultation illustrates how an organization driven by values and a deep sense of mission found itself struggling to have its membership be more diverse.

• • •

Several years ago we were hired as external consultants to help a coalition become a more inclusive organization. The coalition had been founded to provide leadership in the identification and infusion of gender equity in all U.S. educational programs and processes. The coalition was proud of the success they experienced in achieving this original mission. However, over time the coalition's mandate had grown to include parallel equity concerns, including but not limited to age, disability, national origin, race, religion, and sexual orientation. Their presenting issue was that they were unable to sustain a broadly based, diverse organization of members dedicated to achieving their broader mandate. Most of the membership in the organization was female and white. Despite efforts at programming and recruiting for a broader membership, males and people of color who joined often did not remain members. The coalition wanted our help in achieving representational diversity.

Working together with the board of directors and the officers of the coalition, we formed a small internal team of members to do the following:

- ✓ The internal team will operate as anthropologists to uncover the true nature of the culture of the organization.
- ✓ The internal team will discover what aspects of the basic culture encouraged men and people of color to be active in the organization and what aspects of that culture were barriers to men and people of color staying in the organization.
- ✓ The team and consultants will interview current as well as former members who are male and people of color.
- ✓ The team and consultants will jointly identify the themes about the culture that are conducive to and/or a barrier to inclusion of men and people of color in the organization.
- ✓ The team and consultants will schedule interviews several months in advance to provide the basis for a presentation of results to the annual conference.
- ✓ The team and consultants will prepare and offer a report at the annual conference regarding the themes that surface from all interviews.
- ✓ The team will then brainstorm actions for enhancing the diversity of the coalition.

A number of themes emerged from the analysis. One significant theme was that most members, past and present, currently viewed the organization as being a "dominant white female culture," even though the coalition had no intention of being a "closed club." Several males reported experiencing what they perceived to be male-bashing by some organization members as well as by some conference speakers and workshop presenters. The experiences of some women of color caused them to believe that the issues of women of color were not considered as important as the issues of white women.

In this nonprofit organization, membership was voluntary. The volunteers' livelihood did not depend on them staying in their positions in the organization. When they believed their passions, energy, and contributions were not being valued, they took their membership elsewhere. That was what was happening in this coalition for males and women of color.

The culture's practices, policies, and procedures were heavily influenced and informed by white females. In order to achieve full representation of the diverse identities represented in the organization, these practices, policies, and procedures would need to be reviewed and reassessed. The coalition struggled with whether its original mission of infusing gender equity into the schools would be diluted by putting more emphasis on other dimensions of diversity in its programming. Despite this concern, the coalition moved forward, and one of its first actions was to form a male-issues task force to promote male equity at future conferences and to ensure that presentations did not denigrate males. As the organization began addressing the identified themes from the study, the number of males and women of color participating increased, and the organization moved toward the goal of representational diversity.

As in this case, it is often important for external consultants to help the client explore whether their original mandate/vision is being met or needs to be revisited. Or, whether the practices used to reach the original vision hamper natural growth and the broadening of healthy outcomes.

Often Volunteer-Based

Organizations in the nonprofit sector make use of large numbers of volunteers in order to carry out their mission. The Corporation for National and Community Service (2016) reported that during 2015 in the United States, 24.9% of residents volunteered at a value of $184 billion. Frequently the number of volunteers in nonprofits far exceeds the number of paid staff, and organizations have to vigorously recruit and motivate these volunteers in order to succeed. One of the currencies of power that organizations have with their paid staff is the ability to give or take away the employee's current livelihood. The nonprofit organization does not have this same influence with volunteers and therefore lacks the same level of control over them. Volunteers are generally attracted to, and feel a strong connection to, the primary mission of the nonprofit organization, which is what attracted them to the organization in the first place. Volunteers who come to believe that their own perspectives are not represented may be quicker than paid staff to leave the organization and seek other organizations that do represent their views. In other words, volunteers are more likely to vote with their feet—and to do it with less provocation than paid staff. So, when the passion that brings these diverse volunteers to the organization withers, they leave and the organization is diminished.

The following illustration of how strong the conflict can be between values held by different volunteer members of a nonprofit organization will help to emphasize the kind of effect such conflicts can have. In a suburb of Washington, D.C., community leaders had spent years coming to an agreement for a physical restructuring plan for the "dying downtown" area. Once that plan was completed, these community leaders agreed that there was a need to expand the current, mostly white male leadership in the community to leadership that would be more representative of this richly diverse community. A small nonprofit community leadership training program was designed to help grassroots leaders from various community groups become more influential within their own groups and neighborhoods and to prepare them for broader community leadership positions. We were two of the people asked to join as members of the down-town-restructuring group to develop the training program. When we approached several grassroots groups about opportunities for a member or two from their own community to attend the leadership training program, they requested that the training we were designing be focused on their internal groups. While those needs were validated, the planning group was persistent in insisting that the training include men and women, blacks, Hispanics, whites, members of various immigrant groups, and participants of different ages. The leadership team had labored hard to develop their mission statement and a program to support that mission. However, when they were in the process of writing their nonprofit incorporation papers and bylaws, an interesting conflict developed.

The dispute arose around the wording of the nondiscrimination clause in the organization's proposed bylaws. The model bylaws from which the group was working contained out-of-date language prohibiting discrimination based on "sexual preference." Several members of the leadership team insisted on changing the wording to "sexual orientation," in order to make the language consistent with current research and understanding. This brought the issue to the attention of a male African American volunteer working with the group who held a strong religious belief that homosexuality was a preference and was sinful. He immediately objected to including the language of sexual orientation in the bylaws and threatened to leave the organization if the term "sexual orientation" replaced "sexual preference." Some members were inclined to let him leave, since they felt strongly about the inclusion of the revised wording. It was a test of the very values that were motivating the volunteers to form the organization. In this case, several members of the team took it upon themselves to work with the dissenting member in an effort to have him understand their concept of sexual orientation. One of the Latina members shared with the male who was opposing the language change that her brother was gay, and how she accepted him, and how not recognizing the language change was personally painful to her and disrespectful to her brother. Personalizing the issue was a powerful intervention. In the final analysis, this effort was successful; the term "sexual preference" was changed to "sexual orientation" in the bylaws, and the team continued its work with a broader understanding of the term as it was used in their bylaws and in contemporary scholarship.

Organizations are sometimes faced with a decision between losing a valued volunteer and being out of concert with their mission of inclusion. Although in this example the dispute was resolved, such conflicts can force both the organization and the volunteer to make difficult choices based on their value systems that do not always end in a mutually agreed-upon resolution.

Using Differences to Enhance the Work

When working in consulting and training settings, it is important to always be alert about ways in which differences can be used creatively to enhance the consultation or training. This can take many forms; the competence needed is to be open and alert to the opportunities that present themselves. One such example occurred when, in a week-long diversity training session, one of the participants, who was deaf, was using a small transmitter to enhance her participation. Each time someone spoke, she invited the person to speak into the transmitter, enabling her to hear what was being said. The facilitators noted that this was working as long as hearing participants spoke one at a time. But if the dialogue jumped quickly from one person to another or people spoke over each other, the deaf participant could not track what was happening. The facilitators suggested using the transmitter as a "talking stick" when anyone wanted to talk. This slowed the process down for everyone. As the week progressed, the facilitators checked in on how this was working. Early on, though everyone was willing to accommodate the deaf person, there was some annoyance at the process. However, soon it became one of the norms of the group, and in a short time the participants came to see the value of the talking stick. Slowing the process created a climate where each person's contributions were well thought out and taken more seriously. In the closing feedback, there was agreement from the group that using the talking stick was no longer a burden of accommodation but a benefit gained in the quality of the dialogue.

Compensation

The disparity between the salaries of diversity professionals in for-profit organizations and nonprofit organizations can be illustrated by a study that examined the compensation for chief diversity officers, or CDOs (Association of American Medical Colleges, 2012). Every corporate CDO received basic compensation in excess of $150,000 per year, with more than 70% reporting annual income levels above $200,000. By contrast, 67% of higher-education CDOs reported receiving salaries below $150,000, and only 14% received salaries above $200,000. Diversity professionals can expect compensation at substantially lower levels in the nonprofit world. The compensation rates for diversity consultants working in nonprofits are similarly depressed. As noted, during one year volunteers contributed time and effort valued at $184 billion (Corporation for National and Community Service, 2016). This statistic includes volunteer hours provided by consultants working for a reduced rate or even pro bono out of commitment to an organization's mission.

In general, pay scales for diversity consultants in nonprofit organizations—internal and external consultants—are lower than pay scales found in the corporate world; some make as little as one-half or one-third of their corporate colleagues. Recently we sought to include a diversity consultant colleague in a contract we were pursuing to help a community's efforts to deepen the race dialogue. This colleague's daily rate far exceeded the rate the client could afford, but in this case our colleague was willing to do the work pro bono. In general, diversity consultants prefer doing pro bono work to lowering their fees, as doing the former does not devalue the integrity of their professional work. This practice benefits the client that cannot afford appropriately compensated consultants and allows seasoned professionals to contribute their services to organizations whose missions they wish to support. Alternatively, seasoned diversity consultants have donated their time to nonprofit organizations and received a charity donation letter for tax purposes. In a capitalist society, diversity consultants, like other types of consultants, do not always have the luxury of doing work pro bono, and so they experience the reality of working in a competitive market. This makes their level of expertise important. The complex work of diversity demands professionals with deep knowledge of social science theories, seasoned judgment, visionary thinking, strong business acumen, strategic thinking, and cross-functional capacity. These skill sets are necessary for diversity consultants who work in for-profit or nonprofit settings. Recall that diversity work is diversity work. However, the reality is that most nonprofit organizations are not positioned to compensate competitively for these skill sets.

There is another factor that gets in the way of competitive rates being charged for diversity work. At times delving into diversity issues is not valued by leadership, and they contract for having it done as a result of some type of pressure, whether the pressure is internal organizational pressure from their employee base or external regulatory and compliance obligations. This lack of commitment may prevent leadership from fully engaging in contracting services for a seasoned diversity consultant, or they may want the consultant to offer "the sun and the moon" without providing leadership support and financial resources.

We have known and/or been privileged to work with and learn from many diversity consultants and practitioners. The rate they charge varies, and just like other kinds of consultants and practitioners working in nonprofits, many gravitate to the work primarily out of a sense of personal commitment to the values the organization represents rather than the numeric value of the compensation being offered, and they may accept a lower rate for that reason.

Diversity Consultant's Role in Working with Board of Directors, CEO, and Staff

Nonprofit boards of directors are similar to for-profit boards of directors. For-profit corporations are owned by stakeholders, generate money for the owners, and measure success by profit, and board members are usually paid and can make sizeable incomes, whereas nonprofit organizations are owned by the public and serve the public, and success is meeting the needs of the public. Board members are usually unpaid volunteers, and if they are paid, they make reasonable, not excessive income (McNamara, 2008). The major benefit of becoming a nonprofit corporation is obtaining tax-exempt status. The boards of directors in both types of corporations are responsible for effective governance. Likewise, some boards of directors in both types are referred to as working boards. In our experience being involved in several struggling small nonprofits, where the level of financial assets varied and was not always adequate to pay for sufficient staff to perform the ongoing duties of the organization, the work of the board expanded into assisting with daily operational duties. At times this "help" was perceived by staff members as micromanagement. In addition, it limited the time and energy these nonprofit volunteer board members needed to focus on development and governance. Helping the organizations sort through, prioritize, and decide on the most effective distribution of the varied functions of the board and staff is a very important function of the consultant.

Another very important role of the consultant is to pay attention to the diversity of the board. Even when a consultant is brought into an organization where the presenting problem is not identified as a "diversity issue," he or she needs to be hyper-vigilant about where those issues may be present and unsettling within the organization. That vigilance should begin with how the board itself is viewing the value of diversity and if that attitude is actually part of the problem. What are the diversity values proclaimed by the organization? Does the board itself represent those values? Does the workforce itself represent them? What are the messages about diversity that are imparted to the client base?

In U.S. culture particularly, diversity issues are rarely absent from the mindset of the workforce. Diversity consultants need to be fully alert to how, when, and where they might surface and be prepared to help an organization, beginning with its board, address them openly in an effort to allow individuals and groups to be heard and to work toward mutual representation and respect.

Contracting Clarity

When working with an inquiring client, entering into a contract that is precise and actually workable is critical, time-consuming, and sometimes not as easy as one might think. For example, an individual or a group of people within an organization who are dissatisfied with the performance of a board chair, the CEO, or other person/group may reach out to a consultant because they have failed to influence leadership to rectify the perceived needed change.

On one occasion, after spending enough time to begin relationship-building and to really understand the perspective of the initiating group—clarifying precisely what the problem was, exploring whether the issue was perceived the same way by others in the organization, and exploring the possibility that diversity issues could be involved—it was disheartening to learn that the inquiring party did not have the authority to speak for the organization or access to funds to pay for a consultant, let alone the authority to implement a plan. Of course not every inquiry turns into a contract, but it was a good reminder for us to clarify lines of authority up front in any negotiated contract (Block, 2011).

Sometimes the authority within an organization lies outside of the formal leadership structure. Many smaller nonprofit organizations with short tenures tend to be legacy-based organizations. This legacy is based on the vision, beliefs, wishes, dreams, or practices of the person who founded the organization. The cultural perspective generated by this founder shapes the organization accordingly from the beginning. This "legacy person" may function within the organization as the CEO, a staff member, and/or a member of the board of directors. It is critical to assess how much influence this person has had in the organization and how effective or ineffective that influence continues to be. A founder may continue to exert his or her influence long after the organization has grown beyond the need to receive it, as illustrated in the following example.

While contracting with one nonprofit organization to conduct a strategic-planning process involving diversity issues, it became clear that the key issue in the organization involved succession planning for the CEO-founder. After several decades of leadership, the CEO-founder of the organization was having difficulty letting go. He was caught in the dilemma of how to retire and still continue to influence the future of the organization. He did not favor doing a strategic-planning process that might threaten his legacy.

Some people were in agreement with the way the organization had been run under the founder's watch, but many others were eager to create a strategic plan that could generate significant change. The consultants pointed out how problematic it would be for a group of people who were not top management to try to proceed with a strategic plan without buy-in from the CEO-founder and those who supported him. It was recommended that a first step would entail broad analysis of input from all levels of the organization and reporting out that data in hopes that a more informed analysis could help uncover and deal with underlying issues that were getting in the way of the strategic-plan decision.

Networks and Affiliations

Some nonprofit organizations serve as umbrellas for other affiliated member organizations, which allows these member organizations to network. This networking is a strength across much of the non-profit world. However, it also can work against the accomplishment of diversity goals. Each of the individual organizations is values-driven, and the values between them may conflict. For example, one umbrella organization for women's rights consisted of some member organizations that strongly supported reproductive rights for women, but it also included one member organization that strongly opposed them. The strong, values-driven stance of this one member organization got in the way of women's reproductive rights being addressed and created significant values-driven conflict within the umbrella organization. Of course this conflict concerning women's reproductive rights is a societal conflict that cannot be resolved in the umbrella organization. That societal reality becomes the background for the conflict within the umbrella organization.

Uniqueness of Faith-Based Organizations

Faith-based organizations are a unique category of nonprofit organizations. Their bottom line is highly values-based, with the focus on worship and service. The compensation for those involved in a consulting role may be commensurate with those in other nonprofit organizations. Generally, local mainstream churches are affiliated with a regional body, e.g., a synod, conference, diocese, or presbytery. Differing regional bodies are more affluent than others, and some are able to support a church's request for funds to hire consultants. Some religious systems maintain networks of consultants and/ or have staff within denominational offices that are trained to make organization-development interventions. Other churches' regional bodies simply do not have the funds to do that, and at times churches within those regional bodies struggle to simply meet their ongoing financial obligations out of congregants' donations and have little or no money to pay a consultant.

Volunteers do much of the work of these organizations, and congregations come to expect pro bono consultant work, but while they often do get quality services from their own members, who share the values of their religious faith, at other times the congregant volunteer does not have the expertise to fully address the problem, or as a congregant may be too close to the issue to be objective, or does not have enough volunteer hours available to adequately address the problem.

In addition to congregations seeking professional help from within their own member base, they may believe they can solve their problems simply by being faithful to their beliefs. This can also mean that faith-based communities may be in deep conflict before they are willing to consider bringing in an external consultant. At the denominational or judicatory level the work of a consultant is likely to be more clearly understood and valued. There are a couple of other characteristics of faith-based organizations that deserve particular attention and are discussed in the following sections.

The Special Role of the Clergy

It is critical for diversity consultants to understand an important distinction between clergy and heads of other nonprofit organizations. In many faith-based organizations the members hold clergy to their own highest perceived code of ethics and expect that clergy men and women can, would, or should do no wrong. If the clergy are perceived as being or doing wrong, the feelings are often exaggerated beyond what would be projected on other leaders. Another complexity to explore is that in some denominations, while the clergy man or woman is perceived as the faith-based leader, the congregation or a subset of it is the decision-making body.

A consultation that we facilitated in a congregation of a mainline denomination over a period of about nine months may illustrate some of these issues. Although there was no mention of a diversity issue in the presenting problem, it became clear that indeed there was a diversity issue deeply imbedded in what was being presented.

When a member of the board of deacons of the congregation contacted us, he presented the problem as one of conflict between the pastor and the director of the music program. An issue between two people holding these positions is not uncommon; in fact, conflicts are often projected at the interpersonal level. Music programs and pastoral programs do not always have the same aim, and both generally have a strong following. Music programs sometimes want more of the church's emphasis to be on performance, while the pastors may be focusing on something like serving the poor in the community. Knowing that all conflicts have multiple perspectives, and to ensure that we had access to both of the parties mentioned in the stated conflict, we requested and were granted direct access to both the pastor and the minister of music. When inquiring further about which levels of the organization the contract included, we learned that this local church had a congregational form of government—i.e., the congregation itself had the highest level of authority. We proposed, and they agreed, that the contract would be with the congregation, and we would have access to the members of the congregation as well as the pastor and the director of music, for the purpose of "conflict transformation" rather than "conflict resolution" or "conflict management."

In our first face-to-face interview with our initial contact person and several other deacons, we learned that the current pastor was lesbian and the predominant membership was heterosexual. We were informed that the church was part of a denomination that welcomed gays and lesbians, and they did not see the issue of sexual orientation as part of the conflict. We registered this perception and kept our eyes and ears open to test their assumption.

The consultation consisted of several action steps. First, the pastor and the minister of music were interviewed so we could hear their perspectives. Second, we interviewed selected members of the congregation, and as the consultation proceeded, the opportunity was provided for any congregant who was interested to also offer their perspective. Members of the choir and the board of deacons were interviewed to gain their groups' perspective. Educational meetings about conflict were held to help members become aware of their own reaction to conflict. Our aim was to keep the intervention as transparent and informative as possible while respecting individual confidences, and we reported our findings first to the groups that had been interviewed and finally to the whole congregation.

Early in the intervention, the minister of music decided to resign without explanation rather than continue to participate with the efforts to resolve the conflict. His departure made the process more complicated, and the deacons, in an effort to heal some of the anger and pain throughout the congregation, implored us to continue our consultation. The focus shifted primarily to the pastor's behavior. Our probing continued and more perspectives were shared. We now learned that the pastor had indeed acted in certain ways that caused displeasure not only for the music director, but for some other members of the congregation as well. In the absence of the minister of music, the pastor became the lightning rod for unmet expectations, both realistic and unrealistic. The pastor began to pay attention to the congregation's feedback and agreed to some individual coaching sessions. Those sessions were held away from the church, and with the help of some videotaped simulations, she was able to acknowledge her own contributions to the problems and made commitments to change some of her own behavior.

The depth of the issue stemming from views on sexual orientation began to emerge as the consultation progressed. Prior to the current pastor's presence, the church had made a clear commitment to being open and affirming to the LGBT community. When a previous pastor was invited to serve the congregation, the search committee knew he was gay but did not announce it to the congregation before the pastoral role began. His presence in the congregation, and the fact that his sexual orientation had been withheld, led to conflict that divided the broader community. Rocks were actually thrown through windows. When the church voted to support the pastor and welcome gays and lesbians as part of the congregation, a minority of the members left the church.

At the time of our consultation there were about equal numbers of heterosexuals and homosexuals joining the church, and LGBT individuals were in some of the responsible positions in the church. The deeper issue finally emerged. Some of the heterosexual members were concerned, not about being open and welcoming to LGBT individuals, but about the church becoming one in which heterosexuals were the minority.

The dominant issue all along had been the fear of a shift of power, but LGBT individuals made it clear that they truly wanted to be members of a diverse church community and were not interested in assuming all the governance power. The congregation reached a new level of awareness about what it means to embrace an identity group that has historically been oppressed, and the work became how to make the transition from a church that claims to be welcoming of others to one that not only affirms that diversity but is willing to be influenced by all members.

Effects of Strongly Held Values

Faith-based organizations are driven by their strongly held values and beliefs. As is true for other nonprofit organizations, those values and beliefs can be a driving force toward creating a more truly diverse organization, or they can prevent organizations from becoming empowering for all. The following intervention briefly illustrates an effort that capitalized on diversity values to truly bring a marginalized group into the mainstream. This intervention took place in a regional judicatory of a mainline Protestant denomination.

The regional judicatory had a strong affirmative action program that had blossomed out of the civil rights movement a number of decades before, so the judicatory was pained to acknowledge that the number of black women in positions of power was small. Strong black male pastors in the predominantly black churches tended to hold tight control of the leadership. Women were valued for their supportive service but were not encouraged to become church leaders, and many of them believed that their presence and/or involvement posed a threat to the male pastors. There were very few opportunities for black women to experiment in leadership roles and prepare themselves to move into positions of power and influence.

A program of leadership training and empowerment specifically for black women was proposed. Black women from different congregations joined forces to explore the formation of a yearlong empowerment program. A white consultant took a behind-the-scenes coaching role to help design the program and make the connections to obtain funding for the program. However, the up-front leadership of the program came from one black woman, who provided the energy and focus for the program's success.

A strong learning community developed as the women met monthly for leadership training. This learning community became the basis of support and empowerment for the women. Four separate weeklong experiential training events were delivered by a training organization that specialized in applied behavioral sciences. While the training teams were diverse, the key leaders selected for the training program were black females in order to emphasize the empowerment possibilities of this social identity group. This highly successful program turned commitment into reality.

Throughout this intervention, the regional judicatory of the church was able to act on its strong values to reduce racism and sexism in the church and empower a group of black women to blossom into important church leaders. Within a couple of years, several of the women moved into top leadership positions in both the regional and national church. It was clear that members of the group were empowered to take these roles. One region of this denomination had moved a step closer to becoming a racial- and gender-diverse church. However, this issue continues across faith-based organizations.

Women in black Protestant churches in the U.S. outnumber men by more than two to one, yet in positions of authority and responsibility, the ratio is reversed (Lowen, 2017). Though women are gradually entering the ministry as bishops, pastors, deacons, and elders, many men and women still resist and fear that development. Decades ago

Harris stated that sexism against black women should be addressed by black theology and the black church (1990), but in spite of this call to action, the problem persists. Full acceptance of the talents of all persons is important within each faith community. Another important level for addressing differences across a variety of faith communities is described in the following section.

The Power of Interfaith Efforts

Faith communities tend to reflect groups of the same culture and race. However, bringing together people from all faiths in the community can be a powerful process for creating understanding across differences. One suburban Washington, D.C., community responded to violence in the community by doing just that. Over a period of time, several hate crimes had occurred in the community. A Jewish synagogue had a swastika and other denigrating messages painted on its door, and some actual violent acts were imposed on transgender persons. In another incident, an Episcopal church had a banner out front welcoming Latino/a immigrants to mass, but immediately after the 2016 presidential election, someone defaced it with the words "For Whites Only."

The county executive had the foresight to initiate having all county religious communities join together to address acts of violence such as these. Leaders from different faiths formed a Faith Leaders Response Team, and as they worked together, their sense of community broadened beyond what they had experienced previously. This interfaith response team created the capacity to respond immediately when any hate crimes occurred. For example, within hours of the desecration of the synagogue, a group of various faith leaders, including Muslims, Christians, and Jews, showed up to offer their support, and they again showed up to support the Episcopal church that had the "For Whites Only" sign replacing their welcoming banner. These acts of support are important in creating a safe and inclusive community.

When it was decided that the "dialogue on race" needed to go to a deeper level, three large group gatherings were arranged, at which the faith leaders who were already connected could all participate in the race dialogue under the title *Faith Community Working Group Interracial/Interfaith Dialogue on Racism: Seeing the Divine in Each Other* (International Cultural Center, 2016). Approximately a hundred faith leaders participated in each of the gatherings. The ability to bring together a strong interfaith group for this dialogue was enhanced by the existence of the earlier community-building. It is often difficult to reach across faith communities, but the power of the dialogue was clearly enhanced by having the mix. For example, in one small group of six people attending an interfaith dialogue session that we facilitated, there were two male imams, one female rabbi, one Latina Baha'i, one African American male member of the community's first responders, and one white Methodist Christian clergy-woman. Respectful dialogue across interfaith groups was achieved. Those present pledged to return to their individual faith communities and continue expanding the dialogue on racism.

Uniqueness of School Organizations

Schools are similar to other organizations we have discussed in that they are also motivated by their beliefs and values, i.e., education. Their bottom line is "an educated society." Most teachers and staff remain motivated to do the best job they can, even in less than perfect conditions. School systems employ professional staff and many use volunteers to support the professionals. The customer or client for schools is not as transparent as for many other organizations. The immediate customers are the students attending the school, but the ultimate customers are the parents and the general society.

Multiple Constituencies or Stakeholders

Schools are complex organizations that often can become highly bureaucratic—especially in large school systems. In the United States there are clearly multiple constituencies that are critical; state and local school boards, central office staff, teachers and other professionals, and the students and parents are all important stakeholders. In addition, federal guidelines and entitlement mandates influence some decision-making. When intervening around any diversity issue, not only do the students' and parents' values surface, frequently the whole community feels impacted and gets involved. Differences between different social identity groups often become a point of contention. For example, in the U.S., the dilemma and public discourse that resulted from the request of transgender children to use the bathroom of the gender with which they identify illustrate how many stakeholders beside the students and parents in the community become involved. Once the school board was involved, the courts became involved, and the entire community and nation became engaged. A micro-view from another school system of what it is like to work with multiple constituencies is provided in the following example.

The setting for this example is a middle school in a large suburban school system in the U.S. The school is located in what had been until recently an affluent, primarily white neighborhood of highly educated and actively involved parents. At the time of the intervention, as is typical, white parents who were most active and comfortable in this setting controlled the parent-teacher-student association (PTSA).

As the demographics of the neighborhood changed, and more African American, Hispanic, and Asian American families settled in this area, the disparity between the racial and ethnic makeup of the parents involved with the school and the diversity of the neighborhood increased. In order to address this situation, a new African American principal at the middle school encouraged the formation and development of a separate parents' group of African American parents. This provided the opportunity for African American parents to join together in a productive way. The same opportunity was provided for Hispanics. The smaller number of Asian American families did not form a separate parents' group, and their lack of engagement created concern. In an attempt to develop a more fully engaged school community, an intervention was designed to integrate the three groups. The first step of the intervention was to bring the leaders of the African American and Hispanic parents, referred to as parent advocates for their social identity groups, onto the executive committee of the PTSA. Then the PTSA executive committee, including the parent advocates for the African American and Hispanic parents, decided to conduct a joint meeting of the three groups in a diversity workshop. The diversity workshop was the beginning of the long journey toward increased understanding, acceptance, and valuing of the diversity of the community. In this case, the process of differentiation and recognition of each group was necessary before the critical work involving the collective diverse constituencies could be effective.

Uniqueness of Working at the Community Level

Diversity work at the community level certainly involves the same issues that are present in other segments of our society. Frequently the work at the community level can be addressed through nonprofit or faith-based organizations, as we have touched on in earlier examples. There are, however, a few additional aspects of communities that are important to take into consideration as the professional consultant tackles diversity issues at this level. Perhaps the most important aspect to consider is that communities are much more amorphous than a single organization. Community structures, roles, and boundaries are not easily identifiable and may appear loose or ill-defined, and communities vary in their concepts of leadership and the sources of authority. These aspects are discussed in the following sections.

Loose Community Boundaries and Structures

As the chapter on diversity diagnosis in this text points out, it is often difficult to know where to begin to intervene with the appropriate methodologies for inclusion, especially in a community setting. The loose boundaries and lack of a visible, clear structure make it very difficult, if not impossible, to work with an entire community, regardless of size. Most often, diversity professionals work through community-based organizations, such as the local government, the schools or churches, or one of the many other civic organizations that comprise the civil society. However, whatever the choice, there is always the difficulty that working through one organization will shape whatever intervention or work is done in a way that rules out other groups, options, and opportunities.

A community-organizing approach can be used to help communities fully embrace valuing and leveraging differences. Community organizing is particularly effective in confronting specific issues of injustice against a segment of the community. The work of the community organizer is quite different from the usual role of the diversity practitioner in an organization, but it is possible to use the skills of the practitioner to frame a diversity program and/or intervention in a community.

The following description shows how one group of citizens working with diversity professionals addressed the issues in one community with rapidly changing demographics—from being a predominantly white, upper-middle-class community to one that included many African Americans, Hispanics, and Asian Americans. This initiative to create a thriving multicultural community occurred in Silver Spring, Maryland, an inner suburb of Washington, D.C. As happens in many inner suburbs, the downtown area had significantly declined after earlier prosperity. After a number of years of false starts, an economic redevelopment plan was formulated, and by the turn of the century, the process of renewal of the physical space downtown was underway.

The economic redevelopment had effectively made use of a citizens' advisory committee, and as the work of that committee was coming to a close, some of the members became concerned about how to develop leadership that would be more representative of the increasing diversity in the community. One of the major issues was that different ethnic and racial groups, including new immigrants to the United States, were settling in Silver Spring, but the power structure remained mostly white. In addition, the separate racial and ethnic groups tended to be isolated from each other. Concerned citizens decided they would try to rectify this, but the question was how to proceed. They established an informal committee to decide how to shape Silver Spring in a way that would put a human face on the physical and economic redevelopment. The committee represented some of the diversity of Silver Spring, with white, African American, and Hispanic members. They collaborated with a diversity professional, meeting over weekly breakfasts for many months to determine their direction. There were many ideas—and plenty of conflicts—before they were ready to proceed. The following are some of the questions that needed to be addressed:

- ✓ What is the vision of a diversely empowered Silver Spring?
- ✓ What kind of intervention would be appropriate for addressing the issues involved?
- ✓ What kind of structure or organization would be appropriate to carry out any intervention?
- ✓ Should the group work through an existing organization, or establish a new, separate nonprofit organization?
- ✓ Should the work be primarily empowering individuals, or advocacy?

The informal committee decided to focus on creating a diversely empowered community by connecting the existing leadership and the emerging leadership of various specific ethnic and racial groups. It was decided that this would require leadership training, which raised a set of additional questions:

- ✓ Who should be the target for the leadership training?
- ✓ Should the focus of the training be on the grassroots leadership of specific ethnic or racial groups?
- ✓ Should whites be included in the training program?

Behind each question were differing, strongly held opinions and many pros and cons. When members of the group finally reached a consensus, the decision was made to form an independent nonprofit organization, originally called the Silver Spring Community Leadership Initiative (SSCLI), with the following mission statement:

> Our mission is to provide training for community members of diverse backgrounds in order to develop skills and awareness needed to share power and build relationships that cross racial, class, and cultural lines.

A pilot experiential training program was developed to bring together leaders and potential leaders from all segments of the population, including both people with perceived power in the community and those who perceived themselves without power. This pilot program tested both content and methodology for the training during four daylong Saturday sessions that took place over a two-month period. The participants in the training program represented many of the diverse segments of the community. It was decided that the trainers/facilitators for this pilot program would be selected to represent gender and racial diversity. The volunteer team of facilitators working with the pilot consisted of an African American female, a white female, a white male, and a black male from the Caribbean.

The success of the pilot program led to the development of a nine-month leadership-training program designed to develop both the awareness and skills of participants seeking to make a difference as leaders in the Silver Spring community. This program involved three two-day retreats, monthly daylong Saturday meetings, and one evening meeting per month. All of the sessions involved training components delivered by staff as well as participants, which supported participants' individual passion to develop and implement community-enhancing projects. A unique and critical component of the program was the concept of being a learning community, which in this case meant that the group had to continuously self-assess its individual and group performance as well as help determine its ongoing life and future. The program had numerous successes on its way to achieving the vision of a diversely empowered Silver Spring. At the individual level, it was interesting to note that one of the Latina participants moved quickly into leadership positions, first on the school board of Montgomery County and later on the county council. Within a short period of time, success at the community-wide level was noted, with the various advisory committees reflecting the diverse demographics of the community.

Attitudes Toward Leadership

During the development of the Silver Spring Community Leadership Initiative, an interesting cultural difference in the way leadership was viewed was highlighted. When the leadership-training program was first announced, several Latinos/as reacted very negatively to the word "leadership." As do many other group-oriented societies and cultures, some Hispanic societal groups see the words "leader" or "leadership" in terms of something that is imposed on them. The words represent the oppressor. For them, a true leader is not someone who sets out to be a leader; a true leader is one who arises from within to carry out the will of the group (Bordas, 2013). Given this perspective, the source of authority for the leader lies in the group, not the individual, whereas in much of the United States' society, the leader is seen as the individual who is self-directed and seeks a leadership role. This represents a much more individual-oriented perspective. In the United States and Europe, a strong emphasis is placed on individualism—consequently, the word "leader" carries a more positive connotation there (Lewis, 2016).

In the end, the Silver Spring program was not called a leadership-training program; it was called the Community Empowerment and Involvement Program, to have a better chance of attracting Hispanic and other group-oriented segments of the society. A critical takeaway for any practitioner is to first ask enough, and the right, questions to understand the culture of the client system. Understanding how leader/leadership is perceived by different ethnic and racial groups within their own culture is a primary indicator of what kinds of cultural norms and possible conflicts you will be facing.

Uniqueness of Government Agencies

Public Service

Government agencies, like other nonprofit organizations, have yet another kind of bottom line from that of the corporate world. They often operate with the triple bottom line that combines standard metrics of financial success with those that measure environmental stewardship and social justice. The 3P approach—People, Planet, and Profits—requires thinking in three dimensions rather than just one (Elkington, 2004). The scope of public organizations' missions are often broader and have a more profound impact than those typically found in the private sector. These organizations are more likely to employ individuals whose values and needs are consistent with the public service mission of the organization (Wright, 2003).

Although there are many denigrating jokes about government work, we have generally observed a dedication to the mission of the agencies that is similar to that found in other nonprofit organizations. Repeatedly, public-sector employees tend to place a lower value on financial rewards and a higher value on helping others than those in private sectors (Boyne, 2002).

Admittedly there are some frustrations working within public sectors; government, especially large federal agencies in the U.S., tends to be slow to change. The 9/11 Commission found that government failures to anticipate and respond to the terrorist attacks on that date were symptoms of the government's broader inability to adapt how it manages problems to the new challenges of the twenty-first century (Ostroff, 2006). Even though there is an awareness that the persons at the top in the federal government are subject to change every four years, it appears that the basic commitment to diversity and inclusion has transcended political changes.

Stability and Change

Even though we have observed that, overall, there is dedication in government agencies to taking diversity and inclusion work quite seriously, holding tightly to one's own values and/or positions can create problems. For example, in one federal agency, we found a number of white male senior managers who prided themselves on being dinosaurs and bragged about their unwillingness to change. This resistance to change created a very hostile environment for women attempting to move into management positions. They were at loggerheads; each side refused to see the other side's perspective.

In actuality the situation was a polarity. Polarities are recurring, arising issues that are not simply problems to solve but rather different poles (points of view) that need to be managed. In situations where there is resistance to change, in government or in any organization, polarity management (Johnson, 1992) is a useful tool/process to effectively address that structural context. The polarity of stability/change would be applicable for the agency described above. The white males were emphasizing the positive (upside) aspects of stability: "comfort and predictability." Top management wanted to move to what they saw as the positive (upside) aspects of change: "energy and creativity." Top management also wanted to move away from the downside of stability: "frustrated and stuck." We pointed out that it was important for top management, who wanted the change, to pay attention to the concerns of the self-professed dinosaurs, who wanted stability and only saw the downside of change—"unknown and chaotic"— before that stability group would be able to see the positive aspects of change. Because the agency had been blocked from moving forward by the gap between top management's emphasis on the positive side of change and the senior white males' emphasis on the negative side of change, the women felt oppressed and discriminated against. Therefore it was important for the diversity professionals to facilitate a process to emphasize the positive sides of both poles, stability and change, and also to acknowledge the downsides of both poles.

Federal Laws and Executive Orders

Diversity initiatives have been a part of the agenda of the federal government ever since the civil rights movement of the 1960s. In the United States, as elsewhere in the world, federal law protects many groups that have experienced discrimination in the workplace. Equal Employment Opportunity (EEO) emanated from the 1964 Civil Rights Act, which prevents unlawful discrimination based on race, color, national origin, religion, and sex. Later, in 1990, the Americans with Disabilities Act (ADA) added protections for the disabled. The Civil Rights Act of 1991 provides further remedies to protect against and to deter intentional discrimination and unlawful harassment in employment. In the federal government, an executive order made it unlawful to discriminate based on sexual orientation. Affirmative action was initiated as a national policy with a programmatic thrust; it takes proactive steps to make EEO law a reality. Recently, many programs designed to promulgate valuing and managing diversity have been initiated in government agencies. Diversity issues were reinforced by President Obama's Executive Order No. 13583 (2011). The Obama administration's government-wide Inclusive Diversity Strategic Plan in 2016 outlined the second phase of implementation of his original executive order establishing a coordinated government-wide initiative to promote diversity and inclusion. The priority is there; the work continues.

It is our experience that precisely because the federal government has been committed to antidiscrimination, and takes the above laws, regulations, and programs seriously, it continues to be a preferred place to work for individuals and identity groups that have experienced discrimination in the workplace. For example, blacks represent 19.7% of government workers while they only represent 14.5% of the total workforce in the U.S. (BlackDemographics.com, 2016). The federal government has been better than some organizations in protecting the rights of LGBT individuals. Also, those with religious differences have been valued for their individuality and contributions and are able to display symbols of their faith, as long as they refrain from proselytizing in the workplace. Protection from discrimination allows people to focus more on their work than on defending their values.

When working with the federal government, we find it is important to clarify affirmative action programs. Misunderstanding these programs can confuse the issues when doing diversity and inclusion interventions. For example, affirmative action plans have often been misunderstood as the creation of target goals—designating specific numbers of underrepresented groups that should be hired. To the contrary, affirmative action plans involve data-driven analysis of the workforce profile to guarantee that underrepresented groups are included in the selection process for hiring, retention, and promotion. When utilized effectively, affirmative action plans support organizations in having a representative workforce, which is helpful in achieving the organizations' mission and business objectives (Wikipedia, 2017).

Implementation of these regulations is not void of difficulties. For example, as diverse groups have entered the workforce, competition for jobs has increased, often pitting one social identity group against another, particularly white males against women and people of color. In contemporary workforces the competition for recognition and promotion has increased across all social identity groups. The following anecdote illustrates this point.

During a recent diversity training in a large government agency, a number of white males were sitting together at lunch and talking about their experiences in the workplace. Although all the members of the group professed to be committed to equal opportunity and the goals of diversity and inclusion, several of them were quite vocal about their sense that their own professional careers had nevertheless suffered as a result. It is sometimes a difficult task for the diversity professional to help white males see that the inequality their long-lived, privileged status has produced will not continue, or should not continue. Should a white male truly experience discrimination, EEO law would also protect him; EEO laws are not specific to any particular race or gender.

Although the processes for termination of a government employee may be slow and tedious, the myth that government employees cannot be fired is false. Parts of the general population, advocacy groups, and concerned citizens are hyper-vigilant about pressing state and federal governments to pass new legislation to protect groups that are subject to discrimination or harassment. For example, even though there is no federal law protecting all the civil rights of LGBT persons, the government has considered LGBT individuals to be covered under gender discrimination laws, and many states do have specific laws that protect the civil rights of LGBT persons. Part of the diversity professional's job is to help people understand their rights and encourage them to bring discrimination issues before the proper authority for protection.

Sensitivity to the Culture

Understanding the setting of the diversity work that is engaged is a critical component of organizational assessment. This becomes especially important if diversity practitioners are working in dramatically different settings and/or in different countries. We have been challenged many times in our international work. We have come to understand that humility is the most important stance to take when in a different culture. Hook, Davis, Owen, Worthington, and Utsey (2013) have developed the concept of cultural humility as a step beyond cultural competence. They define cultural humility as the "ability to maintain an interpersonal stance that is other-oriented (or open to the other) in relation to aspects of cultural identity that are most important to the [person]" (Hook et al., 2013, p. 2). Although it is important to have cultural competence by learning as much as possible about another culture, one person cannot have a thorough understanding of every culture that is different from one's own.

Remaining open to learning is helpful but no guarantee that you will avoid making embarrassing mistakes. However, by being open about your willingness to learn, you will probably be able to manage the outcome better. This has been especially true for us when we worked with the United Nations in developing countries. An example from a training experience in Eritrea illustrates this point.

We were in the first day of a weeklong "Negotiation Skills Across Differences" training with the ministers of the government of Eritrea when we made the statement, "You must be proud of your participation in the civil war with Ethiopia." All of the participants had been part of the resistance that led to the freedom of Eritrea from Ethiopia. However, they did not see their fight for freedom as a civil war, and they let us know that. For them it was a war of independence from Ethiopia. The Western press had reported it as a civil war, and that is what we had accepted as a true perspective. This was quickly corrected and put into appropriate perspective. Rather than becoming defensive about their reaction to our statement, we replied, "Help us understand more about how you saw the fighting with Ethiopia." From this we learned a great deal about our clients' life experience and culture. Just the fact of our inquiring, rather than defending or excusing, enhanced the rapport with the client.

Cultural differences can crop up in simple ways and interfere with understanding. For instance, United States slang is likely not familiar in another culture, and when used the actual meaning may be lost or, worse, misconstrued. Also, jokes outside of their cultural contexts are likely to be misunderstood and may send a message that we do not intend. Humility often comes in handy when sitting in a group of folks from another culture who are all laughing heartily about a joke that someone has told, and we are the only ones sitting there not laughing. We have a tendency to sit there and think or hope, "Surely it was not about us."

Considerations for Diversity Professionals

Exploring Imbedded Diversity Issues

As stated earlier in this chapter, having a clear understanding of what is to be included in the consultation contract is critical, time-consuming, and sometimes difficult. The general aim is to successfully address the concerns spelled out by the contract. While diversity may not even be addressed as part of the presenting problem, the consultant is wise to never overlook the possibility that diversity issues could be imbedded within the presenting problem. The client may assure the consultant, "We have no diversity issues here!" However, the consultant will be wise to inquire about the diversity of the groups represented in the organization and at what levels of the organization they are employed. The consultant should be sure there is input from each diverse group in any data-gathering effort. If the consultant senses that there is an underlying diversity issue, the issue needs to be surfaced. The incident below is one such example.

A few years ago we were hired by a long-term client, a small nonprofit organization, to conduct a team-building retreat. In our preparation process we conducted interviews to determine which issues staff members thought would be useful to address in the retreat. Contrary to the executive director's expectations, during the interviews a number of staff members raised deep concerns related to issues of racism in the organization. When we reflected these data back to the management team before the retreat, they were annoyed, and reminded us that they just wanted us to lead a retreat that would help them get along with and work better with each other. They denied that racism was an issue in the organization. We felt it was unwise, as well as unprofessional, to proceed in offering a team-building retreat without including this diversity issue. The contract needed to be read-dressed, and we recommended that they broaden their agenda to work with the diversity issue as a primary, if not complete, topic for the retreat time. The management team took some time to consider this and consulted with some additional diversity consultants. They made a counter offer to us, which included them hiring other diversity consultants, where we would be participants in the workshop. Even though this may have been a good idea, and surely we would have learned some things, we made a different choice. Over the years we had become good friends with the executive director, and that was a known fact in the organization. We truly valued the work of this organization and feared that our perspective might be in question and be counterproductive. We continued consulting with the organization through their re-contracting process with the other diversity consultants and then withdrew. We do know that the diversity awareness process they undertook opened doors that needed to be opened as they continued their ongoing work.

Addressing Conflict Avoidance

Generally one expects to find a strong sense of civility in mission-driven organizations, and for the most part we have found this to be true. That value of civility, however, does not always eliminate a sense of frustration and/or anger at times when strongly held points of view differ from one another. If the people involved have the skills and/or guidance to work through those differing points of view, reasonable

solutions/alternatives can be reached without the egos of the participating parties being bruised. There are, however, individuals who will
not push for something they strongly believe would be in their own
best interest, or the best interest of the organization, because it would
feel too conflictual—and conflict, for them, does not fit with civility.
Sometimes they withhold their own truth to be polite, speak in gener-
alities to avoid being pinned down, or pretend that the individual differences are not important enough to risk getting into conflict. Scott
Peck (2003) refers to this stage of group behavior as Pseudocommunity.
According to Peck, it is necessary for individuals to go through the
chaos of truth-telling, risking the fear that intrapersonal feelings
or interpersonal relationships will be damaged, in order to develop
an effective communication and problem-solving climate of True
Community. When differences are related in any way to a diversity
issue, causing individuals to feel that their integrity is in question, the
conflict can be even more painful and difficult to address. However,
when people are not addressed in an honest way that enhances the
full development of each individual and/or their contributions, the
organization suffers. For example, supervisors sometimes do not provide people of color and/or women with the feedback that is necessary for their growth because they fear it will lead to a diversity-issue
conflict. Developing a culture of honest feedback is very important
for personal growth and for organizational effectiveness (Seashore,
Seashore, & Weinberg, 1997). The consultants' skill in enabling each
person to be heard and respected is critical for that to happen.

Key Aspects of Effective Diversity Work

Diversity work is most effective when it is part of a larger organi-zation-development intervention that is addressing systemic change. There is a constant need for internal and/or external diversity profes-sionals to advocate for this deeper, longer, more systemic training and intervention, rather than settle for one-shot or superficial attempts that may just scratch the surface but fail to represent the rich concepts that can come from diverse groups of people working together.

As Huntley, Moore, and Pierce point out in their daringly honest book, *Journeys of Race, Color, & Culture: From Racial Inequality to Equity & Inclusion* (2017), doing diversity consulting brings us face-to-face with the reality of the inequality in nonprofit and for-profit organiza-tions—as well as in our society.

Frequently there is conflict and emotional stress involved in deal-ing with diversity issues, and it is sometimes culturally appropriate that support systems for different groups accompany any interven-tion. When diversity professionals immerse themselves in the issues and model really hearing each person's perspective, it can lead to oth-ers doing likewise. Additional factors that we believe enhance suc-cessful outcomes are to have people from all represented factions of the organization be included in resolving the issue, and to be sure that in-depth processing occurs around differences of feelings and thoughts. Even though the work is hard, when clients accept a deeper level of understanding, we find our own satisfaction.

Summary Table

Types of Specialized Settings	Key Points	Interventions
Nonprofit Organizations	Mission-Driven	Utilizing Internal Team as Anthropologists
	Volunteer-Based	Personalizing the Issue
	Using Differences	Using Hearing Transmitter as Talking Stick
	Compensation	Accepting Reality
	Boards of Directors and Staff	Clarifying Roles
	Consulting Contracting	Inclusion of Influential Persons
Faith-Based Organizations	Projections on Clergy	Self-Understanding Coaching
	Broadening Leadership Diversity	Leadership-Training Program
	Using Multiple Organizations	Developing Interfaith Coalitions
School Organizations	Multiple Stakeholders	Engaging All Constituencies
Community Organizations	Loose Boundaries	Engaging All Diverse Groups as Fully Involved in Planning
	Different Attitudes Toward Leadership	Remaining Flexible to Adapt to Different Cultures
Government Agencies	Resistance to Change	Using Polarity Management in Exploring Stability/ Change Polarity
	Cultural Differences	Using Concept of Cultural Humility

REFERENCES

Association of American Medical Colleges. (2012, November). *The role of the chief diversity officer in academic health centers.* Retrieved from https://members.aamc.org/eweb/upload/The%20 Role%20of%20the%20Chief%20Diversity%20Office%20in%20 Academic%20HealthCenters.pdf

BlackDemographics.com. (2016). African American employment. Retrieved from http://blackdemographics.com/economics/ employment/

Block, P. (2011). *Flawless consulting* (3rd. ed.). San Francisco, CA: Pfeiffer.

Bordas, J. (2013). *The power of latino leadership.* San Francisco, CA: Berrett-Koehler.

Boyne, G. (2002). Public and private management: What's the difference? *Journal of Management Studies, 39*(1), 97–122.

Corporation for National and Community Service. (2016). *New report: Service unites Americans; volunteers give service worth $184 billion.* Retrieved from https://www.nationalservice.gov/ newsroom/press-releases/2016/new-report-service-unites-americans-volunteers-give-service-worth-184

Elkington, J. (2004, August 17) Enter the triple bottom line.
   Retrieved from http://www.johnelkington.com/archive/TBL-
   elkington-chapter.pdf

Exec. Order No. 13583, 76 FR 52845 (2011, August 18). Establishing
   a coordinated government-wide initiative to promote diversity
   and inclusion in the federal workforce. Retrieved from https://
   obamawhitehouse.archives.gov/the-press-office/2011/08/18/
   executive-order-13583-establishing-coordinated-government-
   wide-initiativ

Harris, J. H. (1990, June 13–20). Practicing liberation in the black
   church. Religion-Online.org. *The Christian Century.*

Holvino, E. (2010). Intersections: The simultaneity of race, gender
   and class in organization studies. *Gender, Work & Organization,*
   17(3), 248–277.

Hook, J., Davis, D., Owen, J., Worthington, E., & Utsey, S. (2013).
   Cultural humility: Measuring openness to culturally diverse
   clients. *Journal of Counseling Psychology, 60*(3), 353–66.

Huntley, R., Moore, R., & Pierce, C. (2017). *Journeys of race, color, &*
   culture: From racial inequality to equity & inclusion. Laconia, NH:
   New Dynamics Publications.

International Cultural Center. (2016). 1st interracial/
    interfaith dialogue on racism: Seeing the divine
    in each other. Retrieved from http://www.theicc.
    net/programs/community-building-programs/
    faith-in-community-working-group-fcwg

Jagpal, N., & Laskowski, K. (2016). *The state of social justice
    philanthropy.* Washington, D.C.: National Committee for
    Responsive Philanthropy. Retrieved from https://www.ncrp.
    org/wp-content/uploads/2016/11/PhilanthropicLandscape-
    StateofSocialJusticePhilanthropy.pdf

Johnson, B. (1992). *Polarity management: Identifying and managing
    unsolvable problems.* Amherst, MA: HRD Press.

Lowen, L. (2017, November). The role of African American women
    in the black church. *ThoughtCo.* Retrieved from https://www.
    thoughtco.com/african-american-women-black-church-3533748

Lewis, R. D. (2016, February 23). 6 leadership styles around the
    world to build effective multinational teams. *CrossCulture.*
    Retrieved from http://www.crossculture.com/uncategorized/6-
    leadership-styles-around-the-world-to-build-effective-
    multinational-teams/

McNamara, C. (2008). *Field guide to developing, operating and restoring
    your nonprofit board.* Minneapolis, MN: Authenticity Consulting.

Ostroff, F. (2006). Change management in government. *Harvard Business Review, 11*(5). Retrieved from https://hbr.org/2006/05/change-management-in-government

Peck, M. S. (2003). *The road less traveled: A new psychology of love, traditional values and spiritual growth* (25th anniversary ed.). New York, NY: Touchstone.

Seashore, C., Seashore, E., & Weinberg, G. (1997). *What did you say?: The art of giving and receiving feedback.* Baltimore, MD: Bingham House Books.

Wikipedia. (2017) Retrieved from https://en.wikipedia.org/wiki/Affirmative_action_in_the_United_States.

Wright, B. (2003). *Toward understanding task, mission and public service motivation: A conceptual and empirical synthesis of goal theory and public service motivation.* Retrieved from http://citeseerx.ist.psu.edu/viewdoc/download?doi=10.1.1.573.4836&rep=rep1&type=pdf

CHAPTER TWELVE

Diversity Leadership: There's More

Ollie Malone, Ph.D.

PRIOR TO THE AGE OF TEN, children are fascinated by differences, much in the same way they are fascinated by a box of sixty-four crayons when those choices are compared with the familiar four crayons they might receive with their coloring sheets upon arriving at a restaurant. "Wow," I imagine them saying. "What could we do with all of these colors?" The possibilities of representing endless shades of reality through this box of sixty-four are mind-boggling. Faced with this dilemma of multiple options, some children still favor the cellophane-wrapped pack of four colors, having no clue what to do with the crayons beyond the standard four-option package.

The "Box of Sixty-Four"

The challenge of diversity leadership may be reflected in this simple metaphor of having been given a metaphorical box of sixty-four crayons. How does the leader engage in exploring the options that are not as familiar as other choices? What could otherwise wise and insightful leaders be missing by presenting "art" that is comprised of the same crayon choices when so many other colors are available? In other words, how does a leader incorporate the multiple and intersecting identities present in today's workforce? When does it become imperative for a leader to realize that in the short term homogeneity may support the organization in achieving its business objectives, but in the long term, it may make the organization less competitive?

Changing this mindset is challenging for many seasoned professionals. Aligned with lifespan-developmental processes, by the time individuals reach adulthood, most have a clear sense of who they are and what they like. This is no less true for leaders of organizations. In their leadership-development process, they often have fixed ideas about managing people. For example, here are some people preferences that might be expressed:

"I like people who say what they mean."
"I like people who make room for the opinions of others."
"I like folks who listen well."
"I like folks who will fight to the end for those things they believe in."

These "likes" extend into leadership style and influence how a leader manages and supports diversity in its many dimensions. The dimensions of diversity include age, race, gender, height, weight, physical ability, ethnicity, geographical origin, sexual orientation, marital status, personality type, perceived intellect, and countless other identity expressions of humankind. Inherently, there is nothing "good" or "bad" about any of the identities; they just are *different*. Yet unconscious (and sometimes conscious) bias toward certain "likes" may prohibit leaders from being able to lead with vision, purposefulness, and optimism for creating an inclusive organization.

Social Loadings

Although a box of crayons may provide a useful metaphor for a simple explanation of how individuals approach differences, on a deeper level historical underpinnings have influenced how we conceptualize differences in profound ways.

- Race: Decades after Brown vs. Board of Education, segregation in school systems remains. Research continues to reflect inequities in school systems, despite equality being the law of the land for well over fifty years (Heckman & LaFontaine, 2010).

- Gender: Dramatic differences exist in the educational processes for girls and boys, particularly as they relate to subjects like math and science. These disparities were first reflected in Teen Talk Barbie, which was introduced in 1992 and had to be recalled due to the PR nightmare. The programmed voice box of four phrases, one of which stated, "Math class is tough," underscored the perception that the role of women was to be slim, look pretty, but not necessarily say or do anything of substance or importance (Driscoll, 2008). Smart women were encouraged to be nurses, teachers, and secretaries, while smart men were encouraged to be doctors, lawyers, engineers, or anything else they desired to be (DePree, 1990).

- Ability: Until recently, those differently abled were largely out of sight of general society. School children with disabilities rode smaller buses, distinguishing their mode of transportation from other transportation provided for children without identified disabilities. They attended special schools and often had special classes, even though many possessed areas of intellectual parity or even intellectual superiority compared to their counterparts in traditional schools. Those with physical challenges were to be pitied and provided for, not challenged to reach the full extent of their potential.

- Sexual Orientation: Until recently, men and women with same-sex orientations were "in the closet" and shunned, publicly abused (often without consequence for the abusers), and disconnected from many mainstream activities.

- Class: Those with economic means greater than others have historically enjoyed higher perceived status in our society. An Ivy League education is perceived to be better than a state school education. Those who attended private boarding schools are often assumed to be of higher intellect and to possess better capabilities than those who attended public schools.

- Thought and Expression: Even those who thought differently encountered their own levels of isolation and verbal abuse. Negative nicknames emphasized the fact that individuals who thought and expressed themselves differently from the mainstream would be considered "other."

- Who's on Top? Our heroes were white, male, straight, and under forty years of age. American young men grew up wanting to be John Wayne, GI Joe, and Babe Ruth: all white, all male, and all believed to be straight. Even the appearance of such role-model breakers as Jackie Robinson and Arthur Ashe created such a national stir that additional personal security to accompany them was often warranted.

These historical underpinnings permeate America's understanding of differences today and form a baseline for our current thinking. Our systems, the sacred structures that define our existence in America, have also created strong racial, ethnic, ability, sexual orienttion and gender messages. Consider the following:

- Religious Institutions and Structures: Martin Luther King, on an April 17, 1960, *Meet the Press* episode, stated: "I think one of the tragedies of our nation, one of the shameful tragedies, is that eleven o'clock on Sunday morning is one of the most segregated hours in Christian America." Regretfully, that reality has not changed much, despite the exponential growth of some churches and the creation of what has come to be known as the "megachurch." Many churches may have become significantly larger, but the demographic mix largely remains unchanged (Lipka, 2015).

- Women in Leadership: The number of women in leadership roles in schools, religious organizations, businesses, and many social service organizations (excepting those targeted toward women) is still significantly lower than that of men.

Their compensation continues to fail to equal that of men (Catalyst, 2017).

• Politics and Political Office: Following the highest political office in the land being held for two terms by Barack Obama, it has been purported that the subsequent election of Donald Trump is a direct racial backlash (Coates, 2017).

• The Media: The media, in all its forms, have also served to shape our understanding of diversity, whether through the social identities of the media announcers, who is or is not included in the stories, or the tone and tenor of the reporting.

The consistent and profound effects of these historical underpinnings have resulted in our lack of diversity competence as a society. Although we value diversity, we typically shy away from its management, in part due to sticking with old ways. As the late Edwin Friedman, author, rabbi, and family therapist, states in *A Failure of Nerve: Leadership in the Age of the Quick Fix*, "myths, emotional barriers, and learned superstitions, because of their hold on our imagination, keep our thinking processes stuck and preserve 'old world' views, thus limiting our horizons and range" (Friedman, 2017).

Without leadership development, leaders are prone to stay with the familiar box of four colors. Developing leaders to direct organizations of diverse individuals has been largely indirect and nonspecific when it comes to diversity management. With the increasing complexity of managing diversity well, leaders can and do greatly benefit from taking advantage of educational workshops to enhance cultural competence. Most organizational leaders hire chief diversity officers

(CDOs) who support these efforts and sit on their leadership teams, helping to shape and direct diversity strategy. Many executives retain coaches to provide individual guidance, boost personal effectiveness, and provide necessary feedback on critical issues. Yet even with these support mechanisms in place, moving leaders from diversity champions to visionary leaders of diversity can be a daunting task (Plummer, 2010).

Leadership at the Core

My contention is that the challenge for many who would lead diversity is the need to construct a clear and compelling core. By "core" I mean those beliefs about difference that represent deeply held beliefs about diversity in any of the many ways that "difference" can be expressed (i.e., gender, race, ability, age, sexual orientation, and other dimensions). What is it that I, as an individual in this key leadership role, believe about this organization and the diverse backgrounds, talents, and gifts that are present in the organization?

Several years ago, a direct report (whom I'll call Cindy) relayed a conversation she had held with the president of one of the divisions in our organization. This company, a Midwest manufacturing firm, had been historically led by white males. The former CEO, largely influenced by his wife and daughter, had become a strong proponent of diversity, and had challenged his senior executives, comprised of all white men and one white woman, to embrace diversity as a key organizational driver of excellence. Cindy (a multiracial woman, who visually could be perceived as white) was interviewing one of the division presidents as part of another organization change initiative. "Yeah," the division president said, "I see we're all worked up over this diversity thing."

"What do you think of that?" Cindy queried.

"Well, I figure it this way: for the past three hundred years, white men have screwed over women and blacks, so for the next three hundred years, we got it coming back."

An awkward pause followed, while Cindy attempted to process this response. She was a bit shocked that this division executive spoke as freely as he did and wondered if that thought was shared by the other executives. The leader didn't smile, snicker, or chuckle as he said it, leading Cindy to think that he was not kidding and that he understood the organization's diversity efforts as retaliation for historical grievances. The fact that there was an absence of women or people of color in any significant leadership capacity further led her to believe that diversity initiatives were misunderstood and not appreciated in the organization by its executive leadership. This exchange provided a good opportunity for the leaders to dig a bit deeper and examine their assumptions about diversity. It also presented an opportunity for dialogue and examination of the core.

Your (Lack of) Diversity Is Showing

The 1996 case of Texaco, Inc., is a classic example of a company that through regulatory compliance of racial equity learned the value of diversity. While discussing a pending discrimination lawsuit citing bias in the company's succession plan, people of color and women became objects of open derision and humiliation during an executive leadership meeting (BLB&G, 2018). The meeting was taped by a male employee charged with taking minutes who routinely taped the sessions to ensure the accuracy of the minutes. When the case was brought forth and the account of what was said at the meeting was disputed by Texaco, the employee provided the tapes to the plaintiff's lawyers. In retaliation, the employee was fired by Texaco (Eichenwald, 1996).

The recorded messages verified the negative experiences of the African Americans at Texaco. Interviews with African American employees captured their responses: "We knew this all along." "This just confirms what we always felt." "We knew we were not crazy." The widespread impact of the unexamined core beliefs held by executive leadership was significant and expanded to other areas of corporate interest:

- The board of directors—their support or lack of support for diversity-related initiatives (Fields, 1990);
- Executive leaders—their ability to set the type of standard essential for the creation of a barrier-free organization for all employees (Editorial, 1996);
- Middle managers—their ability to manage the workforce in such a way that issues of discrimination were not present in hiring, promotion, succession planning choices, and compensation;
- Human resources—assurance that company people practices were absent of real or perceived issues of discrimination, and assurance that concerns about discriminatory behavior were dealt with promptly and completely (Williamson, 2002);
- All employees—assurance that these individuals knew Texaco's position on the value of the diversity of its workforce, that diversity was seen as a valuable asset to the organization, and that employment at Texaco meant adherence to this set of core beliefs and values; and

- Public perception. Public sentiment following the revela-
  tion of the Texaco misdeeds was significantly negative and
  created a public relations nightmare, despite the company's
  efforts to address the accusations before they devastated the
  company (Hoger & Swem, 2000; Pruitt & Nethercutt, 2002).

The discovery of the taped messages and the information disseminated was devastating for Texaco. The company's stock price
dropped precipitously, and the company began an effort to stop the
reputational hemorrhaging. The largest racial discrimination settle-
ment to date, of over $175 million, was paid to resolve the federal law-
suit brought by the black employees (Tribune News Services, 1996;
Eichenwald, 1996). It took several years with new leadership and
court-mandated oversight to move the company from being known
as a bastion of racial discrimination to a model for diversity (Labich,
1999). Now the company, which merged with Chevron in 2001, has
received recognition for its diversity efforts from several prominent
and leading organizations, including Glassdoor's 50 Best Places to
Work, Business Insiders Best Companies to Work for in America, and
Catalyst (Chevron, 2018; Texaco, 2016).

Operating From One's Core

Max DePree, former CEO of Steelcase Furniture, relays a compelling story about deepening his understanding of his core in the opening of his classic work, *Leadership Is an Art.* In that opening story, he
relates how, after the janitor at the company, a beloved member of the
Steelcase family, passed away, he spent time with the employee's family and discovered something of the depth of the talent and gifts possessed by his departed friend. He had been invited into this personal

space by a member of the former employee's family, who thought that DePree would appreciate having another view of who this individual was and what the quality of his life had been (DePree, 1990).

To DePree's amazement, the most significant part of this individual's life was not what he had done for Steelcase, but the quality of his skill at art, which was known by his family but largely unknown by those with whom he had worked closely.

DePree's sense of loss is palpable—to have lost someone whose talents and gifts were so rich, but whom he knew so poorly. To develop one's core from a diversity leadership standpoint is to broaden one's understanding beyond the stereotypical messages that often limit our willingness to explore or get to know one another.

The example DePree cites can likely be multiplied a million times within individuals in employment settings (Truss, Shantz, Soane, Alfes, & Delbridge, 2011).

Kip Tindell, chairman and CEO of The Container Store, expresses a similar belief. His company expresses this belief in the phrase "1 Great Person = 3 Good People," stating, "Great employees understand the value of working together to produce the best results. They motivate, inspire, and encourage fellow employees, share credit and opportunities, and help others when needed. They work diligently to connect with all types of personalities, build new connections throughout the company, and keep long-standing relationships strong. They create a sense of community in their own department and other areas of the company. They know the power of wake—that every decision can have an effect on the team, the customer, and other stakeholders" (Tindell, 2014).

As a younger man, I was privileged to work for Sprint in its early days. My boss's boss was a man named Bob: a relatively young, smart, blond, blue-eyed fellow who seemed destined to go places. His nature was friendly and engaging and it was hard to believe that Bob could have had an enemy in the world (except for those for whom Bob's intellect and sarcasm were a challenge). In casual dialogue one afternoon, Bob asked, "What's it like being black here?" Without missing a beat, I turned the tide on him, asking, "What's it like being white here?" Bob stopped dead in his tracks, as though I had hit him in the face with a fifty-pound sack of flour.

"I've never thought about it," came his solitary response.

"Therein lies one difference," I responded.

Bob and I returned to that less-than-three-minute exchange several times during our tenure of working together, sharing more and deeper insights in every dialogue.

The development of one's core as a leader is a critical mobilizer for the work the leader must do. The place where values, passions, beliefs, and (may I say) one's soul collide is where the core can be found (Williamson, 2008).

Debbe Kennedy (2008) advocates clearly stating one's core as a strategy to create more effective harmony and teamwork among those who work together. Kennedy advocates bringing people together with the goal of creating a space large enough for the differences of all those present to be heard and honored. This, she posits, builds a foundation for respect and working together, and from a large field that contains all the differences present, new ideas can be generated and esteemed.

In his book *The Leadership Engine,* University of Michigan professor Noel Tichy (1997) describes a similar central phenomenon, using the term "the leadership point of view." Tichy contends that this leadership point of view, similar to what I have defined as "core", is essential to leadership development—so central that spending time considering it and developing it comprises a significant portion of both the book and of Tichy's public workshops (Thompsen, 1999).

As Socrates says (in Plato's *Apology*), "The unexamined life is not worth living," and I agree that those who would lead diversity must be passionately willing to lead themselves, to discover what they are made of, or what they would like to be made of, and then diligently, through action, reflection, interaction, course correction, and ongoing dialogue, craft the best self possible.

This act, the development of a core understanding of who one is with regard to diversity, is essential. Without it, the leader's ability to impact others and systems is impaired.

In summary, the first step in developing true diversity leadership is for the leader to examine and develop his or her core as it relates to difference. Questions that may be useful for this include:

- What is my relationship to this dimension of diversity? Positive? Negative? Unclear? What conscious or unconscious biases might I hold toward a given group—and in what ways might these biases affect my actions and decisions or color my perspective?
- Why are diverse relationships important to me?
- How does this position agree with or differ from other messages or beliefs that are within me? How might I be inwardly conflicted in ways that cause others confusion? It what ways does this inner conflict reflect a level of inconsistency with regard to my passion regarding difference?
- How broad and how deep is my understanding of this difference? Is my understanding borne of a depth of

experience, extensive reading, and research—or has it been
defined by brief, unexamined exchanges with those who
possess this difference, or with those who don't possess it
but have opinions about it?

- What don't I know—and how might I go about learning
  what I need to know independently or in partnership with
  other valued learners?
- In what area(s) do I need to expand my understanding of
  difference further? *Find Your Why* (Sinek & Mead, 2017)
  proposes a set of questions, thought starters, and ways of
  engaging others that should expand this understanding of
  difference further.

Leading and Learning Across Levels of System

Bringing about large-scale change, from a diversity perspective,
requires more than simply "getting one's own house in order." This
personal introspection is necessary, even critical, but in and of itself
it is not sufficient. Effective diversity leadership requires the leader to
understand and work across levels of system.

When examining the impact of one's behavior in the workplace,
"levels of system" refers to the scope or focus of the leader's attention.
Although discussed in greater detail in the overview chapter of this
book, I find this slightly truncated version useful for leaders' basic
understanding of the concept.

At the *individual* level of system, the leader's focus is on himself or
herself. Imagine an interaction with a colleague of mine who states,
"Men are rude—especially so in business meetings where women are
attempting to speak." As a man, it might be quite offensive to me to
hear such a thing. As an individual, I may perceive myself in a way

that differs from my colleague's description. I may see myself as much more respectful, participative, and facilitative of my female colleague's team membership and, as a result, can't relate to the "rude" reference.

On the other hand, I might have to admit that my colleague has a point. I have seen my male colleagues totally ignore comments of female colleagues in meetings, only to bring them up later and attribute them to someone else. I know the *group* level phenomenon exists—men do behave rudely toward women in business meetings. And as a member of the group called "men," I recognize that this behavior is true for our group.

That exchange highlights one of the challenges when we speak or interact across levels of system. In the example, my colleague is speaking about men at a group level, while I am responding at an individual level.

At the individual level, leaders are most aware of their own actions, behaviors, thoughts, values, ethics, and other identifiers that are unique to them.

For those who have always seen themselves as individuals and not members of a group (typically those in the majority), group membership can be seen as a challenge. Groups tend to have labels and assumptions made about them, which are positive to some but difficult to others.

Level of System	Individual	Team, Group	Organization
Focus	I see/understand the impact of the ism, micro-aggression, or microinequities on an individual.	I understand how this affects different social identity groups.	I understand how this influences entire organizations through rules, systems, practices, or procedures.
Language	Me, my, mine, I	We, top management, middle management, first-line supervisors	The company, our company, the home team
Artifacts	Values, symbols, ethics, totems	Logos, Greek letters, badges, uniforms, rules, secret handshakes	Logos, policies, practices, systems, code of ethics

Given these dynamics of differences across levels of system and the complexities of navigating multicultural workforces, how do leaders prioritize what needs to be incorporated into their leadership repertoire? These fifteen items should provide a useful start:

At the Individual Level

1. *Own your individuality.* Recognize that, as a member of many social identity groups, you retain the right to have your own individual perspectives and worldviews. Do not be afraid to differentiate yourself as an individual. Be who you are and own what is true for you, even when your truth differs from those who share the same social group identity.

2. *Speak from your own informed experience.* Arguably, there is nothing quite as effective as an accomplished leader who shares his or her learning and vulnerability. By chronicling your own journey of challenged living and reflective learning, you allow people to better understand your perspectives, your motives, and your direction.

3. *Recognize others who differentiate themselves from their job categories in ways that provide excellent role models to others.* One executive, for example, rather than parking in his executive parking space, provided it to the person from his group who was voted "Associate of the Month" by others within the group.

4. *Publicly acknowledge your own learning* and how you are growing in the area of diversity leadership. This helps reinforce that the learning process is a journey—and that few are "all the way there."

5. *Provide direct and specific feedback to others (in private) when you see specific actions that need adjustment.* Conversely, provide direct and specific feedback to others (in public) when you see behaviors or actions that are consistent with a climate that values diversity. Invite others to do the same for you.

At the Group Level

Those who enjoy a privileged social status seldom acknowledge membership as readily as those who do not enjoy social privilege. Those who do not represent the organizational prototype often believe they have to assimilate in order to be a full participant in the organization. Assimilation may mean dressing like everyone else, acting like everyone else, eating the same foods as everyone else, or taking on an entirely different lifestyle than those with whom they have grown up. These same individuals often go through organizational experiences fully conscious (occasionally to the point of intense fear) about being different—believing that their experiences in the organization are overwhelmingly shaped by race, gender, sexual orientation, age, or some other dimension of diversity. Deepening one's knowledge of group levels of difference is a key to being able to see diversity in ways that one has not previously experienced it.

6. *In conversation, own your group membership.* Statements that begin with, "As a [white woman, gay man, white man, etc.] ..." provide a lens through which others of like perspective can speak to or relate to the issue at hand. For instance: "As a white man, I've never questioned whether or not I didn't receive a promotion because of my race or gender. Hearing that others think about this daily, and even more frequently, is disturbing to me."

7. *Challenge others to try on the lens of a group membership.* "Could you put yourself in Sue's position for a moment, Ann, and imagine what it would be like to navigate this

organization from a wheelchair? How would that perspective influence your opinion of what it's like to work here?"

8. *Expand your understanding of "group membership" to include the levels of your organization.* What if the executives in your organization, for one week, lived like the lowest-paid employees in your organization? What if you lived in their houses, drove their cars, ate their food, and worked in their jobs? What if the money that is available to you were limited to the money they currently have in their wallets? How would your opinions change about what is just, what is equitable, and what "should" be done? Behavioral scientist Dr. Barry Oshry and his wife, Karen, have done this exercise in their Power and Systems Workshops, which they have run for over forty years. Through these workshops, individuals enter the "system" as an "immigrant" (also known as a "bottom"), as a "middle," or as a "top" (also known as an "elite"). For several days, individuals interact, live, work, eat, and sleep as members of their assigned groups do. They don't have access to their money, their car keys, their credit cards, or other typically available resources. This experience shapes the experiences of participants in ways that a thousand lectures could never accomplish.

9. *Challenge members of your social identity group to flip the lens and think from that perspective.* Ask, for example, "What if I had come to this organization twenty-five years ago with the same degree that my wife had—and with even better grades— and found that she was the one receiving the better offers and

that I was relegated to the 'steno pool'—despite better grades? What would my opinion about my organization be?" Some of the greatest insights that group members receive is not always from members of other groups—it also comes from those who are in the same group(s) as the listener. These individuals have nothing to prove, no axe to grind, making it difficult for the usual resistance to maintain such a stronghold.

10. *Schedule a field trip for members of your group to examine life/ work/family from the perspective of those whose practices may be different.* Encourage field trip participants to withhold conversation and to take in the observations without comments, jokes, or other verbal expressions that would distract others from their thoughts or visceral reactions. Should you undertake this challenge, you should ensure that the "field trip" lasts the appropriate time needed for observation and reflection. Practice multicultural living with a short field trip: shopping in minority-owned businesses or eating in ethnic restaurants that may be different than your common practice. Watching movies with subject matter common to a group different than your own or reading books by authors with diverse perspectives can also be highly enlightening. Short trips encourage participants to extend their learning over longer periods of time.

At the Organizational Level

The organizational level concerns itself with the structures, ordinances, and "musts" that members adhere to in order to be perceived as being well aligned with the organization's mission and direction. Frequently these structures, ordinances, and "musts" provide benefits to one group that may not be afforded to members of other groups. To the degree that they do, and to the degree that there is no performance-based rationale for this benefit, the structure, ordinance, or "must" may be subject to modification or elimination. For example, we'd like to have a workforce that can relocate on demand and is able to respond to organizational challenges wherever they exist, but the impact of certain company policies and practices (e.g., promotion is dependent upon being able to relocate) will be very different on some members of the workforce than on others. This is not to suggest that this "must" should be eliminated, but that there are other ways that qualified, dedicated individuals, who may have life circumstances that don't permit relocation, can still advance and bring value to the company.

11. *Fall in love with listening.* Few leaders have mastered the art of listening. They do a far better job of telling than asking, and a much better job of pontificating than truly listening. In order to create the type of paradigm shift that diversity leadership requires, listening is essential. This is not the "Uh-huh, uh-huh (I can't wait until I get a chance to straighten this misguided soul out)" type of listening, but the type of listening that listens with the singular agenda of hearing the head, the heart, and the gut of the speaker. In the course of the conversation, if you haven't heard these three distinctive

elements, you may want to listen a bit more deeply. If you listen with an earnest commitment, it can be transformational for all parties.

12. *Take a hard, critical look at a few of the policies and practices that drive opportunity and advancement in your organization.* Ask yourself, "Does this policy favor one group over another?" For example, if yours is an organization where a great number of organizational decisions are made on golf courses or in social clubs, might this favor one identity group over another? This doesn't suggest the total elimination of this practice, but that other practices might include a wider pool of the organization's members and give them the opportunity to contribute.

13. *Ask members of different groups in your organization, "What's it like to work here—honestly? What things do you particularly like—and what would you change?"* Leaders who are committed to making the organization better for all often ask this question. After the question is asked, it's important that one listens. Listening may feel like an eternity, but providing time for the candid response will serve to project that one's intentions are sincere and that the response will be taken under serious consideration.

14. *Take action on something you have heard.* There is nothing quite as frustrating as having spilled your innards out to someone masquerading as a listener, only to find that he or she has discovered a newer bright and shiny object to pay

attention to and has moved on. Having created a good connection through listening, leaders must be willing to take bold and committed action to move the dialogue forward. This bold and committed action needs to be taken as quickly as is reasonable. This prompt attention to an identified challenge says that the listener shares the sense of a need for change and that she or he will use the power of her or his position to move forward with regard to the concern. Such action creates an organizational rippling effect that is sustainable over time.

15. *Touch base with those to whom you have listened.* Do they see, feel, and experience a difference? This stage argues for good calibration: Was the solution aligned with the reported need? If there is alignment, take a not-too-obvious bow. You've made a difference. The next step is to repeat this process of listening with different groups until the entire workforce can see that the organization listens and is responsive to their requests.

These fifteen factors, for the leader who chooses to leverage them, can support positive movement for that leader as well as for others. These factors will free the leader from habitual action and serve to open up the possibility for new, deeper levels of dialogue and understanding about diversity. Here are some other potential outcomes:

• Those who feel as if they are on the outside looking in will have the opportunity to step inside and be able to advance as far as their talents, passions, and commitment will take them.

- Those who feel as if they have a "right" to the positions they hold for some reason other than skill and merit will get a wake-up call and see proof that the organization exists for all who are willing to work toward advancing the organization's vision and mission.

- Those who are wondering whether or not the organization's leaders are serious about the diversity-laced rhetoric that is frequently spread like fertilizer will witness powerful examples of the rhetoric turned into committed action. These types of actions tend to be contagious.

Cathy Lamboley: A Case Study in Managing the "Box of Sixty-Four"

During my time as an independent executive coach, a name I often heard on the topic of diversity was that of Cathy Lamboley, the vice president, general counsel, and corporate secretary at Shell. I was honored to work with several leaders in Cathy's organization, and as a part of that work—and other work—I was able to interact with Cathy.

As a college student, she participated in protests and demonstrations for causes she felt deserved a level of justice that had not been realized. A secondary education major, she did not immediately discern the path that would lead her into corporate law, but thanks to the input of an uncle who was himself an attorney, Cathy was able to reach this professional destination.

In her twenty-eight-year history with Shell, Cathy distinguished herself as a competent, respected member of the leadership team. Beginning as a staff attorney, she migrated to the commercial marketing department for a three-year stint as vice president—a role seldom held by lawyers.

Taking on the role of general counsel in 2000, Cathy began working on the initiatives that have made her quite familiar to Shell lawyers and those in the legal community in Houston, Texas.

Her first significant order of business was to evaluate the over six hundred legal firms doing work for Shell and to determine, through this analysis, how much of the work being done was being done by female attorneys and attorneys of color. This initial review pared down the list to only forty-four firms. Ultimately the list included twenty-seven firms who met Shell's expectations for diversity and inclusion. Throughout her tenure as general counsel, Cathy and her leadership team met with the selected firms, ensuring that their rosters of active attorneys on Shell business included women and people of color who were doing challenging, resume-building work as well as work of noted quality, cost effectiveness, and professionalism.

Within Shell's legal department, Cathy made sure the company's intern program was populated by a significant number of women and people of color who met or exceeded Shell's hiring standards. These roles were typically the feeder roles through which individuals were offered permanent positions with Shell.

Coaching and mentoring were also active parts of the new employees' experience. Coaching was available through both formal and informal means. Cathy took an active role in the development of these high-potential lawyers, including one lawyer who worked closely with her to gain a better appreciation of the general counsel role and the activities and perspectives appropriate for high-level legal work.

Active feedback was also a part of these lawyers' experiences, ensuring that they received, on an ongoing basis, the type of feedback that would make them both stronger lawyers and stronger leaders in the organization.

These individuals were also given consideration for projects, choice assignments, as well as opportunities for promotion that might emerge.

As Shell's general counsel, Cathy was one of seventy-two signers of "A Call to Action: Diversity in the Legal Profession," a document authored by Rick Palmore, general counsel for Sara Lee Corporation at the time, that reaffirmed these general counsels' commitment to diversity in the law profession and to taking action to ensure that corporate legal departments and law firms increased the numbers of women and minority attorneys hired and retained. Other signers of this bellwether document included general counsels from organizations such as American Airlines, Boeing, Lockheed Martin, Eli Lilly, Honeywell, Starbucks, Tyson Foods, and Walmart.

Although she retired in 2007, Cathy's commitment to the growth and development of women lawyers and lawyers of color continues. She is the founder of the University of Texas School of Law's Center for Women in Law, and in 2011 she received the American Lawyer Lifetime Achievement Award.

Conclusion

Although Cathy Lamboley held the general counsel role for seven years, her efforts reflected many more years of commitment, self-development, coaching, and influence. Using these well-honed skills, she was able to significantly enhance the box of sixty-four available to her. In this manner, she not only spoke about diversity leadership but demonstrated it in ways that affected her employer, Shell Oil, as well as the entire legal community and beyond.

How will the leaders of today and tomorrow respond to the opportunity that remains? What can be drawn from leaders like Cathy and others who recognize the opportunity that awaits them and, rather than use it for self-gratification only, use it to significantly affect the present and future of lives within their spheres of influence?

Leaders seldom see the world as acceptable the way it currently exists. They see the opportunity for change; they hear the call to do so. And they leverage every opportunity to make something significant out of the box of sixty-four with which they have been entrusted.

REFERENCES

BLB&G. (2018). Roberts v. Texaco [Summary of 1994 case]. Retrieved from https://www.blbglaw.com/cases/00081

Catalyst. (2017, August). Statistical overview of women in the workforce. Retrieved from http://www.catalyst.org/knowledge/statistical-overview-women-workforce

Chevron. (2018). Diversity and inclusion [Page from Chevron website]. Retrieved from https://www.chevron.com/corporate-responsibility/people/diversity-inclusion

Coates, T. (2017). The first white president. *The Atlantic*. Retrieved from https://www.theatlantic.com/magazine/archive/2017/10/the-first-white-president-ta-nehisi-coates/537909/

DePree, M. (1990). What is leadership? *Strategy & Leadership, 18*(4), 14–41. Retrieved from http://emeraldinsight.com/doi/abs/10.1108/eb054292?journalcode=plr

Driscoll, C. (2008). We girls can do anything, can't we Barbie? In C. Mitchell & J. Reid-Walsh (Eds.), *Girl culture: An encyclopedia* (pp. 41–42). Westport, CT / London: Greenwood.

Editorial: Racism at Texaco. (1996). *The New York Times*. Retrieved from http://www.nytimes.com/1996/11/06/opinion/racism-at-texaco.html

Eichenwald, K. (1996, November 4). Texaco executives, on tape, discussed impeding a bias suit. *The New York Times*. Retrieved from http://www.nytimes.com/1996/11/04/business/texaco-executives-on-tape-discussed-impeding-a-bias-suit.html

Fields, M. A. (1990). The wealth effects of corporate lawsuits: Pennzoil v. Texaco. *Journal of Business Research, 21*(2), 143–158. Retrieved from http://sciencedirect.com/science/article/pii/014829639090049j

Friedman, E. H. (2017). *A failure of nerve: Leadership in the age of the quick fix.* New York, NY: Church Publishing.

Heckman, J. J., & LaFontaine, P. A. (2010). The American high school graduation rate: Trends and levels. *The Review of Economics and Statistics, 92*(2), 244–262. Retrieved from http://ftp.iza.org/dp3216.pdf

Hoger, E. A., & Swem, L. L. (2000). Public relations and the law in crisis mode: Texaco's initial reaction to incriminating tapes. *Public Relations Review, 26*(4), 425–445. Retrieved from https://wmich.pure.elsevier.com/en/publications/public-relations-and-the-law-in-crisis-mode-texacos-initial-react-3

Kennedy, D. (2008). *Putting differences to work: The fastest way to innovation, leadership and high performance.* San Francisco, CA: Berrett-Koehler.

Labich, K. (1999, September 6). No more crude at Texaco. *Fortune.* Retrieved from http://archive.fortune.com/magazines/fortune/fortune_archive/1999/09/06/265322/index.htm

Lipka, M. (2015). The most and least racially diverse U.S. religious groups. Pew Research Center. Retrieved from: http://www.pewresearch.org/fact-tank/2015/07/27/the-most-and-least-racially-diverse-u-s-religious-groups/

Plummer, D. L. (2010). Moving leaders from champions to visionaries. *Diversity Executive Magazine.* Chicago, IL: Media Tech Publishing.

Pruitt, S. W., & Nethercutt, L. L. (2002). The Texaco racial discrimination case and shareholder wealth. *Journal of Labor Research, 23*(4), 685–693. Retrieved from https://link.springer.com/article/10.1007/s12122-002-1036-0

Sinek, S., & Mead, D. (2017). *Find your why.* New York, NY: Portfolio/Penquin.

Texaco. (2016). About [Company history]. Retrieved from http://www.texaco.com/about.html

Thompsen, J. A. (1999). Review of *The leadership engine: How winning companies build leaders at every level,* by N. M. Tichy. *Human Resource Development Quarterly, 10*(4), 391–394. Retrieved from http://onlinelibrary.wiley.com/doi/10.1002/hrdq.3920100409/full

Tichy, N. M. (1997). *The leadership engine: How winning companies build leaders at every level.* New York, NY: Harper Business.

Tindell, K. (2014). *Uncontainable: How passion, commitment, and conscious capitalism built a business where everyone thrives.* New York, NY: Grand Central.

Tribune News Services. (1996, November 16). Texaco ends bias suit with $176 million. *The Chicago Tribune*. Retrieved from http://articles.chicagotribune.com/1996-11-16/news/9611160085_1_texaco-chairman-peter-bijur-bari-ellen-roberts-black-cultural-festival-kwanzaa

Truss, C., Shantz, A., Soane, E., Alfes, K., & Delbridge, R. (2011). Employee engagement, organizational performance and individual well-being: Exploring the evidence, developing the theory. *International Journal of Human Resource Management, 24*(149), 2657–2669. Retrieved from http://tandfonline.com/doi/full/10.1080/09585192.2013.798921

Williamson, J. T. (2002). A Case Study of the Texaco Lawsuit. In *Diversity in engineering: Managing the workforce of the future*. National Academy of Engineering, Washington, D.C.: The National Academies Press.

Williamson, T. (2008). The good society and the good soul: *Plato's Republic* on leadership. *Leadership Quarterly, 19*(4), 397–408. Retrieved from http://sciencedirect.com/science/article/pii/s1048984308000672

INDEX

About the Editor

DEBORAH L. PLUMMER is a nationally recognized psychologist and diversity management thought leader. She currently serves as vice chancellor for diversity and inclusion and chief diversity officer at UMass Medical School and UMass Memorial Health Care, where she has primary responsibility for developing and executing a coordinated and comprehensive diversity plan that cultivates in an inclusive academic health sciences center. As professor in the Departments of Psychiatry and Quantitative Health Sciences and in the Graduate School of Nursing, she continues her research on diversity metrics, cross-racial friendships, and health-equity researcher competencies while teaching cultural competence in health care and strategies for reducing health disparities.

Dr. Plummer has held past roles as staff psychologist, hospital-system chief diversity officer, and university professor, and is the founding director of Cleveland State University's graduate degree program in diversity management. She is principal consultant for D. L. Plummer & Associates, which has provided diversity and change-management strategies for over seventy organizations in the U.S. and U.K.

In addition to being the editor of *Handbook of Diversity Management*, Dr. Plummer is the author of *Racing Across the Lines: Changing Race Relations through Friendships* (Pilgrim Press; Half Dozen Publications), which received the Pilgrim Press' Mayflower Award for best publication in the category of Church and Society, and *Advancing Inclusion: A Guide for Effective Diversity Council and Employee Resource Group Membership* (Half Dozen Publications). She has authored several book chapters and published numerous journal articles to the professional community on racial-identity development and managing diverse work environments. She is the lead author in the design and development of the Diversity Engagement Survey (DES), a tool for measuring diversity and inclusion in organizations. She has also written two books of fiction and an essay in the women-of-color anthology *All the Women in My Family Sing*. Her latest release, *Some of My Friends Are...: The Daunting Challenges and Untapped Potential of Cross-Racial Friendships* is published by Beacon Press.

About the Contributors

JIM HENKELMAN-BAHN AND JACKIE BAHN-HENKELMAN are principals in Bahn/Henkelman Consultants. The breadth of their organization-development (OD), leadership-development, and diversity-management work has focused on both for-profit and not-for-profit organizations. The nonprofit work has been in the arenas of schools (including higher education), community and social justice organizations, government and international agencies, and faith-based organizations. Their international work with the United Nations took place in over twenty countries. The scope of their work has included OD interventions and training in conflict management, executive-leadership development, diversity management, negotiation skills, and coaching.

Following their full-time careers, they partnered in the start-up of three different nonprofit organizations: Opportunity Associates in Romania, IMPACT Silver Spring in Maryland, and the Center for Emotional Intelligence and Human Relations Skills (EQ-HR Center) in Maryland. All of these organizations were involved with the empowerment of individuals and communities. In addition to being founding members of the EQ-HR Center, they each served several years as board chair and in other leadership roles. They have been involved in the development of diversity programs and materials; for example, they were two of the authors of *Becoming a Servant-Leader: A Workbook for Bringing Skill and Spirit to Professional and Personal Life.* During Dr. Henkelman-Bahn's career on the faculty of the University of Maryland College Park, he initiated and directed an experiential doctoral program in human-resource development and is currently an emeritus associate professor in the College of Education there. He was also a member of the graduate faculty of Cleveland State University and the Lutheran School of Theology at Chicago. He earned his doctorate from Harvard University and later a master's degree in applied behavioral science from Whitworth College. As a member of the NTL Institute, he has served as a trainer in their Human Relations Laboratories and as co-steward of the Diversity/Inclusion/Social Justice Community of Practice. He was recently honored as an Emeritus Member for his contributions to the field of applied behavioral sciences. He is passionate about and continues to lobby for social justice issues at the local, state, and national level.

Dr. Bahn-Henkelman earned her doctorate from the University of Maryland College Park and a master's degree in applied behavioral science from Whitworth College. She also graduated from the Organization and Systems Development Program, the Group Development Track, and has a certificate in coaching from the Gestalt Institute of Cleveland, Ohio. She was the academic dean for MODA International, an organization in which she also participated as consultant, trainer and coach for multiple United Nations agencies. Prior to her UN work, she worked as a protective service social worker and then as a psychotherapist. As an OD consultant, she also collaborated with a large telecommunications organization and served as an interim executive director of the Servant-Leader Center. She has extensive coaching experience with executive leaders in the

United Nations, NTL Institute, American University, and the EQ-HR Center. Her perspective is in demand because of her unusually sensitive instincts and understanding of persons and their organizations.

PATRICIA BIDOL-PADVA is an international organizational development (OD) consultant and mediator of complex multi-party and multi-issue disputes. Her diverse experience includes consulting with clients in the United States, Canada, Europe, Asia, and Israel. She has facilitated complex public-sector mediations with multiple stakeholders on issues such as environmental justice, siting of roadways and airports, provision of services for children and families, and environmental protection for natural systems such as the Everglades.

Dr. Bidol-Padva specializes in organizational transformation and renewal, shared leadership development, and facilitating multi-party/ multi-issue initiatives that enable participants to jointly create actions that achieve equitable outcomes. Her OD consulting practice focuses on assisting leaders of systems to design and implement inclusive change initiatives that result in the sustainable and equitable achievement of desired outcomes through the use of:

- transformational change processes designed to create and sustain changes in an organization's culture;

- leadership development that enhances individual, team, local, system, network, and organizational capacities for collaboration toward achieving desired goals;

- large-scale change approaches, customized for organizations and communities, that result in the creation of consensus-based action planning and implementation;

- inclusive and appreciative processes that enhance an organization's capacity to support and engage all of its diverse employees and other stakeholders.

LAURA CASTILLO-PAGE, Ph.D. is senior director of Diversity Policy and Programs and Organizational Capacity Building at the Association of American Medical Colleges (AAMC). Dr. Castillo-Page is responsible for strategic planning, setting priorities, staff professional development, and for managing the day-to-day operations of the Diversity Policy and Programs unit. Dr. Castillo-Page also leads the organizational capacity building portfolio of work to promote the infusion of diversity and inclusion throughout academic medicine to support member institutions through services, tools, and resources that strengthen their policies and processes and address diversity issues at the institutional level.

TAYLOR COX, JR., is founder and CEO of Taylor Cox & Associates, a research and consulting firm specializing in assisting organizations with the challenges and opportunities of a culturally diverse workforce. He holds a PhD in business administration from the University of Arizona. During a twenty-year career as an academic, he served as a faculty member and administrator at several universities, including Duke University, the University of North Carolina, and the University of Michigan.

Dr. Cox is the author of three books and more than twenty-five journal articles. Several of his publications have won prestigious awards. He is recognized internationally as a leading expert on cultural diversity in organizations, as indicated by numerous speaking engagements throughout the U.S. and in other parts of the world. As head of Taylor Cox & Associates, Dr. Cox has consulted with dozens of organizations, including Alcoa, Exxon-Mobil, Phelps Dodge, Ford Motor Company, the U.S. Department of Justice, and the Academy for Educational Development.

JENNIFER ELIASON, EDM, is the lead research analyst with the Diversity Policy and Programs Unit of the Association of American Medical Colleges. With the AAMC, her portfolio of work includes research, reports, and special projects that address institutional-level diversity and inclusion issues. Ms. Eliason's work particularly focuses on culture and climate assessment in medical educational and academic health centers. Her research area of expertise is diversity, inclusion, and equity in medical, professional, and graduate education, with a special emphasis in the faculty-career pipeline. Her work has been published in select peer-reviewed higher education and medical education journals, including the *International Journal of Doctoral Studies* and *Academic Medicine.*

Ms. Eliason holds a bachelor's degree in history and nonprofit management from Lesley University, a master's degree in higher education from the Harvard Graduate School of Education, and is currently a PhD student at the University of Maryland, College Park.

BERNARDO FERDMAN is distinguished professor emeritus of organizational psychology at Alliant International University in San Diego and a leadership and organizational development consultant. He is a SIOP and APA Fellow and consults, writes, speaks, teaches, and conducts research on diversity and inclusion, multicultural leadership, Latinos and Latinas in the workplace, and bringing one's whole self to work. Dr. Ferdman is the co-editor of *Diversity at Work: The Practice of Inclusion* (Jossey-Bass).

MELANIE HARRINGTON is president and CEO of Vibrant Pittsburgh, a nonprofit economic-development organization that was established to build a more diverse and inclusive Pittsburgh region by spearheading initiatives to attract, retain, and elevate a diverse workforce.

From 2001 to 2010, Ms. Harrington served as the president of the American Institute for Managing Diversity, a national nonprofit diversity think tank founded by Dr. R. Roosevelt Thomas, Jr., and based in Atlanta, Georgia. From 1995 to 2001, she served as general counsel for D. J. Miller & Associates, a national management consulting firm that specializes in serving federal, state, and local government agencies. And from 1992 to 1995 she served as a senior associate at the Ewing Group Law Firm, specializing in employment litigation.

She currently serves on the boards of Sustainable Pittsburgh, the Downtown Pittsburgh Partnership, the YMCA of Greater Pittsburgh, and the Diversity Collegium (an international think tank of diversity practitioners). She is a graduate of both Leadership Pittsburgh and Leadership Atlanta and serves as an adjunct professor at the University of Pittsburgh's Graduate School of International and Public Affairs.

Ms. Harrington received her JD from Emory University School of Law and her bachelor's degree in psychology from the University of Pennsylvania.

C. GREER JORDAN serves as chief diversity and inclusion officer at University of Wisconsin Medical College. She also holds a faculty appointment as assistant professor of health and equity. She leads initiatives to engage faculty and students in efforts to advance inclusion as an enabler of institutional strategy and a driver of institutional excellence. Her research and writing interests are in the areas of inclusion and high-performance workgroups and organizations. She also lectures and speaks on generations in the workplace, cultural competency, and skills for managing across differences. Prior to her career in academia, Dr. Jordan worked in the automotive industry for nearly twenty years, in engineering and management positions at Ford Motor Company and General Motors.

Dr. Jordan received a PhD in organizational behavior from Case Western Reserve University, earned an MBA from the University of Michigan Ann Arbor, and earned a bachelor of science in electrical engineering from the University of Detroit.

JUDITH KATZ is executive vice president of the Kaleel Jamison Consulting Group. Fueled by her passion for addressing systemic barriers, Dr. Katz has distinguished herself as a thought leader, practitioner, educator, and strategist for more than forty years. Recognized with the Organization Development Network Lifetime Achievement Award (2014) and as one of 40 Pioneers of Diversity by *Profiles in Diversity Journal,* she has been a leader in inclusion, diversity, and organization development for over forty years. As executive vice president of the Kaleel Jamison Consulting Group—one of *Consulting* magazine's Seven Small Jewels in 2010—she has helped organizations around the globe to leverage people's differences, increase engagement, and transform workplaces.

Together with Frederick A. Miller, she has co-created many key concepts in her fields, including the 12 Inclusive Behaviors, a foundational tool for creating inclusive, collaborative workplaces and achieving higher organizational performance. As the author of five books, Dr. Katz's writing has broken new ground in OD and other fields. Her landmark book *White Awareness: Handbook for Anti-Racism Training* (1978) was the first systematic training program to address racism from a white perspective. Her courageous autobiographical work, *No Fairy Godmothers, No Magic Wands: The Healing Process After Rape* (1984), was among the first to assist rape survivors in the recovery process. She has co-authored with Mr. Miller three books on diversity, inclusion, and individual, team, and organization performance, most recently *Opening Doors to Teamwork and Collaboration: 4 Keys that Change EVERYTHING.*

Many organizations have honored Dr. Katz with awards and accolades. In addition to the Lifetime Achievement Award, OD Network has also awarded her with the Outstanding Achievement in Global Work Award (2012) and the Larry Porter Award for Communicating OD Knowledge (2009). The International Society of Diversity and Inclusion Professionals named her a Legend of Diversity in 2012. An accomplished speaker, researcher, and educator with more than one hundred presentations to her credit, she has been a GDIB reviewer since the founding of the Expert Panel.

MARILYN LODEN is an author and change-management consultant. For over three decades, she has worked with corporations, government agencies, universities, and professional firms, conducting research and implementing programs to maximize the contributions of all employees. Her clients have included Astra Zeneca Pharmaceuticals, Chevron Phillips, Citibank, the Federal Reserve Bank, Genentech, NASA, Neiman Marcus Group, Ortho-McNeil Pharmaceutical, Phillips 66, Rohm and Haas, Shell Oil, the University of California, and the United States Navy.

Prior to establishing her consulting practice in the 1980s, Ms. Loden directed the organization-development function at New York Telephone, where she was responsible for executive education and consultation to senior managers on strategic change issues. She was also the originator of the term "glass ceiling," which she first used in a presentation at the Women's Action Alliance Conference in New York City in 1978 to describe the invisible barriers to advancement that many women managers still face.

Currently, Ms. Loden works with organizations to increase innovation and competitive advantage through the effective utilization of workforce diversity. She has developed a comprehensive diversity training curriculum for several corporate clients aimed at building cultural competence and support for diversity, recognizing and reducing the impact of unconscious biases, and leveraging the principles of inclusion, cooperation, accountability, and mutual respect to create diversity-friendly organization cultures. Ms. Loden also advises diversity councils and corporate diversity planning teams, applying change-management concepts to accelerate acceptance and ensure project sustainability.

Ms. Loden is the author of three diversity-related books: *Feminine Leadership or How to Succeed in Business Without Being One of the Boys* (Times Books, 1985), *Workforce America! Managing Employee Diversity as a Vital Resource* (Irwin, 1991), and *Implementing Diversity* (McGraw-Hill, 1996). She has also authored numerous articles on topics related to leveraging diversity and gender equity. Her work and writings have been featured in national news media such as the *Boston Globe, New York Times, Newsweek, Wall Street Journal, USA Today, Washington Post*, and *The Today Show*.

Ms. Loden is a graduate of Syracuse University. She was a fellow of the NTL Institute for Applied Behavioral Science from 1979 to 2015 and served as an adjunct member of the graduate faculty for the NTL/AU Master's Program in Washington, D.C. In 1993, she was named Joyce Barnes Farmer Distinguished Guest Professor at Miami University in Oxford, Ohio, for her work and research on gender, leadership, and diversity. In April 2016, she was awarded the USN Superior Service Medal by Admiral John Richardson, chief of naval operations, for her twelve years of work assisting the U.S. Navy in efforts to better manage and leverage the diversity of talent within its civilian and uniformed ranks.

OLLIE MALONE, JR., having spent more than forty years in the field of diversity and inclusion, is a rare bird. He began his career as a teacher and therapist with hearing-impaired students and has the distinction of directing the first all-deaf production of *The Miracle Worker* with seniors at the Kansas School for the Deaf, where he was a teacher, coach, and full-time champion of the needs and potential of the hearing-impaired. Upon moving into the private sector, Dr. Malone joined AT&T, following its Consent Decree, which opened opportunities for women and people of color at unprecedented rates. His career has included major roles within corporations, where his focus included diversity and inclusion, leadership development, and organization development. Dr. Malone has written, published, taught, presented, and facilitated conversations on difference in a variety of settings in the United States and abroad. As someone who has held executive roles in major corporations, he understands the unique challenges and opportunities that diversity- and inclusion-competent executives hold in organizations—both from the executive's individual role and task responsibilities and from the opportunities for leadership and influence the executive's role affords.

As a researcher and academician, Dr. Malone has studied and published on diversity-relevant topics such as the potential of hearing-impaired workers in business-related roles, the psychological type differences between men and women in organizations, and the psychological type differences between minorities and majorities in organizational settings. His writings on leadership integrate questions and insights for those who would create diversity-competent organizations.

Dr. Malone holds degrees in communication (BA), education of the hearing-impaired (MS), business administration (MBA), adult learning and development (PhD), and transformational leadership (DM). He currently serves as vice president of human resources at the Dallas–Fort Worth International Airport and is a member of the Society for Human Resources Management, the Dallas Area Industrial and Organizational Psychologists, the Gestalt Institute of Cleveland, and the NTL Institute for Applied Behavioral Science. He is the author of four published books, three unpublished ones, as well as several published articles in refereed journals.

FREDERICK MILLER, a past member of the board of directors of Ben & Jerry's Homemade, currently serves on the boards of Pinchot (one of the first graduate schools focused on sustainability), Day & Zimmermann (a $3 billion family-owned business), the Sage Colleges, Rensselaer Polytechnic Institute's Center for Automated Technology Systems, and Hudson Partners (a real estate investment trust fund). Mr. Miller was the first person to serve on all three boards of the most prestigious organizations in his field—ATD (formerly ASTD), Organization Development Network, and NTL.

Cited as a forerunner of corporate change in *The Age of Heretics: A History of the Radical Thinkers Who Reinvented Corporate Management,* Mr. Miller has been honored as the OD Network's youngest Lifetime Achievement Award recipient, as one of the 40 Pioneers of Diversity by *Profiles in Diversity Journal,* and as one of the Legends of Diversity by the International Society of Diversity and Inclusion Professionals.

A frequent and much-sought-after speaker at international conferences and author of more than one hundred articles in journals such as *The OD Practitioner, HR Professional, Chief Learning Officer,* and *Executive Excellence,* Mr. Miller was managing editor of the classic *The Promise of Diversity* (Irwin, 1994) and co-author, with Judith H. Katz, of *The Inclusion Breakthrough: Unleashing the Real Power of Diversity* (Berrett-Koehler, 2002), *Be BIG: Step Up, Step Out, Be Bold* (Berrett-Koehler, 2008), and *Opening Doors to Teamwork and Collaboration: 4 Keys that Change EVERYTHING* (Berrett-Koehler, 2013).

As CEO and lead strategist of the Kaleel Jamison Consulting Group—named one of *Consulting* magazine's Seven Small Jewels in 2010—Mr. Miller specializes in developing workforce utilization strategies that accelerate results to deliver higher individual, team, and organizational performance. A pioneering change agent and thought leader in the field of organization development, he has led transformative change interventions in Fortune 50 corporations, large not-for-profit organizations, and government agencies throughout the United States, Europe, Australia, and Asia, including Merck, Allstate, United Airlines, Toyota, Eileen Fisher, Northeast Utilities, Singapore Telecom, the McArthur Foundation, the City of San Diego, and many others.

LAURA MORGAN ROBERTS is an author, professor, executive coach, and organizational consultant who helps leaders unlock pathways for constructing, sustaining, and restoring positive identities at work. Dr. Morgan Roberts is a Teaching Professor of Management at Georgetown University's McDonough School of Business. She is also a faculty affiliate of Antioch University's Graduate School of Leadership and Change, the Center for Positive Organizations (University of Michigan, Ann Arbor) and Harvard Business School's Gender Initiative, where she formerly taught. She is the editor of *Exploring Positive Identities and Organizations: Building a Theoretical and Research Foundation* (with Jane Dutton) and *Positive Organizing in a Global Society* (with Lynn Perry Wooten and Martin Davidson).

Dr. Morgan Roberts earned a BA in psychology (highest distinction and Phi Beta Kappa) from the University of Virginia and an MA and PhD in organizational psychology from the University of Michigan.

NORMA IRIS POLL-HUNTER is senior director of human capital initiatives in diversity policy and programs at the Association of American Medical Colleges. She leads a portfolio of career and leadership development initiatives focused on advancing diversity and inclusion across the medical education continuum. She also serves as the deputy director for the Robert Wood Johnson Foundation Summer Health Professions Education Program, and leads research and evaluation projects focused on an array of diversity, inclusion, cultural competence, and workforce topics.

Prior to the AAMC, Dr. Poll-Hunter practiced as a bilingual psychologist in New York. She attended the University of Albany, SUNY, where she earned her PhD in counseling psychology.

HERB STEVENSON is CEO/founder of the Cleveland Consulting Group. He has thirty-five years of experience in gestalt-based global consulting. His clients range from $25 million family-owned businesses to multi-billion-dollar global organizations. He has worked in Europe, the Middle East, and South Africa. His practice involves individual and team coaching for executives and C-suite officers as well as large-scale change in international schools. He has developed executive development training programs for the federal government and global corporations. His clients include U.S.-based Exterran, E-Trade, First Merit Bank, National Cooperative Bank, the World Bank, Fannie Mae, the Defense Intelligence Agency, NASA, Vitamix, and Seaman Corp. Global companies include Kentz (Ireland), SNC-Lavalin (Canada), Orascom Construction (Egypt), Pepperl + Fuchs (Germany), and AISR (Netherlands).

He was chair for the Gestalt OSD Becoming an Effective Intervener program. Presently, he teaches coaching at the point of contact at the Gestalt Institute of Cleveland. He is a certified professional coach, certified executive coach, and certified diversity professional. He has published several gestalt coaching and consulting articles in the *OD Practitioner, Gestalt Review,* and the *Cleveland Consulting*

Group Newsletter. He is a member of the Organization Development Network, the International Coaching Federation, the Society for Organizational Learning, and the Academy of Management.

APRIL THOMAS, as a music composer, performer, and conductor, brings a unique approach to diversity management by merging the technical and creative concepts found in high-performance orchestras with the award-winning methodology of her father, the late Dr. R. Roosevelt Thomas, Jr., who was hailed globally as the "Father of Diversity."

Ms. Thomas recognizes that the ultimate question organizations ask is, "How do we get our work done effectively?" As the chief solutions officer of SDMS 360, she has helped numerous organizations answer this question by creating effective business solutions that equip clients to meet the demands of constantly changing requirements and objectives. This has included refreshing and further developing SDMS 360's online content to expand clients' training options.

Ms. Thomas graduated magna cum laude from Wellesley College with a BA in Japanese studies and economics and summa cum laude from Berklee College of Music with a BM in jazz composition and film scoring.